PELICAN BOOKS
A608

THE INSECURE OFFENDERS

T. R. FYVEL

T. R. FYVEL

The Insecure Offenders

REBELLIOUS YOUTH IN THE WELFARE STATE

PENGUIN BOOKS
In association with Chatto & Windus

Penguin Books Ltd, Harmondsworth, Middlesex
AUSTRALIA: Penguin Books Pty Ltd, 762 Whitehorse Road,
Mitcham, Victoria

—

First published by Chatto & Windus 1961
This revised edition published in Pelican Books 1963

—

Copyright © T. R. Fyvel, 1961, 1963

—

Made and printed in Great Britain
by Hazell Watson & Viney Ltd
Aylesbury and Slough
Set in Linotype Georgian

For my daughters,

HANNAH and SUSAN

Contents

Acknowledgements

GRATEFUL thanks are due to the authors and publishers for permission to quote from the following works: Mark Abrams, *The Teenage Consumer*, London Press Exchange; Herbert E. Block and Frank T. Flynn, *Delinquency*, Random House, New York; J. K. Galbraith, *The Affluent Society*, Hamish Hamilton; Virginia P. Held, 'What can we do about J.D.?', *Reporter*, New York; *Juvenile Delinquency in Post-War Europe*, The Council of Europe; George Orwell, *Shooting an Elephant*, Secker and Warburg; Richard Perlman, 'Delinquency: the size of the problem', *Annals*, Philadelphia; Elizabeth Stucley, *Teddy Boy's Picnic*, Anthony Blond; Richard M. Titmuss, *Essays on the Welfare State*, Allen & Unwin; John Townsend, *The Young Devils*, Chatto & Windus; Barbara Wootton, *Social Science and Social Pathology*, Allen & Unwin. Thanks are also due to *Education* for permission to reproduce the graphs from the issue of 1 June 1962 which appear on page 16.

CHAPTER I

Introduction: From a View to a Theory

Into the wilderness

IN the period preceding the writing of this book I often used to watch a London street-scene which seemed to have its special significance.

I was then living in a top-floor maisonette in an area near a London park round which much slum clearance was in progress, and for a while the windows of my back room provided a wide open view of a new public housing estate – locally simply known as 'the Estate', already a sprawling conglomeration dominating the district, but still expanding steadily. There were times when I felt that this vista reflected the precise spirit of the age: the bold aims of modern architecture watered down by the anonymity of local government. The big blocks of flats, seven to eleven storeys high, embodied the early ambitions of the post-war Welfare State – against the background of surrounding slums they looked clean and functional, yet with all the thought that had gone into them they somehow failed to look attractive.

There was too much asphalt; the entrances and hallways had a cramped look; there was an impression of just so much provided in accommodation and no more. Still, I knew from all my contacts that, apart from the normal complaints about high rents, practically all the families who had moved into the flats from the demolished surroundings considered themselves fortunate enough. The big buildings certainly teemed with life; laundry hung above the small, concrete balconies; especially towards evening the sounds of commercial television or the Light Programme seemed to drift from everywhere through windows, doors, and ceilings. Quite a few cars stood parked on the surrounding concrete, mostly small and bought secondhand, but lovingly tended and increasing in number almost week by week. In fact, general opinion had it that with all their much-discussed defects, such as the high rents and lack of soundproof walls, the flats provided their London working-class occupiers with better homes than the majority had known before.

With one fairly notable exception: the adolescents, the teenagers living in the flats, who spent a good deal of their time in hanging about the stairs and courtyards. And, for some years, each Saturday and Sunday towards dusk, I used to witness a curious procession. From my distant window I could see the small, dark figures of boys and half-grown youths, drifting off in twos or threes or larger groups, and all of them, it seemed to me, wearing the identical Teddy-boy suits at the time in fashion. All of them, as if drawn by a magnet, also made off in the same direction, towards the main streets beyond the big railway stations: an untidy area of converging streets and crowded traffic, of shops, cinemas, public houses, and bright lights, aesthetically a God-awful wilderness, but to the boys obviously representing life with a capital L.

I sometimes thought that one could see the social waste-land through which they wandered in actual visual terms. North of the estate lay row upon row of squat nineteenth-century slum streets, with bomb gaps of fifteen years before still showing, an area mostly condemned and waiting only for demolition. So it should be, one felt, yet for many of the youths from the estate these grimy houses had been origin-ally their parents' homes. Now they stood condemned and so were harshly degraded, like a whole way of life to be put out of mind, together with memories of worn doorsteps, dark passages, mother at the sink, and father shirt-sleeved in the kitchen with his newspaper – a whole world of work-ing-class childhood memories now shattered. On its other side, the estate was bordered by a network of crescents and terraces which up to the thirties had been a solid upper-middle-class neighbourhood, a focus for the whole district. Now the tall terrace houses stood subdivided, stucco was peeling from porticoes and façades, untidy cards marked the bells at the front doors; from this vista, too, all its former social authority had fled. So it had from the two local churches, whose dull angularity suggested only the dead aspirations of the Victorian era.

Between these areas, as a replacement crammed with new life and expanding all the time, stood the estate itself. But I felt it represented another question mark. Though the lines of the flats were clean and straight – their main asset – those blocks which were half a dozen years old already seemed to reflect a certain weariness of the spirit. Perhaps it was that skimpy detail spoke of the accountancy of remote public bodies; the entrances and stairways had already the neglected air of a place not loved; the whole impression was of too much public anonymity, of a space-saving set of buildings for those lucky enough to get in, but which proclaimed no satisfying new way of community life.

Not, anyway, to the young. For them, as was clear, the one source of satisfaction they understood perfectly lay in the crowded high streets beyond the big stations. It did not matter that in its back streets this was a dispiriting region of blank warehouses, untidy street-markets, and sleazy lodging houses. In the main streets, at any rate, the young felt surrounded by a full tide of confident life. The confidence of the age was reflected in the ultramodern layout of the chain stores; in shop windows crammed with radios, television sets, record-players, streamlined tape-recorders, and musical instruments; in others offering modern furniture to make any young couple happy at only so much down and so much per week. Confident commercial voices addressed the young from newspaper headlines, cinema posters, and perhaps most insistently from the skilfully designed glossy pop-record sleeves: here were Elvis Presley and Frank Sinatra, and all their temporarily starred British equivalents, expressing sentiments of love, anguish, and desire, and explicitly for you, if you were young. Here, too, was the neighbourhood pleasure ground: the plush cinemas, the modernized dance halls, the pubs with a singing trade, the late-night cafés with jukeboxes blaring and girls to be talked to at the tables. For many of the boys from the estate, this London, offering its pleasures freely to those with money, spoke with the only voice of authority that mattered. The importance of their homes had dwindled; work meant little. Their one emphatic link with society lay through its entertainments, from the new betting shops to the Top Twenty juke-box records: these they understood and clung to. One could gather this from the boys themselves or the leaders of the struggling local youth clubs where on occasion they drifted in and out.

It was also not hard to see the basic defects of their link with the new culture of the streets. It was not so much because the latter was primitive, but because by 1960 it had become so many degrees more commercialized and deceptive and artificial, so that it seemed dangerously easy for young minds cut off from other influences to see all society in terms of caricature: that is, a society where newspapers were concerned solely with sex, sensation, and betting, where television dealt only in violence and get-rich-quick quiz programmes and the popular film was a gangster film; a life of recurring boredom where nothing mattered but money and the smart thing at all times was to give as little as you could for as much as you could get; in short, as they saw it, a distorted materialist society without purpose. On this soil, luxuriant visions could flourish, where fact and fancy were apt to mingle:

Ordinarily we'd just stand at the coffee stall at the corner – some of the blokes would stand there until two or three in the morning – but some nights we'd all pile into a taxi and drive down to the West, you know, Greek Street and Charing Cross Road. There's cafés there and hot dives. We'd go there looking for mysteries – that's what we call the girls – or some fellow had a job, that'd be thievin', picking up a few easy pounds. No, it wouldn't be what you'd call real crime. One time a bloke offered us £5 to beat a fellow up but we never did anything: it was a Greek offered us the money and we didn't like him. We'd try to pick up prostitutes after they had finished work. They didn't mind taking a young Ted home for the night. We'd pick up some of the club hostesses too. Beautiful girls they were, and they'd come home with a young bloke if they liked him. We didn't have to pay, there was no money in it at all.

But the fanciful flight from boredom could also lead too smoothly to violence.

No, we don't have so many fights any more. We used to have them, with knives too. Well, it was the excitement! I've seen our blokes heave a fellow they didn't even know through a plate-glass window – I tell you I couldn't stop laughing. I remember one time six of us went to get one of the Blacks; I didn't know what he'd done but anyway he was a Spade, but then the coppers chased us but we all chucked our knives away as we ran and when they searched us they found nothing. When they finished we all got into a taxi and went down West. We just didn't care: it was the excitement, different from going every night to the pictures where nothing ever happens. One time we used to go regularly to the Angel where there's a lot of cafés and we aimed to start trouble with the Greeks and Turks, start a punch-up. They're Cypriots, you know, grease monkeys we used to call them – our chaps all hated them.

The young man who freely confided these fancies to me was a good-looking young café regular, dandified in dress, who not long after was up before the Court and on his way to Borstal for a spell of re-education at the state's expense.

Criminals or victims?

The shortcomings of the housing estate, the culture of the streets, the steady growth of Britain's Borstal population – it is my assumption in this study that this *ensemble* has its significance, that the current unrest of youth is a new phenomenon, illuminating aspects of our society at which it is worth looking very carefully.

To start with some definitions. It is no accident that the problems of youth have been so much in the news.

We can no longer think of generations in traditional terms [said a recent U.N. report]. Interests and activities are today changing so fast that sets of young people not more than seven or eight years apart in age may be as far apart in their thinking and behaviour as the generations once were.

This swiftness of change is in itself significant. Every age is one of transition, but there are times when the gap between generations seems particularly sharp. Just as in the early years of the century (when the young followers of Shaw and Wells set fire to the Victorian lumber-room) so it seems that today, in the age of the nuclear bomb and the affluent society, youth has turned sharply from the outlook of its elders, less perhaps in actual beliefs than in its whole way of thinking, feeling, and reacting, which may be even more important. This secession has on one level found expression in the writings described as by 'angry young men', in the successive 'new waves' in literature, drama, and the cinema, in the beatnik interlude (which has influenced the clothes even of Soviet poets), perhaps most of all in the exceptionally vivid sense of the young of being a 'generation'. All this is not here my subject: but another aspect of the unease of youth, lower down, may be even more significant. This is the wave of youthful lawlessness, expressed both in mob hooliganism and, more seriously, in a steady rise of juvenile-crime figures, which since the war has been experienced simultaneously in a number of countries.

How much significance should we read into this wave? There may be still some who doubt its magnitude. But as far as Britain is concerned, British juvenile-crime figures have certainly shown one of the steepest increases of all, and the chief point is that they have risen against a background of steadily expanding welfare services. As Mr R. A. Butler (Home Secretary for much of this period) put it sorrowfully, the rise came 'after years of the most massive social and educational reform for a century'. This rise has also already dispelled some traditional views on the causes of crime. A generation ago it was still widely held that even if poverty was only one among the main causes, the delinquency figures would at least roughly follow the curve of economic dislocation and unemployment. Today this link has clearly been severed.

Introduction : From a View to a Theory

Economically the years from 1953 to 1960 were a phase of distinct progress. They were years of full employment, higher wages, and rising mass consumption, especially on the part of the young. These years also saw well over a million new houses built – by 1960 a quarter of the population was living in council houses or flats; they saw around a million new cars on the roads, and several million more television sets in the front parlours. That is, the massive movement of the British working classes away from their former drab slums into a new suburban council-estate life with its novel gadgets and respectability, continued apace. Nor was the expansion of state education and child care and other welfare services noticeably halted. Above all, the replacement of old primary and secondary schools by new schools housed in functionally designed modern buildings was steadily continued, even though there was quite a way to go before the replacement would be complete. Yet the figures of juvenile crime did not go down during these years as had been hopefully predicted earlier, at the end of the war-time hangover. On the contrary, after an initial drop the statisticians' curve showed a sharp and alarming upward turn. The figures in Table 1 tell the story.

TABLE 1. Male offenders convicted of an indictable offence in England and Wales

Year	14 to 17 age group	17 to 21 age group
1938	11,645	10,131
1955	13,517	11,269
1956	15,029	13,425
1957	18,149	16,962
1958	21,628	21,232
1959	23,059	22,342
1960	24,749	25,068
1961	28,244	27,667

Percentually, this meant that in 1959 just over two per cent of youths in both age-groups were convicted of an indictable offence. The figures of the convicted for breaking and entering tell a similar story (Table 2):

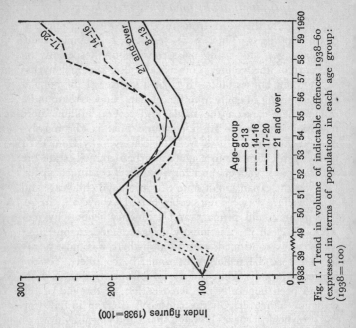

Fig. 1. Trend in volume of indictable offences 1938-60 (expressed in terms of population in each age group; (1938=100)

Fig. 2. Male crime-rate per 100,000 population by age-groups, 1938 and 1960 (all offences excluding non-indictable motor offences)

Introduction : From a View to a Theory

TABLE 2

Age-group	1938	1956	1957	1958	1960	1961
14 to 17	2,770	3,895	5,000	6,931	7,789	9,037
17 to 21	1,396	3,051	3,934	5,513	5,872	6,733

Similarly, the figures of those convicted for offences of violence against the person (Table 3):

TABLE 3

Age-group	1938	1956	1957	1958	1960	1961
14 to 17	80	461	576	787	1,238	1,416
17 to 21	163	1,248	1,635	2,084	2,762	3,006

These figures appeared to surprise even the most experienced social and penal workers. For example, the unforeseen increase in delinquency in the male seventeen to twenty-one age-groups was reflected by an equivalent rise in the Borstal population which went up from 2,800 at the beginning of 1956, to over 5,000 at the end of 1960. Unprecedented measures had to be taken to absorb this new clientele, and Mr Butler's White Paper of January 1959 accordingly introduced the biggest prison-building programme for young adult offenders for many years, including plans for the building of eight Borstals, together with eight of the new detention centres, designed to administer 'a short sharp shock' to the evidently more recalcitrant young offenders of the new age.

These figures of actual law-breaking are only part of the post-war story. Equally noticeable during the fifties was the appearance among a section of working-class youth of a more intensified gang life, characterized by a hostility towards authority in every form, which could flare into violence upon a trivial cause. Coupled with it went a sort of stylized warfare between the gangs themselves, especially those wearing exaggerated Teddy-boy suits, and a fashion for carrying improvised offensive weapons. In fact, if one regarded only the outward picture, a disturbing dichotomy seemed to be at work. As British working-class youth was becoming more urbane, as more modern schools and housing estates went up, so more boys seemed to drift into the new gang warfare and to walk about carrying flick knives or such things as bicycle chains 'for defence'. Defence against whom? The wave of unrest reached one climax in such large-scale disturbances as the 1958 race-riots in Nottingham and Notting Hill, which were largely started by working-class adolescents, which outraged public opinion in Britain and abroad and brought the Law heavily down upon the offenders through the resurrected concept of 'causing an affray', used for the first time for many decades. Not long after, early in 1959, the charge of 'causing an affray' was used again after two large gang fights at dance halls in which two young men were stabbed to death, one of them a policeman.

These events of 1958–9 seemed to represent a definite climax in the wave of youthful violence. Well before this, however, as far as the popular Press was concerned, juvenile delinquency had for the first time in Britain become elevated to the status of a national problem. More than that, it seemed to have become curiously stylized, to have become a fashion. The emphasis in newspaper stories was on what was loosely called Teddy boys (until the word itself went out, or became derisory). Popular Press reports picked for their headline value should be treated with caution, yet there was an insistent similarity about the reports as they told about gang fights, about attacks on cafés, about armed robberies perpetrated by callous youths, about strange armouries of improvised weapons piled up in Court after gang encounters. All in all, it was hard to resist the conclusion that there was something new afoot among a section of British youth, a new and considerable wave of aggressiveness of which the Teddy-boy movement was only one expression.

The Teddy-boy international

This development stands out all the more because British experience has been far from unique. From about 1950 onwards, an increase in juvenile delinquency and gang life has occurred in a sufficient number of countries to justify its description as a 'wave' and to arouse attention as an international problem.

First of all there are the disturbing reports from the United States. The antics of the adolescent gangs of the sidewalks of New York, ready to use even firearms in their feuds, have been given world-wide and highly romantic publicity in such a musical as *West Side Story*. The melting-pot of New York may present a special case. What has worried the American authorities more, however, has been the apparently steady spread of juvenile lawlessness even into small towns and suburbs, with such revelations as that in a single year some five per cent of young Americans can get into trouble with the courts or the police or that youngsters under twenty-one constitute over half of those arrested for theft and robbery.

The whole *malaise* among a section of American teenagers has been well documented. What is not so well known, because more recent, is that developments on the Continent of Europe have been rather similar. In the last ten years, at any rate, with the new economic boom, the figures of juvenile crime in nearly every European country have been rising steadily. More than that, the riots of American youngsters and England's Teddy boys have had their counterpart in similar mass outbreaks on the Continent, occurring now here, now there. In 1956–8 the focal point was in West Germany and Austria, where gangs of dressed-up *Halbstarken*, the Austro-German equivalent of Teddy boys, staged destructive riots in such cities as West Berlin, Hamburg, Brunswick, Essen, Vienna, and Graz. At the time the general view in France and Italy was that such things could not happen there. In 1960, however, gangs of *blousons noirs* staged disturbances in Paris and on the mid-season Riviera on such a scale as to bring the French police out into the streets in vast force: by this time, police *razzias* to round up adolescent gangs had already also taken place in Italian cities like Milan. Revealing reports have also come from Sweden, neutral during the war, enjoying the highest living standards and most developed Welfare State in Europe: yet the rate of juvenile crime in Sweden has gone up steadily since the war, reaching a high point in 1958 in the form of adolescent mass disturbances in Stockholm and other cities which led to massive attempts at social counter-action by the startled Swedish authorities.

Nor is this all. To show that not only capitalist countries are involved, the following story from the Soviet newspaper *Moscow Komsomol* (22 January 1959), one of many which could have been quoted, shows that conditions in Leningrad parks are at times not so altogether different from those in Central Park, New York.

Moscow: It is a shocking event that through lack of proper foresight a Moscow youth has been stabbed to death by eight hooligans in a Leningrad park. Our seventeen-year-old Comrade Vadim Trainin of Moscow had gone to Leningrad early this month on a vacation. While there he contacted the Young Communist League headquarters and asked to go on patrol with one of their squads whose task it is to aid the militia in keeping order in the city. Together with two other boys and three girls, Trainin was put into a squad which was assigned to patrol duty in the city's Lenin Park.

In the park, the squad was set upon by a hooligan gang and it appears that the two other boys and the three girls abandoned young Trainin who was thereupon stabbed to death.

In this needless tragedy, it must be said that the Leningrad Young Communist League has evidently treated this killing with an unjustifiable light-mindedness. We find it essential that the perpetrators of this crime should pay the fitting penalty. We further recommend that all Young Communist squads on patrol duty should be of adequate size and should include young people able to handle trouble.

There is, in fact, evidence that what the Communist Press calls 'hooliganism' is a serious problem in the Soviet Union and the East European satellite states. In Communist Poland this is openly admitted. How large the problem is in the Soviet Union is not easy to say. However, the censored Soviet Press only admits defects in Soviet life when they have reached major proportions, so that when Soviet newspapers in 1958 complained about drunkenness and hooliganism among the youth in cities like Moscow, Leningrad, Tiflis, Odessa, Rostov, and Sverdlovsk, it is fair to conclude that delinquency had become a major headache for the Soviet authorities.

To turn to Asia, consistent reports from post-war Japan tell of insubordination at high schools or in the streets in American style and almost on American scale. Figures quoted in 1960 in alarmed articles in the Japanese Press revealed that, as compared with 1938, the number of Japanese youngsters, including students, picked up on charges of vandalism, truancy, and drunkenness had increased just about tenfold. All in all, therefore, the evidence seems to be that there is a new spirit of lawlessness abroad among modern youth, which has found organized and violent expression above all in the advanced industrial countries of our time.

A new phenomenon

Does all this amount to a new social phenomenon, to be studied as such? I think it does, even though some of those working in the field have argued that, when one considers individual cases, there is nothing new in the pattern of delinquency, which is by now well documented. A common *individual* starting-point is insecurity in childhood, due to a broken home or bad family background. A child from such a home, feeling emotionally insecure and unloved, rejects rather than leaves his home. School to such a youngster often appears a mere meaningless accompaniment of the home which has failed him; the one prospect of security, esteem, and status seems to lie in the street gang and defiance of society; and this often is the start of delinquency. This established pattern, it is said, has in no way changed, except in such detail as the fashion for exaggerated costume.

As for the increase in delinquency, it has been argued, this is not as large as often made out, even in the United States, where official statistics hide the concentration of crime among depressed groups like Negroes and Puerto Rican immigrants. Or again it has been said that the flare-up of adolescent violence could in a number of countries be traced back to the effects of war-time disruption of family life and the shocks then inflicted upon small children – this could be true of countries like Britain, Germany, and France, of Poland and Russia and Japan.

All such arguments carry weight, yet they certainly cannot explain the international wave of youthful unrest – they certainly cannot explain its continuous rise. For one thing, the delinquency figures in many countries are simply too large. In Britain, for example, they are much higher than they should be in view of the progress in social welfare on every side. It seems also clear that the aftermath of the war can be only a very partial explanation of the unrest. Neutral Sweden, to quote only one instance, has after all been beset by this same problem. In the United States, again, the figure of young people convicted has risen so regularly year by year – by now uninterruptedly for nine years, with the lawlessness spreading from the big cities into the small towns and suburbia – that the phenomenon must be connected with *current* developments in American society, as indeed it obviously is.

Furthermore, the recent rise in delinquency has some very special features. In most countries it has occurred in conditions of equally rising material welfare, which has caused some German experts to give it the name of *die Wohlstands-kriminalitaet* – 'welfare criminality'. Again, in a general reading of reports, in other countries as well as in Britain the new youthful violence seems to have become curiously stylized, linked with a special gang life and special fashions. Not all those who dressed in Teddy-boy style or in the style of the *Halbstarken* in Germany and Austria were actual delinquents, perhaps indeed not more than a fraction. Nevertheless, the spirit of rebellion denoted by the costume and the rise in youthful criminality have noticeably gone together. And they have gone together rather viciously. In the United States, public opinion has been roused by the fully-fledged gangsterism recently displayed by juvenile street gangs. What brought Britain's Teddy boys their international publicity was not merely their eccentric dress and trend towards violence – in earlier days there was plenty of violence in industrial England – but their deliberate cult of amorality and the brutality with which they set upon outnumbered victims. (Again, without stressing it too far, we can bring a parallel from behind the Iron Curtain. When Soviet newspapers in 1959 carried renewed articles against 'young criminals and bandits' and threatened the death penalty for those caught with flick-knives, it indicated that the Soviet authorities faced a similar problem of youthful amorality.)

Apart from such violent crime, and to go back to youthful lawlessness in the wider sense, it is also significant that in various countries new names were simultaneously coined for these young offenders who were readily identifiable by their provocative dress and attitude. In the United States they have been called 'Rebels without cause', a name which sums up the movement. In Britain, the Edwardian dress associated with the rowdiness gave rise to the name 'Teddy boys' which survived the costume. In Western Germany and Austria, the similar gangs of provocatively dressed adolescent rowdies have been called the *Halbstarken*, the 'half-strong'. In Sweden, troublemakers were referred to as the *Skinnknuttar* or 'leather-jackets', a name originally for gangs of youths obsessed by a craze for motor-cycle racing in the streets. France similarly has her *blousons noirs*, or 'black jackets'. The Japanese, elegant as ever, have coined the name *taiyozoku*, or 'children of the sun', for their new groups of anti-social youth. The Australians, more briefly, have termed theirs 'bodgies'. And it is instructive that Soviet abuse has been directed not only at the lowly mass of hooligans, but also at the *stilyagi*, or 'style boys', a type of defiant, educated Soviet youths whose elaborate hair-styles, draped jackets, and crêpe soles, as well as their addiction to jazz, showed that in spite of censorship they tried to model themselves on the Teddy-boy international.

What does it all amount to? I found myself asking this question one night in Hamburg when by chance I happened to be a spectator of one of the *Halbstarken* mass outbursts. The immediate pretext for it had been a concert by the rock-'n'-roll experts, Bill Haley and his Comets. Earlier concerts by Bill Haley in West Berlin and Essen had already led to mass teenage riots and vandalism, and so it happened in Hamburg. When I came on the scene, a crowd of two thousand adolescent boys and girls, who earlier had stopped the recital and smashed chairs and windows in the hall, was still milling in a dense mob in the square outside. They seemed in a frenzy, yelling insults and in some cases fighting squads of baffled policemen who were trying to clear the streets, at first good-naturedly, but in the end, amidst rising tempers, finding it necessary to disperse hysterical youngsters by use of tear-gas. The whole spectacle was baffling. Germany in a not-so-recent past had seen riots over mass unemployment; later, the political mob violence of the Nazis, but this was quite different. These German teenagers were living in a dull, prosperous Germany; they looked healthy and well-dressed – so what lay behind their excited frenzy, their anger, their trivial rebellion without a cause?

Or, for that matter, what lay behind the violence of the American street gangs or that of the Teddy boys? Or what was the reason for the striking rise in juvenile crime in the 'fifties in so many advanced countries? Adding it all up, it seemed hard to doubt that there was something afoot, that there were some aspects of our materialistic, mechanized, twentieth-century society – something in the way of life, in the break-up of traditional authority, in the values of the news in the headlines, which encouraged widespread youthful cynicism in general and rather violent delinquency in particular. It is against this wider background of the unrest of a generation that I think the Teddy boy should be viewed. However, in each country this unrest has also taken on its own characteristic cultural forms.

PART ONE

REPORTAGE

CHAPTER 2

From the Shallows

WHAT follows is a self-portrait of Ron, a rather troubled and troublesome youth, which I obtained in an interview. Occasionally one meets a case history which reflects a number of the themes discussed in this book – Ron's story seemed to me one of them. Apart from necessary changes for fictionalizing, I have given it, as reconstructed from my notes, if not in Ron's precise words at least an attempt to catch something near enough his flat monotone. If certain fanciful details are derived probably from the imagination of this young citizen of the Welfare State rather than from fact, this, I think, makes them no less significant.

Q. You haven't always lived here at the Elephant, have you?

A. I only came here when I was about thirteen. Before that we lived down Croydon way, my father and my mum, that's my real mother, and me. My father, he's a Master Printer. We used to have a nice house and a garden. He left my mother when I was eight; I was an only son. My mother died when I was twelve. That was a terrible shock to me and I went to live with my grandmother who had a tobacconist's shop, over at Brixton. Then I found out my father had married again and was living here at the Elephant, and he and my stepmother, they came and said it'd be better if I lived with them.

Q. Did you like that idea?

A. I didn't think much about it. But I had a grudge against my father because he told my stepmother they could expect trouble because I was a bad lot.

Q. Now what gave him cause to say that?

A. Well, when I was ten – I was still with my mother then – I was sent to Approved School and my father knew all about it. It was for breaking and entering a shop. It wasn't a shop, really, it was a warehouse for fruit. There were three of us, we were just kids, and at that time we were mad about oranges and we went to get some. When we got to the warehouse, I found money lying on the counter in front of me, so I took it. We took tobacco, cigarettes, and money. There were some of these soap-box trollies about and we loaded one full of fruit and were wheeling it out when one of us knocked over an alarm clock. Two detectives caught us and took us to the police station. I remember my mother cried in Court and broke down when they said I was to go to Approved School, and I cried, too.

Q. If they sent you away, surely you must have been in trouble before?

A. Yes, I'd done a lot of playing truant, going swimming mostly. When I was at junior school I was hardly ever at school. I'd go swimming in the river. There were about six of us; we'd play on the sewage farm, playing in the trucks. My mother used to get regular summonses. They put me away at Stamford House, that's a remand home, but after I was there three weeks they sent me home again. It wasn't so bad, I wasn't frightened, it seemed easy – I'd say now it didn't frighten me enough, 'cos I went on truanting. I didn't like school, because they said I was backward; well, I was at reading. I just couldn't be bothered. I admit I'm sorry now – since I left school, I've practised reading, the posters on the station. I'm not so good at it even now. My mother? I admit she spoiled me, I had all the money I wanted given to me, and the toys; she used to have toys made for me. When I was ten I was sent to that Approved School I was telling you about. That was in Hampshire. I had to do scrubbing and work on the farm and in the fields. It was strict but not so bad; I quite liked it. Sometimes they were too strict, but other times I'd say it was like a holiday camp.

When I came back, I was eleven, and I'd say I was changed all right. I had to live with my grandmother because my mother was working in a hospital, it was a living-in job, but she always visited me. I was quite happy living with my grandmother. I always make friends easy – people take a liking to me because I'm always ready to help somebody out. Then, when I was twelve, my mother died. Yes, I was terribly upset. I broke down; I had to be sent to a convalescent home at Southend.

Q. You were twelve then – what happened after that?

A. I went back to my grannie, but when my father said I should live with them I said I would – I thought, let my family help me. He was in the print, but my mother, my stepmother, that is, she had a dry-cleaner's place; she had the money in the family. When I moved I went to this Secondary Modern School in the Borough. It was a bit of a rough place – if you want to know about the Teds, that's where I first met them.

For about six months, I think, things went pretty smooth, and then, all of a sudden, my father didn't want me hang up a wedding photo of him and my mother – my real mother. He said she was dead and all that was done with, he didn't want it, so one day I found the photo gone. My stepmother said she didn't know anything about it, so I put it down to my father. He said he didn't know where it was, but I never believed him. I had a grudge against him – that's when I started stealing. I said to him: 'You didn't want the photo 'cos you left her. Still, she was better to me than you two ever will be.' So I started stealing a bit from the dry-cleaner's downstairs and my parents – that's my father and my stepmother – they sent me away to boarding school. What sort? Well, it was a special sort of school. It was quite small but it was a private school, you had to pay – all the boys came from decent families.

I stayed there till I was about sixteen. I was happy there, everything was going nicely. But I used to steal a bit from the masters' rooms. All the time I used to say to myself that I shouldn't do it, but I was never found out. Lessons? I didn't like it at first when they said I was backward; it was only that I couldn't put my mind to it.

I said, 'I'll prove it to you that I'm not backward,' and for one term I put my mind to it and I was top of the class. (?) One thing I remember – it makes me laugh. There was that master living there with his wife and daughter and one time I used to slip out of the dormitory every evening and go to that girl and come back early in the morning. She was about seventeen, but she knew a lot. I always found girls easy to get; I could always persuade them to give me what I want. She wrote to me quite a few times afterwards, I never bothered to answer. After a time, I didn't like the school so much. My parents, they wanted me to be a gentleman. I say they went too far, one way and another. So they took me away when I was about sixteen.

[Some fantasy seemed to have crept into these memories.]

Q. And what happened then?

A. Well, I was at home again and after a time I got myself a job in the building. My parents wanted me to give it up, it wasn't good enough, and so one day I said, 'Right, I'm leaving.' I got myself a room near the Elephant and I started going down the Walworth Road. One night, in a café down the Walworth Road – it was a Greek caff – I saw the Greek what owned it hit a young bloke just because he was sitting on the corner of a table. So I said: 'If you hit him again I'm going to bring the boys and you'll get your caff smashed up.' Mind you, I got nothing against foreigners – I just don't like to see a white man hit, I mean a Greek hit a chap of my own nationality. With that, this Greek picked up a chair, and I hit him. The Greeks started coming at me and this other bloke and me, we smashed up the windows and we were fighting with bottles. They made a case of it at the Borough Court, but we denied everything and we got away with it.

Well, when this other bloke got home, he told his mates there's a fellow just come down the Walworth Road, a terrific puncher, and I met their mates and I went to dance-halls and had a few fights. After getting myself well known I met a girl, a nice respectable girl, and she kept me out of trouble. She didn't like the way I was living, she knew I was very hot-tempered, so I didn't let her know when I was out with the boys.

After about six, nine months of fighting and getting known, a bloke said to me: 'Charlie is coming out of prison tomorrow. He's a hard nut from the other side, a ponce.' Well, we went to meet him and I liked him and gave him some money. I started going over West with him and stopped the building work. We used to go to dives where there was all the prostitutes hanging about. Charlie had two girls; they gave him all their money, and he gave me some. I saw blokes were making a lot of easy money, thievin' and poncing. After I'd been going some months – I was eighteen then – I found a girl who took a liking to me and started to live with me. She used to walk alongside the Strand, soliciting.

Q. Did you have any feelings about that?

A. Me? No. Girls – I've had intercourse with thousands of girls. (?) What I didn't like was people talking. They'd say: 'Here comes Ron the Ponce.' Respectable girls didn't like it, they wouldn't go out with you. This girl, this prostitute – they don't call it 'prostitute', they'd say 'I'm soliciting' – this girl used to take fellows in a taxi. There's drivers in the West that do it, they take 10s. a time. The driver stops the taxi in a side-street and goes for a walk, it only takes about five minutes. Some of the blokes give a lot of money; the Yanks, they got no idea of English money; when they're new they think a fiver's the same as a pound note. They don't get the real thing. This girl I was with, she was on the game for sixteen months, she had the real thing only three times. These girls, they know how to move their legs so a fellow doesn't know: they got a way of fixing things so a fellow thinks he's having it naturally when he isn't.

Well, I was with this girl all the time. Sometimes she'd make twenty pounds a night and she'd give it to me. If you're a ponce, the girl is like a wife. They want you more or less to be like a husband to them. She gives you the money and if you're kind you buy her clothes and things and protect her. Funnily enough, this girl came from a very nice family in Croydon. We visited them, making out as if we were going steady. We spent the money on smokes, suits, juke-boxes, plenty of things. We had a flat in the Old Kent Road with a bedroom, a front room, a kitchenette. I was with the girl all the time. I used to smoke a lot; I'd spend a fiver a day on juke-boxes and cafés. (?) The girl went over West and I used to watch. If a policeman comes, you walk up and say, 'I've been waiting here for you for hours,' and he can't do a thing. Of course if he doesn't believe you and he thinks you're poncing, you can get six months.

Well, after some time I got fed up; I was bored with all this night-life and I packed it in and went back to the building. I was nineteen now and getting full rate, about £10 a week clear. Well, after a time, this other girl of mine, I made a clean breast to her and said I was sorry and she forgave me and we went steady again. She was a sales girl in a dress shop and things were going fine and one week-end I stayed with her family. Well, not long after, one day I got the sack, and so I got the hump. I went to the hairdresser with the girl and while I was waiting I got hold of the heater and turned it hot. She was screaming, but I wouldn't turn it off – dunno why – didn't think it was doing her harm, but it burnt half her hair off. I still don't know why I did it. Well, she wouldn't speak to me, so late that night I was outside the Brick and then I walked along with my mate and two other blokes to the coffee-stall at the Elephant. I thought, this is as far as I go, and was just going home when two girls came along. I said to one of the blokes: 'I bet they're on the game over the other side – they must have quite a bit of money,' and he said: 'Thinking of taking it?' Well, we got talking and bought them cups of tea, and then we said to one of the girls we'd walk her home, just to protect her. Well, just before we got to the Borough we pretended some rough fellows were coming and ran with her down an alley – just to rob her, you understand. My mate, he started kissing her, and he took her bag. The next thing one of the other blokes who was with us was practically trying to rape her. Me and my mate started to run and saw he wasn't with us and the girl was screaming. So we went back and had to pull him off her. We ran down Long Lane and went to the coffee-stall when three squad cars came up. We hadn't a chance. They pulled us into the police station where there were twelve detectives and the girl was there and the only one she remembered and recognized was me, 'cos I was wearing a tie with a girl painted on at that time. The coppers started beating one of the other two blokes and we thought we might as well tell the truth. Next day at the Borough Magistrate's Court they remanded us for a week at Brixton.

Q. Well – was that a shock?

A. I'll say it was. I may sometimes pretend I'm a big fellow, but I don't mind saying, that week I cried my eyes out. I couldn't eat any food – I had to sew mailbags – I thought I'd go potty. When we got back to Court, they dropped the charge of rape, it was just robbery with violence. It turned out the girl was a hairdresser! We said we mistook her, we thought she was a prostitute, and that helped us a bit. Anyway, the others got off with a fine but I got sent back to Brixton to see if I was suitable for Borstal training.

I used to cry a lot. After a few days I was made workshop orderly. I wrote to my girl but I didn't hear from her. I thought it was because of the row at the hairdresser, but later on she told me she'd been round to my father and he said she ought to leave me because I was a bad lot, I'd always be in prison, she'd better pack me up. I was in Brixton a whole month. I used to get down on my knees and pray I'd be let off. At the end of the month when I got back into Court they said the Probation Officer gave me a good reference and they'd give me a last chance – so I was free. My girl had a new flat down the New Kent Road and I went there, but she said it was all finished.

Q. So you were on your own again?

A. Yes, from then on I went with the Boys. I'd play dice and billiards with them, play the juke-boxes, picking up jobs. That went on till the middle of last year, when I thought all this was getting me nowhere.

The Boys? Well, our clique we could be about 100, 150. Once we went over to the East End, there were 200 of us in cars and lorries and vans; we went to fight against the Greeks and the Turkish down in the Commercial Road. It was a terrific punch-up. Only a few people got pulled in.

Ordinary way, of course, there weren't so many. Our clique, we'd meet in billiard halls, we'd play dice. For instance we might go to the Greek caff and play the juke-box, me and a few mates, and one of us might say, 'Let's go over to Camberwell and have a punch-up.' So we'd all go to a caff down that way, and one of us would say, 'Anyone here thinks he's a hard nut?' and then we'd bring out the Boys and there'd be a fight. Or else we'd try to get somebody out of a dance-hall. We used to stand and look for a bit of bother, you know, someone'd look at us cheeky and we'd get him outside.

Q. What about the fighting – how did you set about it?

A. Well, it'd start with fists like, and then somebody'd get rough. We used bottles and chains and hammers. I never got hurt, not serious, and never caught, either. Some did. There's Tommy, he's inside now, and Sid, he's been in the last six months, he had to have thirteen stitches. Or we'd try to fight the Blacks. We used to shout at them in the street 'You black bastards' to try to provoke them, to beat them up, like. Over Brixton way, we'd try to stop them getting off buses, to frighten them. We'd often go for the Blacks, we don't like them round here, we hate them. No, never met any Jewish boys, don't remember any fights with Jews. Greeks and Turks we used to beat up – smash up the caffs. The police? No, they weren't exactly afraid of us. Some, like the old Inspector bloke round here, he'd come into a caff and say 'Cut it out' and we'd go out. But the ordinary copper, well, if he was alone he'd walk past and look at us and not say anything. Of course some were brave, they'd walk straight up to us; we liked them for that. Course it all isn't what it used to be. The fighting is dying down round the Elephant; over the other side, too. The fellows are all twenty-one now, or twenty-two. There isn't a new lot yet. Couple of years' time, I think it'll be rough again.

Q. Did you yourself like fighting?

A. Ever since I was a little kid I wanted to make people be frightened of me, I was determined to make my name. That's why I liked fighting. I don't want to boast, but all that time I only lost one fight. I'm pretty strong, but you've got to have it up here, you got to be fast, it's the quickness. I'd come in and they'd think I was going to hit them and I'd butt them with my head. You got to guard against kicks. Why do we kick a bloke when he's down? Well, gives him something to remember. But don't get me wrong, I'm not crazy. All along I had the ambition to be somebody. I never had the chance to be somebody – I said to myself I couldn't be a film star or a runner – so I wanted to be somebody by being a boxer, and then when I missed the chance through that accident – well, there was fighting.

Q. What about the clothes?

A. I'd say I had six suits, cost about £20 each.

Q. Where did the Boys get all that money?

A. Ah, that'd be telling, but some made hundreds of pounds. One time I had a special suit of satin, with 14-inch drainpipes, 4 buttons, draped; I'd wear a Slim Jim and creepers. Whole outfit cost about £35. Some of the Boys used to have their hair permed. Don't see anything wrong with it. A girl wants her hair to look nice, why shouldn't a fellow? That's what gets me about ordinary people. The moment you've got your hair done up and

wear a Slim Jim, they think you're a freak, a Teddy
boy.

Q. What about your clique?

A. Our clique? They were mostly drivers, in the building,
packers, in the meat market, some of them just loafers –
you had to have money for it. But they'd always lend you
a few bob. That's what I say, they were not like ordinary
people, not snobbish. They had a lot more decency;
they'd always put you up. If they had the money they'd
share absolutely. Once a couple of buck Irishmen beat
me up and got away with a lot of money. My mates said
they'd look for them if it took a year. When you're with
the Boys they stick by you. When you're inside, they
send you things. They're pretty good, they'll come to see
if you're in Court, and they're always willing to be witnesses; they'll take the risk of bearing witness; they're
a good lot, they stick to each other.

That's why I say, it's the ordinary public that causes
the trouble. If we walk into a café they'd say: 'Sorry, we
don't want none of you in here'; they'd say we're Teddy
boys and they're afraid of trouble. And all the time
you're just perfectly normal – it makes me wild when
people stare and laugh at me. No one is going to look
at the Boys and laugh and get away with it. Don't get
me wrong; we don't take any notice of ordinary people
or old people. If they do nothing, we don't interfere. But
when a bloke gives me a look and he doesn't like the
way I dress and perhaps he says, 'Cor, what a sight,' well,
I swing at him.

I tell you: ordinary people, they're supposed to be so
high and mighty, like having a lot of money; what I'd
say is, 'You think you have everything and we Teddy
boys have nothing; you think we're simple; well, we
could have it twice as good as you if we tried!'

Q. All right – but how did you get out of it all?

A. It was this way, the middle of last year. There were
those letters and photos this girl had sent me when I was
inside. I'd left them in a room and the landlord, he was

an Irish fellow, he didn't want to give them to me. He said I should go to the police, he knew nothing. I went to the police, but they said they could do nothing about it. It made me wild, because I tell you, I worshipped that girl. So I went to the Irishman and I kicked his door open. We had a fight, me and him and his wife, she was screaming. I hit him with a chair and kicked him and I went on smashing the furniture. A few days later they picked me up on a charge of G.B.H. – you know, Grievous Bodily Harm – they said I broke the Irishman's arm. Well, I was on three years' probation so it looked bad, but the Irish fellow, the police knew he was queer, and that helped me. They said I'd made a lot of progress; the Magistrate said I was lucky not to be going for five years, but he'd give me a final chance, and I got a £10 fine. But I'd had a fright. I told the probation officer I wanted somewhere to live that was different, like when I was at home, and he told me to come here to the old Reverend's House. There was four of us young fellows staying there, it was like a family; I was there six months. I'd say it's through that I learned there's more in life than just hooliganism. I got a job now, in a warehouse. I went back for a bit to my parents, but I wouldn't stay. They wanted me to dress different, not to wear tight trousers. I worked hard in the warehouse, but they didn't think I'd changed, they wanted me to be in by eleven every night, so I packed it in.

I've got a room now, but I still come here to the Reverend's once a week, and things are different. I've met a girl, I'm going with her now, going steady. She's a decent girl. I want to get married next year. In the warehouse it's hard work; I make about ten pounds a week, take home clear. I wouldn't say I don't go out with the Boys now and then, but not much. I want to do something better. What I want to say is this: I'm older now, I want to have a sense of responsibility, I want someone I can love and look after and make a home. It's funny, this girl, she lives at Peckham and several times when I've

37

missed the last bus I've walked home to the Borough. I like walking at night. I had that Swiss watch then and for something to do I used to time myself – see how fast I could make it from her home to mine.

So far, society had not made Ron's uncertain uphill struggle easy for him.

CHAPTER 3

Fashion and Revolt

A new starting-point

THE young man interviewed in the previous chapter could be described as a fairly typical Teddy boy. The more I thought about the confused ideas filling his mind and those of similar youths I talked to, the more it seemed to me that the Teddy-boy movement could be seen as throwing light on two developments in English social life of the fifties. The first was the struggle of the bottom layer of young unskilled workers for social emancipation, for a place which should be their own by right within the new classless mass culture. The second development was the growth of a new type of violence which seemed to be associated with this drive.

To start with the positive side. If the Teddy-boy movement is looked on in this way as a symptom of proletarian rebellion, a piece of defiant flag-flying, then it is interesting to note that the actual post-war Edwardian fashion was from the start a symbol of revolt, but on two extremely separate social levels.

The full Edwardian fashion actually started in Mayfair. It was said to have been launched from Savile Row soon after the war as an answer to American styles. For the young exquisites-about-town, who first and briefly took it up, its extravagance was also like a gesture against the war that was past, against mass culture, the Labour Government, the notion of England's decline. In its exaggerated form (curled bowlers worn over long hair, long Edwardian coats, ultra-tight trousers) the style was also short lived, vanishing from Mayfair as it reached suburbia.

Meanwhile, however, the fashion had utterly unexpectedly been transported across the Thames, to the tough and swarming working-class riverside areas around the

Elephant, Southwark, and Vauxhall, and this was quite an event – a symbol of social revolt on another level, though at first not recognized as such.

To the public eye, the new thorough-going proletarian Teddy boys, standing about at the Elephant in their full regalia, looked at first like music-hall caricatures – and at the same time somewhat ominous. From all accounts, these first pioneers were certainly 'a pretty rough lot'. In terms of age-groups, they still had their links with the older cloth-capped gangs which in earlier periods had dominated areas like the Elephant, keeping the police on the run and razors in their pockets. A social worker from the Elephant area told me, 'As I recall it, the local Teddy-boy fashion in its first bloom had few law-abiding members. It was definitely the submerged tenth who popularized the new clothes. They were the groups who were not respectable, not socially acceptable.' A young man who was briefly in one of the earliest gangs described its members as almost entirely un-skilled workers or just drifters. 'They were market porters, roadworkers, a lot of van boys, all in jobs that didn't offer much – labourers could cover the lot.' Some of them were out of work but had their own methods of keeping up. 'They just went in for thieving. Many of the Teds thought nothing of it: they call it having a bit of business. I remember how they'd always try to bring in words they didn't know the meaning of, like calling somebody they didn't like "bom-bastic".'

Not very promising material from which to start a new 'Movement', yet this is precisely what the first few hundred Teddy boys from south of the Thames achieved. Through similar gangs which soon spread elsewhere in London, they created a subculture whose mark was certainly its utter unexpectedness. There was the dressing-up which among the first Teds seemed simply weird. For one thing, they were still proletarians: their faces did not go with the dandified clothes; they had not yet the smooth look of the later generation of English working-class boys accustomed to money. For another thing, as determined innovators, the first Teddy boys carried the eccentricity of their garb to an extreme which had an effect of masquerade.

Was it, as it seemed, un-English? The influences were mixed. In hair-styles they derived plainly from America and the films. The most common consisted of aggressive sideboards, with masses of hair at the back and a fuzzy shock of it above the brow. Other styles favoured were the jutting Tony Curtis, the Boston, the fiercely shaved Mohican. These fancy hair-styles, involving appointments with special barbers and expensive to come by and maintain, were to their wearers clearly symbols of masculinity. Among the clothes the jacket of the suit, long and fully draped with flaps and velvet collar, came nearest to true 'Edwardian'. With it went knitted ties, plain or flowery waistcoats, tight-fitting trousers or 'strides', and – incongruously at first – blunt shoes with enormous crêpe soles. The whole theatrical outfit might cost upwards of £20: considerably less than such smart clothes cost a few years later, but in this first phase, when cash and credit were not so easy to come by, an unprecedented sum for a low-paid young manual worker to spend on himself.

Given the ingrown conservatism of English working-class life and its hostility towards any dandyism or hint of effeminacy it must have taken special determination for the first Teddy boys of south London to swagger along their drab streets in their exaggerated costume. What lay behind their impulse? The rest of the charade gave the clue to this act of self-assertion. For with the clothes went a special Teddy-boy manner – dead-pan facial expressions which delighted caricaturists, and an apparent lassitude of bearing which seemed a cover for the tensions among the gang. It was a point of honour for Teddy boys to be more interested in themselves than in girls. In dance-halls – this was before the arrival of rock-'n'-roll – they did not deign to dance, or only in a condescending manner. This lassitude was, of course, only a surface affectation. If girls were scorned as real companions, they were very much in the Teddy boys' minds as objects and as prey. In fact, one could say that this whole dressing up in groups by young unskilled wage-earners was only a means of furthering the usual aim of such young men – the nightly prowl for girls. And, just as the sartorial fashion was like a romantically stylized assertion of being important, 'being somebody', so the primitive romanticism which inspired the clothes was applied to the night-life, too. The result was the organization of Teddy boys in gangs, some quite large, to defend territories defined as 'theirs'; or, when the mood came, to raid those of other gangs for girls. In this way the police and public around 1953 and 1954 first became aware of a new type of Teddy-boy disorder in the late night hours. This disorder was also formalized, rather like a ragged fantasy of warfare. A bus conductor told me that in a certain public house at the end of his run, which was something of a frontier post, he could on Saturday nights see huddled groups from different gangs watching each other like cats, or in the words of the old song 'Tread on the tail of my coat'.

In fact, before long the Teddy boys seemed to have created a little world of their own: a subculture with its own laws of dress, behaviour, and territory, in which they strutted about, looked challengingly at outsiders, chased girls, occasionally fought each other, and planned the occasional larceny. There were perhaps a few thousand of them in inner London, and in its peculiarly organized form the cult went on for a few years. On the whole, it was a primitive performance. The early Teddy boys were working-class youths with an itch to assert themselves against society – this was the new element – but since their little 'anti-society' did not help them to get on, it remained in this respect unreal. There might be some satisfaction in the obsessive banding together, in wreaking violent vengeance against anyone who disparaged the uniform, in the occasional large-scale fights, in baiting the police and being in on the knowledge of local crime: but since all this did not help the individual Teddy boys to get anywhere as adolescence passed, most of them, in fact, led a dreary life. A young man who had belonged to one of these first gangs in East London until he went for his national service into the Navy gave me the following picture of its life, put down here from my notes in the form of question and answer.

Q. Where did they hang out?

A. They used to collect at Arcades or in a caff.

The pictures, too. They were always going there. In the afternoons they'd bump their way in without paying; evenings too, and Sundays. Then they'd go back to a café and sit there till closing time.

Q. What did they do with their time?

A. Sometimes they picked up girls. There was a place they used to call the 'kitchen'. Five or six fellas would go in and watch each other perform. The girls? They were just about the lowest, the scrapings.

Some Friday or Saturday night, perhaps, they'd get into a car – there was always a car – and go down West.

In the cafés there was always talk about what they'd call 'business'. Everybody'd know; I used to, myself. It didn't pay to miss anything because you had got to be topical in conversation ... it was like a message going through everything. The fellows would know all about the fighting; it was a sort of broadcast: there might be a fight, so all meet at the so and so place, because you'd want to go in with a nice team.

The fighting? They didn't carry knives much: it was usually lumps of wood or bottles.

Girls? There never were any girls in the gangs. Fellows had girls, but they didn't mix ... they didn't mix fighting and girls.

Q. Otherwise ...

A. It was sport, mostly. Some fellows went in for boxing and weightlifting and swimming ... a bit of football would creep into it. The fellows would play in their suits every Wednesday in the park. ... It'd be without a referee, about fifteen a side, pretty rough.

They used to make jokes. When a mob got on a bus, they'd play the conductor up. They'd all say someone else was paying. One time I saw about forty fellows all flag a taxi, then everybody'd say it was somebody else.

Q. And what happened to these original Teds?

A. Some were put away. Borstal, quite a lot went to. What happened to most of the others was exactly what happened to ordinary people in ordinary life – mixing with the opposite sex and sooner or later they'd go steady and they'd end up pushing a pram. When I got back from the Navy I found the top men married and settled down, to my amazement. Fresh fighters had taken over, but I though they were not as tough as the old 'uns – they'd been a rough mob. . . .

Viewed in cold retrospect, the story sounds dismal. Most of the early Teddy-boy groups probably led much the same unconstructive life. Driven on by boredom, by the need for spending money or just by anger against society, a good many of them landed up in the dock and went on to Borstal or prison. Others vanished vaguely into adult life, and that was the end.

Winds of change

It was easy enough to scoff at the whole performance, as most people did, yet in view of what has subsequently happened in English society it is now possible to see it was more than a joke – that the early Teds were on to something, early figures in a process of far-reaching social change. The way in which these working-class youths maintained their stylized dress and gang-life for several years, regardless of what society thought or the jeers they encountered, showed that the winds of change were blowing not only through Africa but through the English slums. The very fact that the early Teds came from the 'submerged tenth' was significant: it showed that in the new post-war English generation even unskilled young workers were no longer ready to be excluded from society and what were deemed its pleasures.

For the chief point about the Teddy-boy cult was that it

went on: the dandyism it had brought into working-class life remained there. True, the sartorial fashion itself changed. Step by step, through various deviations, the clothes and haircuts grew less eccentric and extreme, until at the end of the fifties they had become unified in the rather attractive 'Italian style', which had become normal walking-out wear for the working-class boy; and by 1960 this had blended with 'conservative cool', or just very ordinary but well-cut clothes.

By this time, it is true, the strange pioneers, the original Teddy boys, had long been superseded. Their gangs had broken up, the very term 'Ted' had become one of derision, denoting ill-mannered behaviour. Yet it was also possible to see what the movement they started off had finally achieved. Towards the end of the fifties one could say that for the first time English working-class youths had in their great majority become meticulous about their persons and highly fashion-conscious. This dandyism, moreover, was not one in which they imitated their middle-class betters. Quite the contrary, it was rather more in line with what was worn by young people on the Continent. Other barriers, too, were being lowered. English working-class youths had also broken away from the old shirtsleeves or Sunday best into the week-end informality of jeans and sports clothes. Altogether, this added up to quite a revolution, illustrating the new affluence of working-class life, and it is interesting to see how far this social revolution went down the rigid English class-scale. My young informant from east London, who as a teenager had been among the early Teddy boys, found when he came out of the Navy at the end of the fifties that his area was still a tough working-class 'manor', yet the whole atmosphere had subtly changed.

The gangs were definitely smaller. For one thing the pin-table Arcades where the fellows used to hang out had mostly disappeared. And a good thing, too. They had been depressing places, dirty and moribund.

The fellows in the gangs were different, too. Where early on it had only been about two out of ten, now five out of ten of all boys were dress-conscious. I noticed flick knives had come in much more, but I still think most of the fellows carried them only out of bravado. Mostly they happened to know someone who knew how to use a knife genuinely, who'd got a name for it, so all the others would back him up.

The big change was, the average fellow had more money – you had to have more money now to be in the swim. Things cost more but there was a lot more cash about. For one thing, all the chief gangs now had fellows with cars and motor-bikes. The special motor-bike mob who wore black leather jackets thought of themselves as the top lot; they met by themselves in their own pub. In general, the fellows now met not only in cafés but in dance-halls and saloon bars, and the older ones had started drinking again. You could go to all kinds of clubs – that was new, too – and there were lots of parties. Some of the fellows had record players and you'd have a party going on all Sunday, with fellows and girls and drink and dozens of records.

That is, even in the dead-end districts of London, there had been radical social change. Boys and youths working in unskilled jobs were no longer loutish but searching to take part in ordinary mid-twentieth-century city life. This was the positive side of the social revolt whose flag had been raised by the Teddy boys half a dozen years earlier. But, as some of the accounts I have quoted above show, the movement had also gone round strange corners to produce other results denoting not progress but regression.

CHAPTER 4

The Destructive Element

The cult of violence

THERE were also some very obviously unpleasant sides to the Teddy-boy movement. From the start, it was mixed up with a rather ugly streak of violence and a general hostility towards society which often overlapped with actual criminality.

Perhaps this was also not immediately recognized. However, as the gangs of Teddy boys spread outwards to the London suburbs, this unpleasant side of the phenomenon impressed itself fairly forcibly on the public mind.

There were a number of reports of Teddy boys causing wanton damage to cafés. Incidents occurred where pedestrians were terrorized in the streets. Frequently, youths not belonging to a gang were fiercely beaten-up; the typical Teddy-boy assault seemed to be in odds of five or six against one. At the same time the police authorities in certain areas became aware of a marked increase in thefts and burglaries and the evidence indicated that some of these operations at least were being planned in the cafés and other hangouts where the Teddy boys gathered.

In fact, in certain Teddy-boy circles, complete disregard for the law seemed to have become an accepted feature of a new sub-culture. This statement needs qualification. The majority of the youths who, on leaving school, bought the Teddy-boy uniform and tried to become junior members of a gang, were not delinquents and had probably no intention of engaging in more than a spot of brawling and collective bravado. But because the original Teddy boys had come from the submerged tenth, there was an overlap between their movement and the criminal world. As the police saw it, in each large Teddy-boy gang, in each regularly frequented café, there were usually some hardened young characters with police and prison records to be found, and there was also something in the whole atmosphere of deliberate defiance cultivated by the Teddy-boy movement which made it easier for this minority to establish their authority.

The extent to which the Teddy-boy groups were mixed up with criminality probably varied greatly with the district. A probation officer in the north London area who had witnessed the arrival of the very first Teddy-boy gangs in his district and later saw quite a few of their members in the dock and among his clientele, told me that he had recognized them from the start as a danger which ought to be stamped out, or at any rate stamped on. The danger of the movement, in his view, was that it brought together two distinct anti-social attitudes. The first was simply that of the usual adolescent rebellion, although he thought the Teddy boys represented a new concentration of lads whose antagonism against teachers, employers, and the State was quite abnormally tense. However, the second attitude which the Teddy boys had also made their own was the outlook of the typical criminal area where lawbreaking was part of ordinary life and the police were always the enemy. By associating the spirit of adolescent rebellion with criminal traditions, by giving it the glamour of a special uniform and gang life, the Teddy boys were in fact spreading this criminal area outlook far beyond its usual confines, and therein lay the danger. Young boys in his district had joined the gangs simply because they appeared romantic. The collective cynicism and the uniform offered psychological security and status. It seemed daring and exciting to sit in a café where the conversation amongst older youths ran on who was a good man with a knife and how much the boys had got away with in the latest case of breaking and entering. But before long one youngster after another appeared in Court, sometimes on charges which resulted in their being sent away, and many of these were boys who, but for the attraction of the Teddy-boy fashion, might never have joined such company. In fact, said this probation officer, the connexion between the spread of Teddy-boy culture and that of criminality seemed to him pretty direct, at least in the sector of London he knew. As soon as the large gangs had staked out their territories, his case load began to lengthen and so did the number of local lads sent off to Borstal and detention centres. Some lads were in this way started off on criminal careers for which they had not been by temperament predestined: they had simply been sucked towards crime by this sinister fashion and not been clever in getting away with it.

Since the first Teddy boys were drawn largely from the more lawless areas of London, this overlap with criminality was in a way explicable. Rather more surprising was the additional neurotic streak in the cult of violence. There was a peculiar, nasty viciousness in Teddy-boy assaults – a blend of gangster methods and of a touchiness towards imagined insult which seemed to denote a basic insecurity. The movement also presented another puzzle. One could see why this swaggering gang life had its attraction for certain particularly unstable types of youths. Yet why should the number of such youths have suddenly increased so much?

One explanation put forward by many social workers was that these adolescents of the early fifties belonged to a generation which had suffered unduly from childhood disturbance during the war, and so threw up an unusually large proportion of psychologically disturbed boys and girls.

How much weight to give to this theory is not easy to say, but it would also explain some other features of the Teddy-boy cult. For instance, it could be argued that the combination of obsessive violence and obsessive interest in personal adornment betrayed not only a social but a sexual unsureness among the gang members in general. It was certainly the case that in the inner Teddy-boy circles homosexuality was regarded as one of the ubiquitous facts of life. A shrewd Irish observer, who had knocked around with the London Teddy boys for some years, gave me his view that if one picked any hundred of them, especially from those who had been to prison, seventy-five would have had some homosexual experience, some of them, as he said, 'just for cash, some out of curiosity, the majority out of sheer boredom'. This ambivalence would not necessarily be in contradiction with the main aim of the majority of gang members, the monotonous nightly prowl for girls (if necessary, prostitutes would do). It could also be argued that this deadly promiscuity also showed a continuous need to demonstrate a masculinity which was felt to be threatened without such demonstration.

A similar interpretation of a sexual twist in the make-up of Teddy boys could be ascribed to their excessive interest in their own and each other's clothes and hair-styles, such as the habit of the early Teddy boys of having their hair permanently waved. The interesting stock answer given by Teddy boy dandies to inquiring journalists about this usually was: 'If the girls do it and make themselves look nice, why shouldn't we?' My Irish informant was sure that this revealed a basic effeminacy and nothing else:

If you look into the motive you will find it was largely jealousy – jealousy of the girls for being the centre of attention. They just couldn't stand not having it all to themselves. If you had listened to these Teds as I did when they stood about in dance-halls, all you would hear about was clothes and style. One would say: 'I paid seventeen guineas for this suit at so-and-so's,' and the other, 'I paid this new Jew tailor nineteen guineas for mine.' They could talk literally for hours about styles and cut and prices, the way you usually only hear women talk. But even if they all weren't effeminate, though I know some of them were, the main thing with these Teds was that they had to outshine the way the girls were dressed by the way they themselves were dressed. The Teddy boy himself was always the person who had to stand out.

Perhaps the notion that the Teddy-boy movement was a belated result of wartime disturbance does throw some light on its character. If it is accepted that many of the Teddy boys were disturbed adolescents who were always impelled to prove their manhood, then to them their violence was not senseless. As they felt about it, such a thing as a disparaging remark about their appearance, even if only made jokingly, was not trivial but an attack upon their very *raison d'être*, upon their insecure manhood, and to be reacted to as such.

But if the notion that the flare-up of violence in the early fifties was the expression of a particularly disturbed generation, a delayed effect of the war, makes some sense, it still remains only a partial explanation. It does not explain why this type of violent reaction should have perpetuated itself among successive further generations of adolescents, so that it had become simply part of the social climate at the end of the nineteen-fifties. In this perpetuation some other factors were surely at work which will be discussed in subsequent chapters. At this point it may be enough to say that the tradition which the Teddy boys bequeathed to their adolescent successors was that group violence could be part of ordinary street life; and that by a special new subcultural code it was in order for them to take the law into their own hands. If a certain youth was objectionable to a gang, it was both possible and the expected thing to ambush him and teach him a lesson, and, if cleverly organized, this could be done almost with impunity. Even after the original large gangs had disintegrated and the nervous tension which had been part of the original Teddy-boy life had quietened down, the tradition of reacting violently to an alleged insult survived, as illustrated for instance by the following report (with names omitted) of a case of assault in a Thames-side suburb, a favourite gathering place of the second and third generation of Teddy boys.

A gang of Teddy boys flung a man through a quarter-inch thick plate-glass window of a shop in X High Street during the night, after attacking him and beating him almost unconscious. The man, Mr B., aged thirty-eight, was taken by ambulance to hospital where stitches had to be inserted in wounds in his head, right leg, and back. Mr B. was on his way home after a darts' match. He had just left a friend's car in the High Street when the gang stopped him. This is how he described the attack:
'The Teddy boys were shouting and pushing each other. I

went to walk past them when one of them asked me if I was swearing at them. I told him, "I've not said anything to you, cocky", meaning "cock" in a friendly manner. He said to me: "Call me mate, not cocky", and then took a vicious lunge at me. The whole gang then jumped at me and I went through the window. I must have been almost unconscious. I can only just remember crawling out of the window and then being kicked.'

Mr B.'s friends in the car and two other men saw the attack. They ran to help Mr B., but the gang had scattered before they reached him.

After which, if any of the high-spirited youths were identified or arrested, they ran the risk of sentences ranging from conditional discharge to being sent to Borstal or a detention centre. Only rarely were prison sentences imposed, for the authorities had the good sense to know that few consequences would be more dangerous than to expose such disturbed youths to the company of seasoned criminals. It was more reasonable to hope that they would within a few years grow out of this adolescent gang life, either through the break of military service or in some other way, and get married and settle down as ordinary citizens, which indeed mostly happened – but not always, and this was the important point.

It was in 1954 or thereabouts that the authorities noted that the tide had changed and that the figures of juvenile crime, which for some years had been subsiding from the post-war peak, were again taking a sudden sharp upward turn. More than that, the Teddy-boy movement was unmistakably linked with this rise.

In the popular Press, enough reports of such violence were coming in to add up to a general new heading of 'Teddy-boy stories'. In London, traditional trouble-spot areas in the East End, around the Caledonian Road, the Old Kent Road, and Wandsworth Road, were becoming the scene of night-time fights and disturbances in which quite regularly large mobs of rowdy youths were involved. Impromptu weapons were used, stabbings occurred, and as a rule police squads had to be rushed to the spots to break up fights – their arrival was usually the signal for the participants to scatter. Enterprising reporters managed to ferret out that some of these disturbances had been Teddy-boy gangfights on a territorial basis of one area against the other, and produced stories of how Teddy-boy gangs up to a hundred strong had been mobilized for a 'punch-up' involving coshes, bottles, and knives; mostly it was only the threat of knives, but in some wilder clashes they were actually flashed and used.

Nor did the gangs only fight each other. Cafés were damaged in actions of revenge against their proprietors, especially against Cypriots. For a certain period, bus conductors on late-night routes were molested, and in one or two cases beaten up and left badly injured by Teddy boys who vanished into the night. Another disturbing trend was the violent hostility of Teddy boys against certain youth clubs, which became the target for recurring raids and vandalism. Because of running disturbances, well-established institutions were forced to make new regulations barring youths in Teddy-boy clothing. Some smaller clubs had to be temporarily shut down. Club leaders, in interviews, confessed themselves at a loss how to cope.

The Teddy-boy movement was also spreading outwards from the centre of London. Dressed-up youths who congregated at week-ends in large gangs were creating new trouble spots in outer suburbs like Kingston, Croydon, Barking, and Finchley. Other centres of congregation were open spaces like Blackheath and Clapham Common. Gangs also made a nuisance of themselves on the Saturday-night trains to Brighton and Southend. Similar reports came from the provinces. Among cities which became centres of Teddy-boy life were Birmingham, Nottingham, Liverpool, and Bristol. Another development was that the movement appeared to be attracting boys at a younger age. Schoolmasters in secondary-modern schools in London working-class areas complained that some of their boys were losing interest in school life at the age of thirteen and fourteen, because their minds were already stuffed with wild tales about the doings of Teddy boys in their district, the romantic café life, the tooling up, and the battles, and their whole attention was already fixed on the acquisiton of suitable outfits for themselves and the day when they might join as cadet members of the gangs. In fact, the impression which a foreign correspondent in London might have got from his reading of the British Press in, say, 1955–6, was that the Teddy boys and their violence were already a small but significant and alarming part of English life.

Seeing the problem in scale

This was probably seeing the problem in false scale. England was, and remains, a relatively law-abiding country. Even at the peak of the movement the number of Teddy boys in the Greater London area did not exceed a top figure of 30,000 (some observers thought it only half or a third of this figure), and most of these spent probably most of their time in boredom rather than activity. Nevertheless, the net result of their arrival was that lawlessness was going up. In spite of the change from unemployment to Welfare State, Britain was more lawless in 1955 than in 1935, and above all among juveniles and young adults this lawlessness showed some definite new features.

It was becoming clear that, within not more than two or three years, the primitive gang life of the 'submerged tenth' had under the impact of the Teddy-boy movement become more organized and sophisticated. The street corner was going out and superseded by the café as the centre of the new 'anti' groups. Secondly, the Teddy-boy fashions undoubtedly gave these groups an added cohesion. Some social workers saw this very early on as a new danger.

A third difference between this juvenile crime-wave and preceding ones was that the 1950s ushered in the new age of mass publicity. The Teddy boys were therefore not only news in the Press, on television and radio, but they *knew* that they were news. Many social workers felt this was one of their main troubles. An example was the publicity given to the wave of rock-'n'-roll riots in British cinemas in 1955. These began at the Trocadero Cinema at the Elephant, where a mob of young people broke up a performance of a rock-'n'-roll film featuring Bill Haley and his Comets. To the accompaniment of delirious yells and shouts, seats were torn out, attendants molested, and the performance brought to an end. A social worker from the area told me that after these first riots at the Elephant he was not surprised to see them repeated elsewhere. Anyone could see that the excitement and sense of destruction were fed by publicity. The gangs felt that such behaviour was almost expected of them.

You had the feeling that they had read all about themselves in the papers – actually, quite a few of my boys had already had personal contact with the Press, and one could see that they were affected: they began to behave more defiantly, to show off, to be 'big-heads', to become what they thought the public wanted them to be – cosh boys, Teddy boys. It was as if they were being sucked into violence by something bigger than themselves.

In other words, Press publicity itself sharpened the lines of conflict between society and Teddy boys. The cinema riots, which were repeated in a number of forms, were in themselves no profound event. Another incident, however, which illustrated to the public how far these fantasies of a spurious youthful gangster life had spread in England, was the so-called Clapham Common murder case of 1954.

This took place on Clapham Common, on a peaceful summer evening, at a spot where a band was playing. The audience sat listening on park chairs while some young people were dancing on the concrete. Lounging on the seats were a seventeen-year-old youth called Beckley and three of his friends, who sat smoking with their feet up on other chairs. Because of this they became involved in an altercation with another boy, only sixteen, but already the leader of a gang with an unpleasant reputation in the neighbourhood. Seeing this whole gang converging on them in force, Beckley and his friends tried to get away, but the gang closed in. The astonished bystanders on Clapham Common were witnesses of a silent and desperate struggle in which flick-knives were flashed and two boys held Beckley on the ground while a third kicked his head. Next, dirty and bleeding, Beckley and one companion were running across the grass for their lives, with their enemies streaming in pursuit. At the edge of the Common, the fugitives jumped on to a bus, but as the bus stopped the gang surged forward. Beckley, his friend, and the conductor were dragged off. Before the passengers could intervene, Beckley lay stabbed to death on the pavement, his companion was badly wounded, and the assailants had scattered to the winds.

It was of course not long before they were picked up and the ringleaders stood trial at the Old Bailey. The nineteen-year-old who had wielded the fatal knife, and now stood white-faced in the dock, was sentenced to death, and then reprieved, while four other youths went to prison for common assault.

A fight on the Common – such a spot of trouble could easily occur whenever boys and girls were congregated. However, the new traits illustrated by the incident, and not easy to explain, were the neurotic concentration on points of gang insult, the complete disregard of surroundings and bystanders, and the deadly use of knives, all part of the gang-life fantasy in the minds of these youngsters.

The public reaction

While at first they had been treated as a joke or curiosity, a new and understandable development of the late fifties was a sharp public reaction against the Teddy boys and their aura of violence. In the worst-affected areas they were barred from cafés, cinemas, and certain public-houses. Dance-halls imposed rigid rules about dress and behaviour permitted on the floor. In some parts of the country the legal authorities also reacted forcibly. A probation officer from a Midland town told me that it was in 1956-7 that he and his colleagues felt suddenly that they were up against something new in juvenile lawlessness. With the spread of Teddy-boy cafés and 'big ideas' imported from London, they felt they were moving towards the sort of situation which existed in some

American cities, where the juvenile gang leader held the field as a successful opposite number to the probation officer. This development demanded countermeasures before it got out of hand. My informant put it something like this:

We had to show both the leaders and their followers that crime was not an automatic passport to probation, and so we recommended that certain characters we had had our eye on should at the first chance be packed straight off to Borstal, even without previous convictions against them. This not only gave a sharp shock to the young gentlemen themselves, but it also had the salutary effect of stunning everybody else in the gangs and so giving us in the probation service the necessary breathing space to get on with our individual case work. These sentences were quite a departure, but we felt it was the only way. The thing we had to do was to strike sufficiently quickly, to get at the cynical, anti-authority, couldn't-care-less elements whose motto was 'What have I got to lose?'; to sort these out and hit them in a way to demonstrate that they had plenty to lose.

At the same time, as far as the general public was concerned, the causes of the whole phenomenon seemed to remain inexplicable; wasn't incomparably more being done for the education and welfare of young people than ever before? It was not surprising that the late fifties also saw the start of that inconclusive public debate about the morals of the young generation, which is still in progress. On the one hand, some fairly strong charges were made against the young, and by implication against their teachers, and repeated from Westminster, from the Bench, and in editorial columns. The attacks were apt to be rather sweeping, singling out not only the Teddy boys but the generally obnoxious way of dress and behaviour of a large section of youth. Blame for these shortcomings was laid on lack of parental authority, on too much easy money, on pampering by the Welfare State, the general decline in morals, and so forth. On the other hand, it was noticeable that almost all teachers and social workers in actual touch with the young strongly rejected these general charges against youth as ill-informed and prejudiced. After all, what were the many-coloured clothes but a challenge cocked at a dull and materialist society? One of the most experienced youth workers in Britain, Dr Josephine Macalister Brew, protested in her book *Youth and Youth Groups* against what she considered an unprecedented degree of ignorant prejudice against the whole young generation, based on exaggerated reports of isolated incidents:

> Young people have never been under more heavy fire; their manners, their spending habits, their love of modern dancing and modern music, have all been the subject of abuse, and for the first time in the history of this country a section of the community has not been able to dress as it pleased without virulent attacks and suspicion. In spite of the fact that the *rise in delinquency consequent on the war years has been halted*, the relatively few cases of unquestionably violent gang behaviour have been magnified out of all proportion to their incidence.[1]

The italics in the above quotation are mine. It was very natural to make this misjudgement. Without the slightest doubt, the general social and educational standards of British youth were rising year by year. The parallel phenomenon of rising lawlessness and violence followed a little later in the fifties, but was unfortunately equally real. Far from being halted, the upward trend in the juvenile-crime rate persisted steadily. In 1955, the total of those found guilty of indictable offences in the male seventeen to twenty-one age-group in England and Wales numbered 11,269. In 1956 they were 13,425; in 1957, 16,962; in 1958, 21,322, and at this figure stood at well over double the 1938 total. The number of youths in this age-group convicted for violence against the person showed an equal rise from 745 in 1954 to 1,595 in 1957, and 2,051 in 1958 (in 1938 the figure of such convictions had stood at 147).

By 1958 this new development was also apparent to the legal authorities. For example, in London and the Home Counties one magistrate after the other made comment on the fact that the criminal minority among young people had

1. J. Macalister Brew, *Youth and Youth Groups*, Faber & Faber, 1957.

become noticeably both larger and more criminal. Noting that crime in Berkshire had in the course of two years gone up by a third, the Chief Constable of that rural county said (9 April 1958) that the average age of those responsible for burglary and other breaking-in offences was under twenty. At Wokingham, the Chairman of the Magistrates said (19 March 1958):

I have no hesitation in, saying that the children of this part of the country are guilty of more serious crimes than the adults. The juvenile crimes I have had to judge are more like a calendar at the Old Bailey.

As Chairman of Quarter Sessions in neighbouring Bucks, Lord Birkett said (15 April 1958):

There are thirty-six prisoners and of these there are no less than twenty-two who are twenty-one and under: among these, one is nineteen, two are eighteen, seven are seventeen, and five are only sixteen. Everyone reviews such a state of affairs with a profound taste of dissatisfaction, in these days when so much is done for the care and protection of the young.

The Chairman of Middlesex Quarter Sessions, Sir Ewan Montague, Q.C., said a few days later (24 April) that the proportion of young offenders who had just come before him was quite appalling: of eighty-nine cases of dishonesty on the calendar no fewer than forty-four of the defendants – or one half – were under twenty. One youth had the almost inconceivable record of eleven previous convictions at the age of twenty, a second, six previous convictions at eighteen, and a third already four at sixteen years.

The third wave

If these absolute figures were not really so large, they were all the same unmistakably indicative. What they showed, when broken down, was that among a fairly large minority of youths, criminality was quite steadily becoming not less but more widespread. In 1953–5 this minority had been dominated by the very large gangs of Teddy boys with their heads stuffed with romantic notions about dressing up and gang loyalties. In the later fifties this was much less the case, but the rise in juvenile lawlessness had not been halted. Quite the contrary. A perceptive observer, the Rev. Douglas Griffiths. who directed a youth club in a particularly 'difficult' area of Lambeth, described what he saw in fifteen post-war years as follows. During this period he had seen three separate 'waves' of adolescents organized in gangs in the dead-end areas of London. The first had been that of the old cloth-cap gangs of tough razor boys in the years immediately after the war. Next came the Teddy boys, washed and spruced up, strangely and expensively dressed, moving about in large gangs, lawless and dangerous in their way, yet driven on by recognizable social urges and ambitions.

By 1955-6, however, the height of the Teddy-boy cult was passed, certainly in London. The very word 'Teddy boy' had become a term of derision. 'Teds', 'a mob of Teds' was the more common description. The next, or third wave of adolescents who now took over were certainly more sophisticated. They went about in much smaller, more purposeful gangs; their special clothes in the Italian style were not particularly formalized; but among those who tended towards criminality the lack of any standards or restraints had become, if anything, even more marked.

In Mr Griffiths's view, this deterioration was in a paradoxical way even linked with the break-up of the original Teddy-boy fashion of distinctive clothes and very large gangs.

The Teddy boys in their early large gangs, at the height of the vogue, had had a fierce sense of being an outcast community. They cultivated this sense, they depended on it, their revolt had its *esprit de corps* and went with rigid loyalties of members towards each other. However, when large numbers of boys took up the fashion, so that it was no longer easy to tell who was 'a true Teddy boy' and who was not, the Teddy boys themselves were no longer a community 'which stood up against society in loneliness'. As the wearers of the garb became more numerous, the original gang spirit and cohesion was lost, and the large groups broke up into smaller groups linked by definite aims.

According to Mr Griffiths, this had its negative results. The anti-social attitude cultivated by the Teddy boys remained; what was lost was the sense of outcast pride and fair play that had existed alongside. As Mr Griffiths saw them, many of the members of the new and smaller gangs which now appeared

lived in a social situation in which conscience or ethics played no reasonable part. They had therefore even less inhibitions against violence to overcome. While some of the Teddy boys I knew had often been notable for tenderness towards children and gentleness towards old people, their successors in the smaller gangs showed no such saving grace.

According to Mr Griffiths, this total lack of standards was the context in which one should, for instance, see the increasing tendency of young gangsters to attack and rob women and old people. True, the actual perpetrators of these crimes were few in number; but they expressed the steady further coarsening of the spirit in certain areas of London which, Mr Griffiths felt, was a feature of the years from 1956 to 1960.

At this point, one can perhaps draw a rough balance sheet between the opposed features of the Teddy-boy movement. On the positive side, the Teds could be seen as forerunners of a larger movement for the sartorial and social emancipation of working-class youth, in which they were soon left far behind. On the negative side, they had introduced an element of violent lawlessness to which in their own lives they tried to give romantic formal rules. With their decline, these limitations dropped away, but the general heritage of violence remained.

A political event

Several occurrences in the second half of 1958 were to bring dramatic proof of this. The most sensational were the notorious Notting Hill riots in which West Indians and other coloured immigrants were attacked by mobs for four days and nights. Scores of people were arrested, and the riots became a political event in Commonwealth affairs.

Race relations in Britain are another story in itself, and the Notting Hill riots were well documented in the Press, but there are two points about them still worth noting. The disturbances were kept going for so long because, upon hearing the news, gangs of youths armed with knives, chains, and the like, converged from all over London into Notting Hill, where they fought coloured men and the police with equal frenzy. The second point was that the riots were started by nine very ordinary working-class boys, six of them only seventeen, with previously blameless records. Yet upon hearing of previous race riots in Nottingham, the nine armed themselves with coshes and iron bars and, as if in a dream, they began to walk through the streets of Notting Hill and savagely attacked any coloured pedestrians they met, beating them to the ground.

In passing heavy prison sentences upon them at the Old Bailey, Mr Justice Salmon spoke of the nation's horror and disgust at their action and went on with his famous statement:

Everyone, irrespective of the colour of their skins, is entitled to walk through our streets with their heads erect and free from fear. That is a right which these Courts will always unfailingly uphold.

These were ringing words which did much to restore British credit abroad. The heavy sentences also proved a deterrent against further open racial assaults. Yet, after Notting Hill, something in English life was not quite the same again. The question remained unanswered of what had prompted nine ordinary London adolescents to engage in such sudden brutality. Ignorant race hatred seemed only one factor involved. Another was clearly the spread of the Teddy-boy sub-culture, within which gang warfare, the carrying of weapons, and the use of violence were in certain adolescent circles regarded as 'legitimate'. This was largely the view of the west London police, and a leader of a youth club, to which several of the nine had belonged, also told me how large a role accident had played in the whole affair:

It all happened on the night the club wasn't open. Not knowing what to do with themselves, the idea came to them to have a go at the Spades. Yet if they hadn't been at a loose end that night they might never have started. At the club you might have said they were the sort of boys who wouldn't say boo to a goose, but once the excitement started they were swept away by it. When these sort of boys are at a loose end they'll take up any activity to break the boredom. A fight with a neighbouring gang would ordinarily do the trick, only a neighbouring gang isn't so easily recognized. Coloured people are, so on that evening they decided to beat them up – and the rest followed.

Evidence that the colour question was only one expression, if a dangerous one, of new habits of violence among a section of youth was also soon provided from other parts. Before the shock of the sentences at the Old Bailey had been completely absorbed, the charge of 'causing a common affray' was used again, twice in succession, in cases of ordinary gang warfare, that is, only involving white victims.

The first of these affrays was a fight between two gangs remarkable for its surroundings – a dance-hall in a quiet suburban street in Barking – in which a nineteen-year-old youth, Alan Johnson, was stabbed to death. The second and ugly case, in the last days of 1958, arose from a similar brawl between armed gangs outside a dance-hall in Holloway, in which a slightly older man, Ronald Marwood, dashed into the mêlée and stabbed to death a young policeman, Raymond Summers. Because of the debate over capital punishment, the Marwood case became a *cause célèbre*, involving petitions in Parliament, banner headlines in the popular Press, an editorial in *The Times*, and more frenzied mob scenes, enacted in front of assembled foreign correspondents outside Pentonville prison, as Marwood was executed. . . .

In conclusion: everything has to be seen in proportion; these highly publicized cases were of course only isolated incidents in British life. All the same, by the beginning of

1960 it could no longer be denied that certain parts of London at night were dominated by a new spirit of insecurity. If the total number of crimes of violence was nothing like as dramatic as headlines suggested, still the number was going up year by year. There were other signs of the current trend.

In April 1959 a Private Member's Bill was discussed in the Commons to prohibit the sale of flick-knives. That enterprising national institution, the *Daily Mirror*, was running its own campaign for the voluntary surrender of weapons by youthful members of gangs. After a week the newspaper's office had received hundreds of items ranging from army revolvers to home-made weapons fit for a do-it-yourself age. At the same time the Home Secretary admitted to his deep regret that in 1959, just as in 1952, there were still 6,000 men sleeping three in a cell in Britain's antiquated prisons, the reason being that the additional accommodation built during those seven years had been entirely swallowed up by the increase in the number of inmates.

At the beginning of the 1960s, the overall number of people in British prisons and Borstal institutions was still not much over 30,000. Though this was easily an all-time record, it could perhaps be said that organized crime in Britain was still not the major social problem it was in certain other countries. But it looked well on the way to becoming such a problem. At any rate, by 1960 it was also apparent that British public opinion had woken up to the existence of an alarming streak of violence among a section of youth; that is, to the strange problem of the Teddy-boy type of society in its midst.

CHAPTER 5

Café Society

Past and present

IN a sense, the new state of insecurity appeared like a historic regression. The remarkably law-abiding character of twentieth-century English life had often been commented on. Looking back in 1940 on an era which he felt was ending, George Orwell wrote:

Perhaps the most marked characteristic of English civilization is its gentleness. You notice it the instant you set foot on English soil. It is a land where the bus conductors are good-tempered and the policemen carry no revolvers.[1]

Orwell associated this gentle quality of the common English people with their deep-rooted dislike of militarism and war and their extraordinary respect for legality, the general belief in 'the Law' as something above the State and the individual.

Everyone takes it for granted that the law, such as it is, will be respected, and feels a sense of outrage when it is not. Remarks like 'They can't run me in; I haven't done anything wrong', or 'They can't do that; it's against the law' are part of the atmosphere of England.

This picture of the law-abiding England of pre-1940 was one which most foreign visitors carried away with them. Today the picture has already a somewhat dated look, but to be quite accurate, it was never a complete picture. Even the gangs of Notting Hill and Holloway had their immediate predecessors. The Industrial Revolution came to Britain much earlier than to the rest of Europe. Its impact was harsher and it left behind a heritage of historic slums and of some primitive gang life, which lingered into the inter-

1. George Orwell, *The Lion and the Unicorn*, Secker & Warburg, 1940.

war years. If London had its Hoxton Terrors, provincial cities had their equivalent. In the steel city of Sheffield, particularly badly affected by the depression, cloth-capped gangs with hundreds of members, such as the Mooney Boys and the Garvin Gang, haunted the drab streets of the Park, Crofts, and Norfolk Bridge districts of the city, defying the police and rendering the districts unsafe for several years. The razor gangs of Glasgow were as notorious as that city's tenement areas, and equally a product of economic depression. Well-known early gangs like the Redskins, the Black Hand, and the Beehives were recruited from the great army of unemployed created in Glasgow by the economic crisis after the First World War.

If the Teddy boys of Notting Hill and South London therefore had their predecessors, the studies of Sir Percy Sillitoe and others also reveal the difference between the two periods. The older gangs were basically a product of poverty, of mass unemployment and degraded slum life like that of Glasgow. The gang leaders were not adolescents but older men, who were often also notorious criminals. The gangs were strictly confined to certain areas; their ascendancy rested on primitive brute force, and an intelligently directed opposing force of picked and aggressive police officers was therefore enough to shatter their ranks. On the other hand, the Teddy boys of today are adolescents rather than adults, and represent a widespread new way of life found throughout the country. Or one might put the difference as follows. While the cloth-capped pre-war gangs of Sheffield and Glasgow were a survival from a cruder past and could be dealt with as such, the Teddy-boy gangs – and this is the disturbing point – are a direct product of today, a by-product of a new economic revolution which has put spending money on a scale not known before into the pockets of working-class boys and girls. Spread as it is throughout the country, the Teddy-boy society seems like a distinct, recognizable little stratum of society.

The pages which follow include some personal impressions of this society. They are based on conversations with youngsters involved in this life and with social workers in contact with them. The conclusions are not meant to be expert and exhaustive. They are, in fact, 'impressionist', and my excuse in putting them forward is that in a field where so little is documented even an outsider's views may be of value. Perhaps it should also be stressed that the descriptions apply to a period when the Teddy-boy fashion developed by the early large gangs had already receded. What I am writing about is the present society of the smaller gangs who have followed the Teds. However, since the words 'Teddy boy' and 'Ted' have become general currency, it seems convenient to go on using them.

The Teds and boredom

A good start for any study of the Teddy-boy society is its habitat, the café, or caff. The spread of café life among working-class boys and girls has surely been among the more interesting developments of the post-war years, and it has also been spontaneous. Whether one looks in on such a café in London, a small country town or seaside resort, the impression is much the same. The usual picture is of a long room with a counter for the sale of coffee, soft drinks, and snacks, and tables placed close to each other. Young men, all dressed up, will look challengingly at the intruder, the girls appearing less certain of themselves. A new and shiny juke-box will usually be giving forth its sounds. If the décor is contemporary, this adds to the popularity of the establishment. In fact, an atmosphere of garish gaiety, warm coffee steam, contemporary décor, and the noise of the juke-box seems to have become for many young people an antidote against the emptiness of their lives. And why not? Here I come to a subject on which I have some very personal views, namely the pall of boredom which has for so long hung over much of English social life and especially the lack of social amenities for young people in working-class areas.

Adolescence is a time of life when young people feel uncertain and expectant, driven on by urges they do not fully understand; when they feel the need for gregariousness and for places where they can come together informally, to meet the opposite sex, to drift, to experiment, to feel their own way towards adult life, and this without supervision from their elders. Urbanized industrial society is in general deficient in providing such opportunity, but I think that in England (up to about 1950) this shortcoming was more noticeable than anywhere else.

I always felt that after dark the average English town had a dead and shuttered look found nowhere else to quite the same degree; for the bored lads at the street corner there was probably no choice but to spend the evening at an isolated milk-bar, coffee-stall, or pin-table arcade, or else once again at the pictures. To be sure, there were pubs, but it is probably time that the brewers' legend of the public house as a modern community centre was done away with. By today the majority of public houses have become little more than commercialized outlets for a few multi-million brewery combines, while the State has also stepped in to make the consumption of beer and spirits a highly taxed pastime. The pub was also not a place to which a young man ordinarily took his girl. But then, where else? In some districts, though not all, there might be a club, but this usually demanded the special effort of joining in some activity. For the majority, who did not want to make this effort, there was often nowhere to go but the anonymity of the local cinema with its latest American film, or else the dark back alley.

The juke-box café

The last ten years have seen a fairly vigorous attack against this void on the part of the young generation. This has expressed itself in a variety of new ways; for instance, in the fact that working-class boys and girls now go in growing numbers on holidays abroad; in the persistent teenage demand for a new urbanity which has produced the luxuriously equipped Mecca dance-halls, and caused youth clubs to be rebuilt with attractive canteens; in such spontaneous movements in their time as skiffle and the cult of rock-'n'-roll and the twist; and, above all, in the spread of the young people's café and its variant, the espresso-bar.

The drift of the young generation from pub to café reflects a considerable change in habits. Youths of today who believe themselves mature at sixteen or seventeen are put off by licensing restrictions and the fact that they cannot take their girls to public bars. In most pubs they are not welcome in groups and the pub is not the place for their kind of noise, which is connected with the world of juke-boxes and 'pop' records. On the other hand, the average little café answers their demands. The price of coffee is cheap, there may be music, and above all the ordinary café is a small enough place for a group of young people to be able to regard it as 'theirs'. 'When a bloke goes to the same café every night, well, I mean he's known – he's somebody.' A group of tough sixteen- and seventeen-year-old London youngsters (with already quite a few police records among them) told me what they would regard as their ideal for life after dark: to have a choice of several cafés in their own neighbourhood, which would be nice and cheerful places, modern in decoration, with tables for those who wanted to sit, and room enough for others to dance, and which would stay open till midnight!

Needless to say, this ideal is not found very often; in the case of these particular boys there was actually not a single late-evening café open in their area. One reason is that it is hard to make such places pay. It may well be that the English working-class young have staked their demand for café life rather too late in the day. In an age of advertising and large-scale entertainment of every kind, the running of a small café purely for the entertainment of young people has already become a doubtful proposition in many localities. In many places one finds that the young complain that there are not enough cafés open after dark, while the proprietors maintain that there is no economic demand to justify them.

Within these limits, however, a working-class café life has

developed in several distinct forms. The most common is the development of the original rough working men's 'caff', which provided cheap, simple, hot midday meals and has now extended its hours to provide coffee and juke-box music to the young. Of other forms, the less successful is probably the milk-bar or soda-fountain in a newly built-up area. Through a peculiar English lack of skill in this trade, this has never achieved the efficiency of the American drugstore counter. A more successful development is that of the espresso-bar, whose popularity has its cultural significance. While the sophisticated may deride espresso-bar glamour, to the majority of British working-class youth this glamour, which goes with the 'Italian style' in clothes and films, seems precisely part of that modern life they want to aspire to. In some parts of London most of the cafés catering for the young are today run by Cypriots bent on making them paying propositions.

Another decisive import from abroad has been the American juke-box. This instrument is, of course, the product of a large entertainment industry, and as soon as one speaks of the juke-box one is involved in an argument of pros and cons. To the refined middle-class ear, the raucous sound of an infernal machine blaring out something like 'Jailhouse Rock' at deafening volume in a small, confined space, i.e. a small café crowded with overdressed Teddy boys and their girl friends, may seem like a good idea of hell. And yet, and yet ... talking to those in touch with these young people, I have always felt that there is a good deal to be said for the juke-box. First of all, it has made the café a place to which girls can come on their own. The music provides justification; they can sit and nod to the rhythm as they sip their coffee without appearing too obviously waiting to be picked up. Conversely, the juke-box enables the boys to express their personalities at sixpence a time through the individual choice of records. Moreover, behind the loud noise the youngsters genuinely respond to the catchy rhythm. As against this, the voices from the juke-box speak in American or pseudo-American accents, and therefore incessantly conjure up a world of fantasy which to the listeners must remain unreal, and at its worst the din may merely help to kill time in an hypnotic way. As one graduate from the Teddy-boy society confessed to me, while the juke-box was playing, 'the fellows don't have to think, they don't have to talk, they can just sit there with a dazed expression.'

While all this is true, it does seem to me that the positive side perhaps outweighs the other. For its adolescent habitués, the juke-box café or espresso-bar with music does satisfy the need for a rendezvous and social life after dark which is so strongly felt. Often it is an obsessive need. For many youngsters their most vivid link with contemporary culture is through the lyrics of 'pop' music. The juke-box café, especially if featuring the Top Twenty, fits with this emotional attitude. To the Teddy boys of today and their girl friends, it is like a magnet, drawing them evening after evening to its lights and music, a primitive substitute for the Continental café and wine, women, and song.

That at any rate is the romantic ideal. In practice, in London, the number of cafés available or permitted to keep open into the night is very inadequate. This was my experience when one night, with a young companion, I made the round of the cafés still open in the later evening hours in one extensive London area. As a starting-point, there was just one single café-restaurant with agreeable modern décor and a classless atmosphere, frequented by Teds, by students, by anybody. Next, there were two dim 'caffs', where I was told one could pick up interesting local news, but where I saw only groups of young men sitting silently at tables with an air of killing time rather than anything else in a dingy setting. Next, there were two fairly similar, narrow dives, with the juke-box at work and every chair occupied by over-dressed boys and girls from fourteen to fifteen upwards. Last of all, there was one larger establishment, an obvious local rendezvous, with two tough-looking Cypriots serving behind the counter, with a noisy and mixed crowd at the tables, boys of school age putting coins into gambling machines, and down a passage a second, rather grimy room with more pin-tables, a small space for jiving and, some wild-looking girls ('not much cop,' said my young companion) waiting to be picked up. And that was all: apart from a few milk bars which closed early, these six cafés after dark served a London area of about 200,000 people, which probably contained upwards of a hundred public houses. And a café-round like this could, I believe, be undertaken in any similar urban area of England.

At the moment the lack of balance between the adolescent demand for facilities for social life and the supply of such facilities undoubtedly creates social strains. Because cafés kept open into the evening for young people generally don't pay, there are too few of them. Because they are so few, youngsters have no choice where to go and as often as not end up in cafés taken over by the Teddy boys, whose gangs in this way enjoy undue influence and draw in recruits.

In other words, the rise of the new café life and of the Teddy-boy movement are not identical developments – they only overlap somewhat. But against this, the availability of cafés where members could meet night after night has given the young gangs a cohesion they might otherwise not have possessed, especially in keeping up their sense of outlawry from society. Conversely, the knowledge that well-known gang members could be met at certain cafés has often given these places a romantic local attraction and thus made for a steady stream of new recruits. In this sense, the Teddy-boy society has been very much a café society, a product of the curiously belated, in some ways beneficial, in others sordid, development of the café as an institution of English working-class life.

CHAPTER 6

A Spot of Sub-culture

Untender is the night

WHEN one returns from the wider topic of café life to the narrower confines of Teddy-boy society, one soon comes up against its problem of dull boredom. One does not require many encounters in this society to discover that its culture is one of incessant efforts to fill an empty expanse of time. So, perhaps, is that of many city dwellers of today. The distinction is that for the Teds this problem can become obsessive, and the means of killing time therefore take on the same importance.

Side by side with rivalry over girls, it is, I think, this underlying sense of boredom in Ted society which is responsible for some of the continuance of gang warfare. In the original heyday of the Teddy boys in the early fifties, this was pretty elaborate. Some of the gang leaders-in-chief were called 'governors'. Their local subordinates were the 'assistant governors'. It was a point of honour for a proper 'governor' to be able to call out a ragged force of a hundred youths for a purpose which as often as not was a mock battle, but sometimes turned into a real one. By and large this phase is over. The smaller gangs of today are more knowing and purposeful, and probably some degrees more criminally inclined. But to judge from incidents reported, the spirit of this warfare still goes on. In the boredom of the night-time cafés, insults by one group against another are still brooded over. Evening after evening the rancour grows, until tempers are worked up, telephone calls are made, the boys tool up, and a punitive expedition is organized.

This warfare remains the Teddy boys' special little contribution to culture. But, in the main, in their outlook on leisure they are affected just like others of their generation by the current mass media. The cinema remains a basic addiction. Television has entered into their lives, but less than one would have supposed; on the other hand, the cult of 'pop' music has become an integral part of their day and night-time life. Apart from this, fashion consciousness has remained a passionate interest and mark of status.

The anodyne of the pictures

Not long ago I sat in a vast suburban cinema alongside three dolled-up Teds and their girl friends. During the pre-liminaries of the performance they had made a nuisance of themselves by exhibitionist laughter and catcalls. All this stopped, however, as the main feature came on. This was a gangster film, put over with that powerful realism which Hollywood direction sometimes achieves. The sordid side of American city life was forcefully conveyed – one felt that those making the film had raked this mud with a venom. Then came the dream-cliché of relentless and nightmarish pursuit. With all hands against him, the hunted killer-victim stumbled round corners and over walls and down alleys. All in vain. As each new avenue of escape beckoned, it was barred by more men with guns. The trap was closed. This was it, the pay-off.

Happening to glance at the lads by my side, I thought that they were watching the climax of pursuit as if the dream were their own. Their silly dead-pan expressions were relaxed. They seemed to have forgotten the girls at their side. For them, too, this was it – the pay-off, their own fears and desires represented artistically, their amateurish ideas of ambushing and gangsterism writ large. When the lights came on, it took them quite a few moments to gather their wits and resume their swagger.

While cinema-going among the general population has under the impact of television dropped by over half during the last ten years, this seems markedly not the case in Teddy-boy society. Here the 'pictures' still supply a basic emotional need – the lack of cinemas is a common adoles-cent grievance in New Towns and outer suburban estates. Small boys seem to play truant from school much as ever before to slip into the 'pictures'. Older youths may take their girls to the cinema twice a week or more. To break the deadly monotony of a Sunday afternoon, they will queue up early in daylight outside the local Odeon. I was often told by youths that when out of work they would spend one afternoon after the other at the cinema. It is not hard to see why the cinemas should remain this ideal time-killer. Its vast, comforting darkness offers not only relaxation but, to a Ted, temporary relief from the strain of being 'somebody'. The cinema is sex-dominated, the sanctioned place to take one's girl to, with sex on the screen and a good deal of it in the auditorium too. The values of the films often approximate to those of the boys themselves. Emotions are there to be gratified. When obstructed by an opponent, the hero uses his fists. When rejected, he reaches for the bottle. The magnified hero and heroine seem to demonstrate how one can live fabulously on any social level. Or, again, there is the gangster film, most popular of all with the Teds and as if tailored for them.

Not for them alone, of course. But it appears a fair assumption that the Teds, as a group of youngsters who have rejected their traditions, are therefore peculiarly open to suggestion from the mass media. The influence of the film on the Teds has the danger, first, that it presents a gaping negative. As my Irish informant put it,

It's not just the violence. A lot of people go to Westerns and gangster films and it makes not the slightest difference. But these young Teds, they've got no standards; in their dim way they're always groping, and the trouble with the films is that they show them a way of life, an American way, which they think they can copy, yet which in reality for them is nonexistent.

There is also the positive danger that the idea is implanted at least in a dreamlike way among the susceptible that they, too, can live fabulously. Only one thing is needed, namely money; and if money is lacking, well, one way of getting it is through breaking and entering, or, if you're a girl, by just a little harmless prostitution. This effect of the films is not direct and measurable, but in talking to the dimmer sort of Teddy boys and listening to their ideas about the desirable life, one can usually note how strongly these have been coloured by film clichés.

The Teds and the telly

By contrast with the cinema, the impact of television on Teddy boy life seems still to be surprisingly small.

Perhaps one should expect this. Viewing usually drops to a low point at the courting age when adolescents, stirred by their instincts, find it far more exciting to collect in the stairway of a block of flats rather than sit at home in front of a television set. Nor has television in England become acclimatized in public places, as in Mediterranean countries. In England there are no sets in cafés, and in any crowded public bar, where people can talk, the occasional shimmering television screen is commonly disregarded. All the same, in view of the staggering statistical increase in British television viewing, I was a little surprised to find Teddy-boy circles apparently little affected by the new medium, and indeed apt to talk of it with a certain scorn.

There appear to be some fairly obvious explanations. Television does not fit in with the sex motif that runs right through Teddy-boy life. There is little point in sitting with your girl in front of some living-room television screen. Either adults are present, in which case you are not at ease, or else, if you are alone with a girl, there are better things to do than to watch telly. Another difference is that television lacks the streamlined sex-appeal of the films, perfected by Hollywood at the cost of so many millions of dollars. The performers in television drama are not 'stars' in the Hollywood sense, but just ordinary English actors and actresses, and so in adolescent eyes conditioned to Hollywood glamour they are vaguely wrong. I also found the boys irritated by the interruptions of uplift or current affairs in television programmes – such interruptions showed that the whole television programme was not 'theirs', that some hostile adults were trying to sell them something, that they were being got at – and similar reactions were even shown towards the advertisements.

In this general disregard of television, some programmes are, of course, exceptions. Those about themselves, that is about 'youth' or 'the Teddy-boy problem', are often watched eagerly by the boys, who find them flattering, and find it natural that they should be discussed. Intermittently popular programmes are those presenting football, boxing, and hot music, though here the basic appeal is that of sport and pop music themselves, rather than the medium of television. Altogether, I vividly recall the comment of one precocious young ruffian who seemed to sum up the whole impact of television on his young life in a few succinct sentences:

It's getting so boys like us can't stay at home any more. It's telly every night: I say it gets boring. You take the television room at the Club. One time it used to be crowded, now you never get more than a few fellows, and then mostly it's kids. It's all those advertisements. They're something horrible. You see a bloke with a gun just going to shoot somebody, and next thing you get 'OMO adds Brightness', and when it starts again you see the police are already in the room.

What could be more concise?

As the reader may have gathered, the above criticisms apply almost exclusively to commercial television, for the good reason that, apart from a few sporting and musical shows, BBC television seemed almost unknown in these adolescent circles. The one reason above all which was given to me was that the BBC voice is still the ruling middle-class voice, that of teacher and of authority, which sends these boys and girls scurrying for cover – or to the familiarity of the brisk and half-American salesman's voice of 'the Commercial'.

Music has charms

While television has made only this little impact, exactly the opposite is true of commercial pop music. Its influence is hard to overestimate. The ordinary Ted's mind responds to the latest catchy tunes, and his body to the rhythm of jive. Here he is no rebel. The point where he feels most at one with the culture of contemporary society is within the commercial musical ensemble, in the world of pop records and record players, juke-boxes and radio disc-jockeys, the whole accompaniment of manufactured voices bawling, yearning, or whispering at the boys and girls, trying either to incite them to movement or else (as I think Aldous Huxley once put it) asking them to swoon on waves of softest syrup.

In their enthusiasm for this brave new world, the Teds are of course only in line with most of their generation. And with its predecessor, too – after all it can be said that the British fought the last war to the sound of the Forces' Propramme left continuously switched on in the Other Ranks' mess. Since then, the gigantic American and Anglo-American musical entertainment industry has made further spectacular progress in these islands, and above all among the young. It is hardly possible to count how many millions of pop music records are sold annually on the teenage market. Lately the possession of a modern long-playing record-player has also become the fashion among the very young. Of the half-million record-players annually sold in Britain, the majority are bought by very young boys and girls. At an average price of £15, which means paying a couple of pounds down and the rest by instalments, they are well within reach as new status symbols.

These facts about the youthful pop-music boom are commonplace. But what I felt was significant was that in participating in this enthusiasm, as he certainly does, the average Ted was for once not in opposition to society, but *sharing* in a positive reaction.

This is shown in a number of ways. Pop music is a pastime where he may often, just like other boys, spare no expense. I remember an occasion when I tried to talk to some young toughs about hobbies and their faces remained bored and blank, as if hobbies were a thing for their old man but no longer for their generation, until I mentioned records, and this changed everything. They all kept them. One sixteen-year-old announced: '*My* hobby is collecting LP's. You have to pay 35s., but it's two guineas for the old stars. I got dozens of those.' Well, perhaps he had them. In darkest Notting Hill, not long after the riots, a youth leader told me:

Record-players are the thing these days among the boys. You just don't find a house without one; they're just about taking the place of the telly, expensive ones, too. Television seems to mean little to the youngsters these days – the only thing they bother to watch is boxing and football – but it's remarkable how well they know the records. Even little girls at the club will ask if we've already got the latest hit, 'Babyface' or something. Tunes are the one subject where you can be sure of getting them to talk.

One can go further. Ordinarily the Teds, as young rebels, are automatically against any ideas of working hard and 'getting on'. Sweat and toil to learn music is one of the few exceptions. A boy willing to devote every evening to practice in a band is not derided for his pains. Even in tougher Ted circles, musical ambition is generally regarded as legitimate. In fact, some of these dim circles show a pathetic longing to be 'in' on jazz-as-art and to be knowing about traditional and modernist style and the rest.

In other words, his love for pop music appears to be the chink in the Teddy boy's armour of non-participation. This is already recognized in the well-meaning efforts 'to talk to the boys in their own language'. I remember visiting a café in the drabbest district in an industrial town which had been opened in an attempt to bring in some large groups of wild and footloose boys and girls. The café had remained almost empty until a manager was appointed who was himself knowledgeable about the Top Twenty of the Month, and what changes to ring on the record-player. As if he were the Piper of Hamelin, his café became a popular centre night after night. When I saw it, it represented the odd spectacle of a crowd of overdressed, bizarre, and desperate-looking adolescents milling around in a confined space, yet

under the spell of music all impeccably on their best behaviour, 'living' themselves into the part of being good boys,
like actors guided by the Method.

Many clubs in difficult areas have had a similar experience. By setting aside a room for records and jiving and
leaving the youngsters in it fairly unsupervised, they have
brought in drifting boys and girls who otherwise might
have stayed resolutely outside. It is true that in club circles
there has already been some opposition to this move. The
sight of an overcrowded, untidy room in which a few
youngsters dance, a far greater number merely stand about,
and the record-player is continuously turned up to top
volume, is not edifying. It is said that if youngsters merely
drift into a club for this one passive amusement and nothing else, very little is really gained, except that they are off
the street.

Even so, I kept on feeling that this musical enthusiasm of
the Teds was something positive which could be the starting-point for contact with them, if only one could understand just what it meant. It is perfectly true that this
enthusiasm is constantly stimulated by the pop-music industry through a skilful sales appeal, whose flattery begins
with the faces on the glossy record sleeves, and ends with
the yearning note in the lyrics directed explicitly at every
boy or girl. But I also felt that the rhythmic music impinged
directly on an aspect in the life of these youngsters to which
they and society had done absurd violence – simply, their
youthfulness.

Some time ago, Humphrey Lyttelton gave me what I
thought a telling explanation why jazz should have become
a modern urban folk-music which appealed so powerfully
to the younger age-groups and only to them. If jazz was a
music of revolt, he said, it was so in a general, youthful,
undramatic sort of way. It appealed to young people coming
up in the world because it demanded no great *expertise*
either to perform or to listen to. It was democratic, in that
on the stand even the band leader was only just another
performer. It was international, in that the idiom was the

same in every country. Lastly, it was an idiom which the young felt their elders did not understand, and they rather liked this.

The reasons for this difference in the reactions of the old and the young to jazz are also fairly simple. Jazz, even in its derived forms, is still a functional music, that of a vigorous and youthful dance, whose basic step is the athletic jive. Hence it remains a lively, almost nervous music, whose rhythm older people find unsettling, but to which the young instinctively respond with their bodies.

If all this applies to jazz proper, it remains true even of its debased forms. When a particularly catchy tune is put on in a juke-box dive, it is a common sight to see even the most passive dead-pan young Teds quicken to life, nod rhythmically to the beat, and look almost eager. The reason is that there is something youthful, appropriate to their age-group in this music to which they can respond, not as pseudo-adults, but as boys – as what they really are. And it always seemed to me that here one was on to something, that this response to pop music also indicated the long-term solution to the problem of the Teddy boys: that they must be enabled, guided, or if necessary impelled to step out of the pose into which some quirk in society has forced them – and made to become boys again.

CHAPTER 7

Thrusters and Drifters

The membership

To turn from the cultural to the social viewpoint – how is the Teddy-boy society constituted and recruited? In trying to answer this question one has admittedly to generalize, lumping together sophisticated London adolescents with a taste for the clubs of Soho with small-town boys and girls in provincial juke-box cafés. All the same, I found that teachers and social workers in different localities usually had a pretty clear idea about the character of their local Teddy-boy society and that the impressions tallied fairly closely.

To those who had to deal directly with the problem of the Teddy boys, and who were often highly unsuccessful in trying to influence them, the cult of deliberate and anti-social irresponsibility among these youths and boys often seemed *sui generis*. In fact they were not so unique.

A friend from Oxford gave me a neat sidelight on this. He had been struck, he said, by the close parallels between the bloods, the top set among Oxford undergraduates, and the South London Teddy boys among whom he did some social work. Both groups were alike in seeking provocative emphasis in dress: there were even traces of sartorial similarity. Both groups, each on its own social level, had similar tastes for women, fast cars, jazz, and the West End life. Above all, both the young Oxford bloods and the London Teds were intent on living irresponsibly – the essence was that they both felt free from social pressures; each group, for instance, felt free to set off on a night's expedition at a moment's impulse.

Situated between these two groups, as my friend saw it, was the great majority of State-aided undergraduates at the university, who never felt free from social pressures. They sat in their rooms and worked, they worried about examinations, about making ends meet and what jobs they might get – in any case, they worried. And this hard-working majority had as little social contact with the carefree Oxford top set above them as with the irresponsible Teddy-boy *jeunesse dorée* below. Each class went its own way.

While the other two groups are, however, well established, the emergence of a *jeunesse dorée* life among unskilled adolescents is still a very new phenomenon. For this reason, probably, one is struck in this milieu by its atmosphere of constant thrust – living for kicks – and of defensiveness towards outsiders.

A second point to note about Teddy-boy society is that it is strikingly youthful. In this respect it reflects the genuinely earlier physiological maturity of the present generation of teenagers. Although the boys themselves are aware of it, this acceleration of adolescence seems a phenomenon about which surprisingly little has been written, perhaps because its implications are so startling. But there can be little doubt about this change. A number of studies in Britain, the U.S., and Germany indicate that, on the average, teenage girls today arrive at biological maturity a year earlier than their mothers (and probably two years earlier than their grandmothers) while the boys have also kept pace.

The causes of this acceleration are still speculative – it is thought to be connected with changes in diet and infant care and the fact that modern teenagers are also taller and heavier than those of the past. Whatever the explanation, the change itself has already begun to create complications: for parents whose sons and daughters at fifteen or sixteen claim an independence which they themselves only enjoyed at seventeen or eighteen; for teachers in secondary modern schools who find themselves – as some have complained – facing 'sex-excited louts and hussies'; for the authorities at approved schools, and so forth.

As for the Teddy-boy society, its age composition also

quite clearly reflects this earlier maturity. A good many Teddy boys, as they leave school at fifteen, buy their uniform from their first earnings. If we take it that in so doing they are proclaiming their open rejection of school and parents and asserting their adult status, the point to note is how early in life this claim is made. As a rule, youths from seventeen to twenty-one are still the actual leaders of gangs – it is they who usually appear in Court – but in many gangs boys of fifteen are already members, adeptly working their passage upwards, and this precocity clearly poses new problems.

Class and the Teddy boys

To return to the class aspect of Teddy-boy society, while its life may illustrate the social advance of working-class adolescents in Britain, it is also clear that its members are drawn from a very narrow class of these young workers, one which under the current new stratification is also a class left over, left behind. Perhaps this is best shown by a process of exclusion. First, through the 11-plus examination, the twenty per cent of grammar school boys are creamed off; they have no truck with Teddy-boy life. The same is true for the minority of boys going into skilled apprenticeship. As young apprentices these don't earn enough money to keep up with the flash café life. On the other hand, once they become skilled workers, they feel it is beneath them: their earnings are then on a level where they are on the contrary pulled in the opposite direction, towards what is today called an 'Americanized' style of working-class life, a life of suburban houses, cars, household gadgets, respectability – in any case, right away from Teddy-boy café society. The latter is thus recruited mainly from those left over, from the young unskilled workers whose earnings are too low and irregular for them to take part in this *embourgeoisement*. But if they cannot take part in this, their earnings are at the same time much higher than in the past and enough for café life and fashions. Without the status of the white-collar worker and the prospects of the apprentice, and probably with resentment on both scores, a young unskilled worker can, at least at the age of seventeen, spend more money than either of the others. This is the economic basis of Teddy-boy society.

Finally, within this changing life of a special class of unskilled young workers, the Teddy-boy society is a still further minority phenomenon – a concentration of the insecure, of unstable adolescents, those with weak family ties and the fewest special interests, who are drawn to this nightly café life as to a drug, to hold back their anxieties.

This cannot be proved precisely by statistics, but all the evidence, especially the experience of social workers, points to the conclusion that the Teddy boys include a majority of insecure youngsters from bad or broken homes. One senior Borstal officer told me that in his experience of Teddy-boy offenders, more than half came from family backgrounds which were 'absolute hell'; another quarter from homes which looked superficially all right but probably were not; while less than a quarter came from genuinely adequate homes. From my own limited impression, too, it seems justified to regard the Teddy-boy society as a new way of adolescent group life which like a magnet draws in the most psychologically insecure among working-class adolescents.

The Drifters

This need to find security in gang life is most pronounced in the case of certain younger members of the Teddy-boy society to whom a social worker in Notting Hill always referred as the Drifters. It seemed an appropriate name. The Drifters, as the term is here used, could be described as a minority within a minority, the extreme wing of the Teddy-boy society, or perhaps more accurately described as its lowest stratum. They are boys and girls who appear adrift, without apparent direction in life, or recognizable moral standards, rejecting all authority, living only for the immediate gratification of desire and the search for security in the mob.

When one goes into the individual background of such youngsters, one usually finds that they come from deprived homes. 'Among these particular youngsters,' one informant told me, 'I have never heard one affectionate word spoken about parents, indeed always the opposite. They are laughed at and ridiculed, sworn at and deceived, and if they are not ready to pass over the easy five bob then it is taken from them.' Usually the same youngsters are also the product of a bad area – Notting Hill is a good example, or the neighbourhood around Kings Cross, where sixteen-year-olds feel already completely worldly-wise, cynically weary of life, with no feeling that there is anything to learn or any attachment to district or country or anything but money. But other special circumstances, too, can produce groups of adolescent Drifters to whom vandalism, promiscuity, and petty crime mean nothing, even on a new council estate, provided determined ringleaders appear and there is no counterpull.

As the lower stratum of the Teddy-boy society, as a problem of today, the Drifters seem to be a recognizable entity. Indeed, the picture built up in my mind from conversations with people struggling thanklessly with this problem was like that of a single unintegrated, defiant, and dangerous problem-child – only this child was in actual fact a collective of adolescents. To me the most remarkable aspect about this collective of the Drifters is that they should exist in London at this present day. Yet the Drifters do exist. What follows is some documentation about them which I have gathered from various places. As elsewhere, I have thought it best not to give names and places too exactly, and the opinions of my informants are given more or less in their own words.

Shiftlessness

The first and foremost characteristic of the Drifters which makes them so intractable is their extreme shiftlessness. Perhaps this is due to the fact that most of them have cut themselves off from their homes and so are in a vacuum.

At any rate, their state of mind is one where it simply does not occur to them that an impulse, a desire which seizes them, should not at once be gratified. This freedom to follow impulse is what the gang seems to sanction: hence its attraction. In this freedom to follow impulse they also find emotional security. Any attempt to guide them, to interfere, is therefore like an attack on their security and at once opposed or evaded as such. This is what makes the Drifters so difficult to deal with and has made pessimistic social workers coin words like 'unreachable' or 'unclubbable'. Youth-club leaders are well aware of this floating antagonism among some of the boys and girls they are trying to draw in. As one leader from a notorious London area told me:

Perhaps this latest generation is even more delinquent than the last in pinching motor-bikes and cars, but what strikes me is the way they do it – the growth of sheer irresponsibility. The other day some of our boys went to the market and simply began to throw goods from stalls all over the place and so they came up before the Court. But for them it was just having fun. They would pinch a car in the same way. You saw what an impressive new club building we have; for a good twenty-five per cent of the fourteen to sixteen age-group it makes no difference. They will never be constructive. They just come in for a game of darts, a coffee, they flit in and out, nothing else. We thought: 'We must give them easy things to do.' Right: we organized badminton groups, judo groups, a snooker tournament, but they never stuck at anything more than half an hour. Then suddenly one of them would say: 'Comin' out ...?' and they'd all flock after him like sheep. If you ask where to, they'd say, 'To the chip shop' or 'Sit in the café.' It's just to be somewhere different, to move about, with no objective.

But then they've got no objective. They've got no faith, no religion, they don't see why they're in this world. Basically, it's a matter of seeing how selfish you can be. They're not interested in their jobs – money is the only thing that counts.

Destructiveness

Another characteristic of the Drifters is their destructiveness, their evidently compulsive desire to smash, to destroy, to harm. Perhaps our age has encouraged some such general tendency. Not long ago, when I watched a rock-'n'-roll session (this was just before the highly organized change from this dance to the twist) which had been arranged in a London Town Hall by local voluntary workers anxious to do something positive for the young, it occurred to me that there was more than a trace of this in the collective exuberance. Inside the hall, the scene had a touch of bedlam; what looked like a thousand boys and girls of ages ranging from fourteen to nineteen were sitting closely packed at the tables, or shoving to get on to the crowded floor, with a resentful and jostling queue outside. The crowd effect, the rock-'n'-roll rhythm and the continuous noise clearly provided a special excitement. The youngsters were enjoying themselves, shouting, laughing, smoking, and pushing past each other to drink coffee and lemonade; the girls had an air of keeping themselves continuously on display; boys were dancing with their heads to one side, seeming not so much interested in their partners as intent on displaying their skill as dancers or their newest suits. But what was distinctly noticeable, in addition to the excitement, was a hint of mob callousness and destructiveness. Youngsters making for the dance-floor shoved their way ruthlessly through the crowd; I saw cigarettes thrown on the floor or stubbed out on the tables; chairs were kicked out of the way or pushed over; at one spot, where crockery was smashed and stewards hurried anxiously to the scene, there were shrieks of laughter.

Now, all this disorder was quite obviously under control. The dancers were plainly nice ordinary suburban boys and girls who would presently grow up into ordinary suburban adults. And yet I thought that an undertone of mob excitement and destructiveness, which is a mark of the age, was distinctly to be felt. Take away the restraints holding it in check on such occasions, carry the urge to an extreme, I thought, and one arrived at that wanton attitude of destructiveness which is a mark of the Drifters, which is let loose above all against public property and from which youth clubs in exposed areas have also particularly suffered.

Since this destructiveness of the Drifters springs from unrestrained primitive emotions which are always there, even a small pretext is enough to set it off. A common cause is the feeling among the members of any such group that they are being deprived or excluded from anything they want. I was told a story of this kind from a new London housing estate where, in spite of the warnings by the local youth leader, the permanent premises for a youth club were given lowest priority and still not built two years after the estate had gone up. As a result, my informant told me, the estate quickly had its gangs of juveniles who tended to become unclubbable; the boys especially seemed absolutely frustrated because they had nowhere to go:

All we had for the Club was a converted air-raid shelter and we had such a long waiting list that there was no point in adding to it. Among those who weren't allowed in was particularly one wandering gang who came to the doors several times, ranging from a girl of fifteen, the youngest, to a youth of twenty-one. One night after Whitsun week it was found that the Club had been broken into on Whit Monday and completely wrecked. The gang scattered tea and sugar, they smashed tables, tore out the electric wiring, they tore books into shreds . . . they were found and caught. Four of the boys with previous convictions went to Borstal or on probation. Another eleven were between them fined £60. Yet my feeling was they were really victims. It all happened because they felt excluded, so their reaction was primitive. They actually agreed that they hadn't intended to do much damage at first – they just wanted to get in, but once inside they got excited and couldn't stop smashing.

It appears that an idea of having been excluded or unfairly treated, which can set off their floating resentment like a spark of fire, often underlies cases of vandalism.

How are these young Drifters to be caught and led back

to a life of conforming with Society? One answer is, through the Youth Services. But here lies the difficulty. The hostility of the Drifters is not only something which flares up when the gang feels thwarted or excluded. It is a basic emotional attitude – the Teddy-boy antagonism towards society carried to a neurotic and dangerous extreme – which makes these youths seem unclubbable.

Given the individual case histories of most Drifters, one can understand, in a way, why they should have an ambivalent attitude towards youth clubs. As they are only boys like others, they like what the clubs offer for almost nothing, namely the chance to drift idly into the premises for a spot of billiards or ping-pong, to listen to records, to enjoy the company of girls in the canteen. The chance to enjoy all this is obviously desirable, and to be excluded from it is to a Drifter not only an affront but a basic attack against his security. On the other hand, they must have these things only on their own terms of freedom to behave as they choose, and again one can see why. The characteristic Drifters of fifteen and sixteen have broken off contact with largely loveless homes; they have consigned their years at secondary modern school to the dustbin and found a temporary security in the calculated egotism of the gang in which each of them can feel 'somebody'. Their attitude towards the authority of a youth club, even a minimum authority, is therefore often an irrational 'So you want to drag us back to what we've escaped from? Don't think you can do it!' This is the point where violence often begins, where a gang of Drifters becomes like part of a 'resistance movement'.

I felt that this came out strongly during some talks with a dozen or so club leaders from council estates in difficult parts of London: their work seemed like a perpetual effort to snare shy game, only this game consisted of London boys and girls. In this social war there have been notable successes, but also enough disheartening failures to demonstrate the extent of the problem.

There was, for instance, Estate A, where the tenants' club

for young people was never even opened through apprehension of the youthful gangs roaming the neighbourhood.

They've never been stopped, they are dangerous and they've bags of confidence: if anything, they're getting worse. They don't carry weapons as a rule, but in case of need are never at a loss where to find them. In one affray we had the lavatory chains torn off to be used as weapons for lashing.

There was Club B, which according to its leader had had a wretched history: started, packed up, started again several times, and then the police called in.

Not the local police – they generally arrived too late. If there's trouble the best thing to do is to dial 999. If you do, however, you can take it you've lost the confidence of the boys, even the good ones. You've shown that you can't cope and it means that you've also done something which in the eyes of the boys takes you right away from being on their side, so that their respect is gone. But what else can you do?

The ways in which such aggression can flare up are also incalculable. There was the young club leader from Estate E in one of London's toughest areas who had made a point of going to neighbourhood cafés to try to get to know boys.

In the café, when talking to me, they would call themselves by different names. Some didn't give any names – never gave them away. If I did find out from someone else and called them by their name they would be startled, suspicious. 'How do you know my name?' They were like half-wild animals.

Perhaps because most of the gangs he met included one or two psychopaths, the old tradition of 'a fair fight' had hardly a flicker of life left.

Many of the regulars in the café thought it nothing to discuss complex methods of violence in front of me, about butting people, kicking them in vulnerable places, and dealing with them.

Fantasy also crept constantly into the idea of aggression.

I remember one boy in a beautiful Italian suit who carried not merely a knife but actually a gun. When I asked him why, he said: 'There's all sorts of Cypriots and Maltese walking about round here ... you've got to put your hand on something.'

The problem of making headway in this social war is not an easy one. Special clubs to attract boys of this type have been formed, but the difficulty is how to cope with their waywardness if ordinary club activities are at the same time not to be completely disrupted. Club leaders with exceptional understanding can do this. For instance, at Friendship House in Lambeth, the Rev. Douglas Griffiths has very successfully turned boys of this type into steady club members, but the following story he told me shows the patience required:

On one occasion, for instance, four boys dashed into the club before it was open and in that very brief visit they cut the cloth on the billiard table and damaged the table-tennis table and a wall. And then they were out again through another door in no time. I followed them very slowly down the street, but just kept them in sight. After a while they stopped and let me catch up with them. I said to them: 'Well now, why have you done this? I just want to understand you.' And they said: 'Well, last night, one of our chaps was hurt in the cinema. The attendant set on him and he's had to go to the doctor today. So of course we're feeling peeved. We've got to take it out of somebody. Wouldn't you?' And they simply thought that it was the most natural thing in the world that they should destroy somebody's property because somebody had hurt one of them. Well, when we knew what the trouble was, we were able to deal with it. ...

Another telling little story – this came from a West London area adjacent to Notting Hill – was told to me by a young professional youth worker who went out in New York style in an attempt to become a street-corner youth leader to a group of rather dangerous and delinquent young Drifters. Making contact was not so difficult, but, as this young man saw it, being with these youths morning, afternoon, and evening was rather like being in touch with mental illness.

He thought these youths were not unintelligent, though secondary modern school had made no impression on them, but in their defiant mood there was no such word in their vocabulary as 'future'. They took casual, unskilled jobs – when out of work they looked to other ways of keeping themselves. When some were convicted and sent to Borstal, the answer to the question: 'Do you realize you may be away for two years?' was merely: 'So what?' When they were destroying property, they were unconcerned about the feelings of other people, unless indeed they did it deliberately to make people angry, just for a laugh. Within the group they egged each other on. The more violent a boy, the greater the respect given him by the others. They were often not aware of pain inflicted on other people because they simply did not see them as people.

I felt the decisive thing in my work with them was to convince them finally that they could not destroy me – that I was not afraid of their behaviour. Things did indeed become a bit different when they got to like me and were sorry if I got hurt. The extraordinary thing was that from one moment to the next they suddenly accepted me. Then they were most concerned about me and my welfare.

Such a picture of 'mental illness' must, of course, be seen in proportion. Adolescent Drifters like this represent only a minority within the Teddy-boy society and they are only a minute fraction of their age group.

Even so, if it is thought that there are no more than a few thousand such adolescents growing up in London, they exist as a recognizable type, a strange product of the Welfare State, and, since many will inevitably graduate into adult crime, their existence poses disturbing problems. To give each group of Drifters the special psychological attention described above seems hardly feasible. Yet something needs to be done. A simple calculation shows that the share of young delinquents in the annual cost of the penal apparatus adds up to a sum larger than the whole contribution by the state and local authorities to the youth services.

And if one wants to know what harm can be done by even a small number of such youths, neurotically equating aggression with 'fun', one need only recall the Notting Hill riots.

CHAPTER 8

Sex and Insecurity

Sex for the asking

PERHAPS the simplest thing to say of the Teddy-boy outlook on sex is that it is like that of the rest of present-day society – only more so.

This can be said not only of the psychopathic Drifters, but of nearly the whole of Teddy-boy café society, including many very ordinary adolescents who by their mid-twenties will have forgotten all about dressing up and have become ordinary young married men. In its structure, Teddy-boy society may be rudely governed by young adolescent males, but the sex drive remains the mainspring of nightly activity. The possession of the right girl to take to a cinema, dance, or back alley is the symbol of status. As often as not, rivalry over girls is the starting-point or pretext for a gang fight – for going out 'teamhanded' for a 'giggle'. Since Teddy-boy society is also a concentration of the troubled, the intensified sexual chase also represents a search for reassurance. Its over-intensity somehow reflects a failure to mature, it is a substitute for lack of success on other levels, it is the topic endlessly chewed over in those night-time café conversations when dingy depression is only just kept at bay.

All this is a very ordinary story. As sociologists have found (and as one knew before), a nightly quest for sexual adventure is the common habit among young males at the bottom of the social ladder. Moreover, in a country like Britain, there is today noticeably far greater freedom in sex matters – this freedom has already spread far into the ranks of middle-class youth. Secondly, sex has never received such massive publicity as today, from the ubiquitous underclothes advertisements to the incessant erotic gossip in the popular Press.

It is not difficult to see the reason for this message. It's good for mass sales, and the advertisers like it. Should one in this framework still speak of a special Teddy-boy attitude to sex? A few points stand out. For instance, the precocity of Teddy-boy sophistication. The typical Teddy boy takes his sexual pleasure where and when he wants it, and without further thought. Intercourse with a girl follows naturally after a dance session, a visit to the cinema or the chip shop, and in the circumstances much of it is back-alley sex. Common enough, but what is probably new is the youthful age of the boys.

By the time a boy today has reached fifteen [Mr Brian Carney has quoted a Birmingham club leader as saying], he is ready for a full sex life – and the Teddy-boy movement, by giving its group sanction to sexual freedom, helps him to get it. Even Teddy boys of thirteen and fourteen boast of their sexual adventures, and I don't doubt their word. Once they don Teddy-boy clothing, the breakaway from conventional morality is complete.[1]

According to many observers, this early promiscuity induced by Teddy-boy life goes with deliberate callousness, especially on the Drifter level.

I remember an odd boozy night. There was a girl well known for her antics. Ten of the fellows queued up for her. It was just an ordinary entertainment for them. Then they got into two cars and drove to a spot five miles out of town, but the girl wouldn't go through with it again, so they drove off and left her – left her in the middle of the night: they're callous, I tell you. . . .

However, such a precocious male sex life demands partners. What of the Teddy girls? In terms of being real gang members, a small number of these can be encountered. They are usually working-class teenage girls in complete revolt against their families and living dangerously and excitedly for the moment. But the more common type of camp followers are rather dumb, passive, teenage girls. In my

1. *John Bull*, 10 March 1959.

glimpses of them they seemed crudely painted up, pathetically young, appallingly uneducated, some of them probably in danger of drifting into prostitution – in any case, as I looked at their expressionless faces, I felt sorry for their future families.

Of course, not all girls in Teddy-boy life are of low I.Q. As a sort of insurance, as if looking for the common exit from this racketing life, many a Teddy boy likes to have a respectable girl in tow, whom he sees separately from his friends in the gang – the pattern is frequent. In any case, in considering the role of girls in this life, one has to take account of what seems to be a fundamental difference in juvenile delinquency between two sexes. If we accept the psychological explanation that a delinquent is frequently an emotionally deprived youngster who 'steals for love', then the equivalent to the boy who does so through stealing or breaking in is the girl who slides into prostitution. The revengeful delinquency is similar: boy and girl are both trying to get something of value while giving nothing in return (which is why the money obtained in this way is so often immediately squandered). The distinction is that a boy up before the Court for theft is always in danger of slipping through circumstance into a criminal career. The delinquent girl who is his psychological counterpart may end up on the streets, or else she may become a slut and an inadequate wife and mother, so perpetuating the evil. But as such she is unlikely to feature much in the criminal statistics, which explains, at least in part, why the proportion of boy to girl delinquents is six to one.

Another distinction is that girls have quite a different attitude to delinquent gang life. They enter it for different motives and so it is always easier for them to get out again. I was given an illustration of this by a young woman teacher in Yorkshire who had successfully kept in touch with a group of girls who, on leaving school, knocked about with a lawless gang of youths in outlandish Teddy-boy garb. The girls, when I saw them in a café, looked reckless yet also more wholesome than their London counterparts, better groomed, more self-confident. Yet they also seemed absurdly young to be leading this life. According to the woman teacher they were members of a large and loose gang, living away from their families; some had lived on their own from the age of fifteen, doing what they liked, accepting no authority. It was like a dream life: they were shop girls, and on the slightest pretext, if any wrong word were said to them, they were in the habit of asking for their cards and walking out. As it happened, the previous year had seen some unemployment in the town, and jobs for young people were no longer plentiful. But these girls still walked out of their jobs on the least impulse – they just could not grasp that they were no longer able to do this, and when they found that there was not a similar job to be got in the shop next door, they simply came to my informant in full expectation that she would conjure up such a job for them. On the occasions when these girls confided in her, she said, it was not hard to recognize the sense of insecurity which haunted these girls beneath their superficial air of independence and their determination to be adrift. She had little doubt that the basic feminine ideal of a normal home life with husband, home, and children was the driving force even in their life in Teddy-boy circles. The danger was that before they knew, they might come to be care and protection cases and normal life more difficult to attain.

Even so, even on the lowest Drifters' level, the chance for teenage girls to step out into a new existence of respectability is much easier, because it can be done through a mere choice of suitor. I found a young London Ted in a moment of self-criticism making this point to me quite explicitly, almost jealously. Women, he said, always have something extra in them a man hadn't got:

You take a girl that's got in with a gang of hoodlums. You think she's just a slut, but one day you will see her walking arm in arm in the High Street with a fellow and not even looking at the gang as she passes. Mind you, the boys would never tell. They might feel sorry for the fellow who didn't know what he'd got hold of, but they'd give the girl a chance to forget.

There is an old masculine code – their own – even among Drifters.

Has the Teddy-boy movement in fact had much impact on the life of adolescent girls in this country? It is hard to give an answer. In 1958 there were by Home Office statistics about 11,000 unmarried mothers of sixteen and under in this country, a small number but double that of 1952. From another angle, about one unmarried woman in eighty in the under-twenty group had an illegitimate child during 1938; in 1958 the figure was one in fifty, in 1959 one in forty. This does show a trend, but the absolute figure remains small – the Teddy-boy movement has been a mainly masculine affair.

To return to the boys themselves, the main harmful consequences of their sexual outlook is that in their violent conduct it is mixed up with deliberate callousness. Not, of course, for ever. In the end, even the wildest Teddy boy as a rule arrives at the point where traditional morality reasserts itself, usually at the point of the shotgun. 'My girl's got a baby coming. Didn't want to get married, but what can you do?' Even so, the Teddy-boy years may have their consequences: one observation to this effect was made by my Irish informant:

The way they live, free sexual intercourse is almost universal. They get it where they want it. They don't care where. They'll go to a dance-hall, pick up a girl, have intercourse, and finish with her, never see her again. The result is they've nothing to look forward to when they get married. These lads are worn out, they've got no excitement left in sex before marriage. So most of them can't make a marriage go and that's where the new trouble begins for them. Have you noticed one thing – these young fellows, at the start they don't drink? They'll stay all night in a café but you don't see them much in pubs. But when they're older, when they've settled down and got married, that's when they start drinking. They're restless, marriage means almost nothing, but if they start going back to cafés the wife will get to know about it. But if they say they're going round to the pub it sounds harmless. They say they're just going round for a game of darts or bridge, but that's where they pick up women and go in for really heavy drinking when they're a few years older.

And it is then that they may also go in for the more dangerous types of crime such as pay-roll snatching.

Teds, Cyps, and Spades

Another revealing relationship in contemporary London is that between the Teddy boys and the Cypriot café owners in whose establishments the Teds spend so much of their time and their money. The post-war immigration of Greek and Turkish Cypriots to London has always struck me as a fascinating accidental consequence of Empire, if probably one of the last of its kind. Here they are, steeped in Mediterranean culture, these emigrants from Aphrodite's lovely island, with its classic shores and Crusaders' castles, its white-washed monasteries and minarets, its fierce sunshine and olives and vines. Now they are in their cafés among the brick and grime in Upper Street, around King's Cross, in the Tottenham Court Road and Hammersmith, swarthy men standing behind their tea and coffee machines, chattering to their families in demotic Greek, to the background noise of the juke-box, as they survey the London Teds and their girls who form the main part of their night-time clientele. What thoughts pass behind their dark brows? The picture to my mind was always one of mutual dislike, each side despising the other: while the Teds look down on the Cypriots as foreigners not regarded as quite 'white', it is not hard to guess how the Cypriots must despise these louts who provide them with custom and at the same time insult them. As it happens, by coming to London and opening a number of late-night cafés, the Cypriots have largely aided the expansion of Teddy-boy café society. But the operation has been attended by little goodwill. In Teddy-boy talk of fighting in North London (that is, talk of battles far from those fought for Enosis), the 'Cyps', who are Greek and Turkish Cypriots, their cafés, and plate-glass windows, featured frequently as 'the enemy'. The hard-working Cypriots in their cafés were 'raking in the money' which the Teddy boys spent. Although they were still new in London, they were rapidly getting on, while the Teds were not getting on. True it might be by their own choice, but then there was always an element of doubt about this choice itself – enough cause for anger.

General prejudice apart, I think the same anxiety lies also behind the fierce hostility of the London Teddy boys against the coloured immigrants. Of course, other factors are involved. On the whole the Teddy boys have much the same amount of colour prejudice as the rest of the British population, sometimes more, sometimes less, but to understand the reasons why the Notting Hill riots attracted Teddy boys from all over London into the battle, one has to try to see what was involved for them. There was, for example, the question of status. To a Teddy boy who insists on a social status of which he is always unsure, it is vitally important that no coloured immigrant should be better than he, or even an equal. The same applies to sexual jealousy: to boys to whom indiscriminate sex is a substitute for all their inadequacies, the sight of a Negro with a white girl may seem like a knife-thrust against their masculinity.

Then there is social and economic jealousy. When listening to the tale of Teddy-boy grievances against the West Indians, I found that one of the first complaints was always that West Indians were making quick money and riding in flashy cars, and this money came from immoral earnings of white and coloured prostitutes. The complaint is revealing. After all, the typical Teddy boys are not against any man who makes money ruthlessly. They rather admire such a person. Nor are they against immoral earnings as such. In the ordinary Teddy-boy café it does not take long to learn the identity of the local ponces, and the information is given without sign of disapproval. No, the rationalizations hide a more basic clash, namely that the Teddy boys and the West Indian immigrants who are working side by side are trying to travel in different directions. As new immigrants the West Indians are to begin with underdogs, but once they make good there are again no underdogs below the Teds. As new immigrants, again, the West Indians are very noticeably trying to get on, to make money and gain status. But the Teds don't want to get on; to join their movement is in fact to oppose getting on, to live in a dream of endless rebellion. In this dream picture, it is essential that the coloured in their territory should feature as lesser beings. Any coloured man who does not stay put but instead rises and buys up houses or a big car destroys this picture of security and so represents a profound threat. It is against this threat that the ranks in an area like Notting Hill have been tightly closed.

The fear of authority

I think that much the same feelings have helped to produce the violent antagonism of the Teddy boys towards the police, about which something ought to be said.

It has been important for the development of the Teddy-boy fashion that the gang should give its members a sense of reassurance. This feeling is, of course, quite irrational, at least as far as the authorities are concerned. Every new arrest exposes the futility of the whole rebellion, and this, in turn, explains their violent antagonism towards the police. A hostile attitude towards the police is, of course, common to a good many working-class adolescents. For historic reasons, the police in England have been for long widely regarded as the defenders of upper-class property against the mobs from the slums, the revolutionary mob, i.e. a good part of the old working class. This hostile working-class view of the police is still strongly held, and much of it has survived slum clearance.

There's little sympathy among that class for the police [said an informant to me in talking about the families of Teddy boys]. In any tough criminal area there is never respect for the police: they are looked on purely as oppressors. When there was that stabbing in Holloway, when a policeman was killed, the one thing everybody said was: 'They'll make damn sure *somebody*'ll hang for it.' Even the older working men in the pubs who usually dislike the Teds were talking in that strain.

It is this anti-police tradition, with its elements of old class struggle, which the Teddy boys have now turned into a social vogue. It goes naturally enough with the other aspects of their rebellion, but I think there is something more than just this tradition involved. Talking to boys of all ages in London, good and bad, Teds and ex-Teds, I found a single-minded acceptance of a state of cold war between themselves and the police which was startlingly uniform. Indeed, in Teddy-boy mythology it was the police who were the enemy aggressors. Like enemies, they were simultaneously despised and feared. They were despised, for instance, as cowards hiding behind their uniform. 'You see a copper walk past a crowd of fellows when he's alone and if somebody calls out a remark it's ten to one he'll pretend not to hear – he'll walk on. They're only brave when there's two of them so they can give evidence.' At the same time the police were feared because it was thought that their primary aim was 'to get the Boys', to knock them about at the station, and to manufacture pretexts for charges. There was a prevalent idea that the police could always spoil a boy's career and frequently were out to do so. 'I'm not afraid of the coppers, but I know, if they possibly can, they will put you on a charge. They will say anything, that you resisted arrest, that you were carrying horrible weapons. Result? You're put on probation. That means you've got a record – you can't get a good job.' The police were also regarded as the enemy who stopped the Boys from leading their rightful and carefree social life. In one area they were held responsible for closing all the late-night cafés; in another, for the break-up of the large gangs. 'It's all the coppers. These days, if they saw a dozen fellows standing together, they'll tell them they'll have them up for an affray. It's getting so they'll tell you to move on if they just see two blokes on the pavement.'

Listening to the plaintive talk, one got a sense that in these adolescent circles a constant state of war with the police was accepted as just one of the facts of life. Now, there may be some partial factual basis to this clash. After all, the juvenile crime wave *is* a reality. As the Commissioner of Police for the Metropolis reported in 1960, two-thirds of all arrests for shop-breaking, warehouse-breaking, etc., involved young persons under twenty-one (and two-fifths juveniles under seventeen). Faced with the rising wave of juvenile crime, and no doubt egged on by their superiors, the police in some areas have certainly taken to chivvying local Teddy boys suspected as being a cause of trouble. How much of this talk of the boys being beaten up at the station ought to be discounted is hard to say – it is by now almost a point of honour for an arrested boy to make this claim. But no doubt a certain amount of rough handling does go on and is a cause of genuine fear. I was for instance told on good authority about one gang of particularly reckless sixteen-year-olds: 'No matter how tough these young fellows think they are, they remain dead scared of the police. They know once the police get them into the cells, they won't be handled with kid gloves – and that knowledge is always in their minds.'

The shock of recognition

Yet, at least for the older boys, the fear of being physically knocked about is not the most important thing. The real and overwhelming fear is that once a boy is arrested and sitting in a cell, his whole illusion, his whole fantasy of being safe as a member of a gang is suddenly taken from him, and it is this loss which is so terrifying. Each time another hero is arrested, a myth is destroyed. The power of the police represents in fact the flaw in the Teddy boy's dream of secure rebellion. The more intense the fantasy, i.e. the more neurotic a boy's belief that as a member of the gang he can live amorally, do what he likes and disregard the law, the more intense also becomes hatred of the police, who threaten the fantasy.

It is of course not only the authority of the police which exposes the Teddy-boy rebellion. Behind the police stand the Courts, the power of magistrates and judges. As the futile young rebels come up against the real strength of the society they had tried to oppose, the result is usually an overwhelming shock. There are of course a minority who remain hardened, but I have often heard the opposite stories of reckless young Teddy-boy offenders who, when they find themselves in the dock, are at first as dazed as young prisoners of war whose entire familiar universe had collapsed. A social worker from West London who had attended the Court proceedings where some of his boys were up on fairly serious charges gave me this picture:

The thing which shocked me extremely was my own lack of preparation for seeing the boys in Court look so differently from what I had thought they were like in their normal social setting. They looked even physically smaller – they were really only infants, suddenly finding themselves completely helpless and without even being able to express it. When I asked them about this they didn't know how to put it into words, but what seemed to me the worst was the sudden awareness on their part that all their fantasy strengths were of no use to them. The boys were now surrounded by police, having to answer to a person who had very definite authority – it was not a matter of their giving this man authority – they weren't asked. I think their helplessness was linked with something else as well, that no matter how many do-gooders there were in their outside world, at this point they could not be helped. Where even that failed, everything had failed them.

Of course, this sense of shock – the shock of recognition – does not last. Youth is resilient and adaptable. Once sentenced, most boys adjust themselves. Even Borstal and Detention Centres become eventually slices of real life, with irksome restrictions but also the positive experience of companionship, and which in any case soon pass. Their reactions to detention naturally vary in many ways, but two points seem to stand out. First, while the present crime wave indicates that the boys have outside become noticeably more troublesome, the authorities 'inside' claim that they are no more difficult to manage than they or their predecessors were before, which seems to indicate that when the sense of insecurity is less, as it nearly always is in institutions, so is the need for defiance. The second point is the striking contrast between the intractability of some Teddy-boy leaders when they are out in the street with the mob and their evident helplessness when they are on their own and have to face an unfamiliar situation. An older ex-prisoner, who had seen a good many characteristic Teddy boys pass through his establishment, put this to me with some contempt (his comments applied to the time a few years back when young offenders were still sent to prison in some numbers, which is now rarely the case):

When they're in a group together, they're ready to tear any place apart, but get one of them on his own – he wouldn't say boo to a goose. He might be definitely against the rules, but the warder would need only take him round the corner and clip his earholes for him and he'd cave in. I've seen them come and go. Once they're inside they're nothing. The first month they always write the same sort of letter: 'Dear Mum, I'm very very sorry for what I did and I won't repeat it. When I come out I want to go respectable. I'm going to go steady with Jeanie down the road, etc.' They'd often cry, too, not in front of the others, but when they're on their own. I got friendly with one who'd been a sort of king of the Teddy boys down his way. I looked in one time through the spy hole – I was a 'red-hand' then – and saw he was crying on and on, though of course he denied it when I mentioned it. The way they're helpless on their own is pathetic in the case of many of them. Immediately they're up against anything really important, any major decision, they're helpless.

That is, unless something – the right girl, the right friends, a job, or merely the advance of time – helps them to pass from their adolescent insecurity.

However, the shock of arrest and the experience of detention can also have the opposite effect. One way of covering up fear and insecurity is by renewed defiance. And circumstances often encourage this. When boys get out, the same environment is often waiting to receive them again, the same street, the life of the pictures, pubs, and pool-parlour; the Boys still at the corner and in the cafés, the same old talk of clothes, sex, fights, and nicking. How quickly before a boy is back in his old ways? With the difference only that what he has undergone has become a mark of higher status in the gang – now he can feel really tough. There is always this danger. As Lady Wootton has written, 'It is easy to underestimate the effect of appearances in Court or of residence in approved schools, Borstal, or prison, in creating a delinquent culture based on common experience.' [1] How far this happens is hard to know. So are the ways of preventing it. But this is another story. To see the current problems of delinquency in proportion. one has at some point to turn to the much greater changes taking place in the surrounding society.

1. Barbara Wootton, *Social Science and Social Pathology*, Allen & Unwin, 1959.

PART TWO

DISCUSSION

CHAPTER 9

The New Society

The passing of the bourgeois age

WHAT is the shape of the society which is producing increased numbers of young delinquents? The discussion of the question may take one rather far afield, but I believe that if we want to see the delinquency problem in its social framework there is no avoiding this.

The belief that we are rushing into a new society is today found all around us, but the definition of the basic nature of the change is less easy. Some would see it in the incessant march of scientific technology. In an industrial country like Britain this revolution is particularly evident. One can see how on top of the historic divisions between the two nations of England in terms of social class a new division is being superimposed – a rift between two cultures: between those who are familiar with the new scientific age and those who are not.

Some again would put the main emphasis on social levelling and the spread of new habits of mass consumption and mass entertainment. In 1960, practically every British household owned a television set; well before the end of the decade the majority of households will probably own a car – in all these respects Britain has already travelled far.

In connexion with this mass culture, some saw the signs of change in the arrival of new figures of authority, the take-over bidders, the advertisers, the gossip columnists, the publicity men. Yet not only these were making headway. A telling sign of social change, to my mind, was the growth of the teenage market and of a mass youth culture. I recall a remark which made a particular impression on me, made to me by the head of a youth club founded half a century ago in what was then still the darkest East End of London: 'Today our motoring club has sixty motor-cycles and thirty motor-scooters. The girl friends act as secretaries. They'll arrange the logistics of a tour to the Pyrenees without any ado.'

Yet on whatever outward signs one likes to put the emphasis, to my mind the essence of the contemporary change is that it is indeed a whole change of social order – the great bourgeois age, which went with exclusive middle-class privilege and middle-class culture, is passing. As it recedes, it is being gradually replaced by a new affluent society [1] which is based on mass consumption, and the increasing *participation* of practically everyone in a new good life and many other things alongside.

Of the fundamental character of this change there can already be little question. It was the age of bourgeois exclusiveness which launched what we know as Western industrial civilization. This bourgeois age has had a long innings, but almost any middle-class European whose memories go back some thirty or forty years knows that a dramatic change has occurred in his lifetime which it is not easy to communicate to the young, and that the world of his own childhood with its large solid houses and its domestic servants lies already in another era. Writing in 1955 about the new look of post-war Britain and Europe, I tried to define what it had replaced:

The causes of Subtopia lie in the social change more far-reaching than the establishment of the Welfare State – in some thing like a change of ruling class.

It is ruling classes which set cultural patterns and for more than a century the dominant culture of Western Europe has clearly been that of the well-to-do middle class, the *haute bourgeoisie*. It was a culture which went with those great English social inventions: the gentlemen's club (and the soft club chair), amateur sport, and the long week-end; with French *cuisine* and finishing schools, German scientific *Tüchtigkeit* and German music, Italian and Viennese opera; it went with family holidays in Scotland and Switzerland and on the Riviera; with large *appartements*, parlourmaids, and the solid house-façades of

1. Even though it has become a cliché, I come back to Mr Galbraith's well-known term as the most apt.

Europe's middle-class cities. It went also with the distinguished European repertory theatre, the great tradition of the European novel (whose last representative was probably Thomas Mann), with liberal individualism, introspection in art, psychoanalysis – anyone thinking aloud could enumerate a similar list for himself. In all its aspects – and this was important – this bourgeois way of life was also a minority culture from which the lower-class majority of the population was by and large excluded.

It is this bourgeois minority culture with its exclusive appeal that has been crumbling. The process has gone further in the United States than in Britain, and further in Britain than in tenaciously bourgeois countries like France or Germany. What we are now entering instead is a social era based on mass participation. The keynote is that culture is no longer for a minority. Everyone must now participate.[1]

Writing the present chapter at the beginning of the sixties, I feel that the revolution has already gone further, and with it new problems are upon us: and, to understand these better, it is as well to see the sort of social structure which has been left behind us.

In terms of what one might call 'ruling-class participation', the bourgeois society which arose in Europe out of the French and the Industrial Revolutions represented a considerable advance on earlier aristocratic eras in which power and fashionable culture had been vested in only a small fraction of the population. The solid upper-middle-class culture, the one which really mattered in the European bourgeois society, was shared in by perhaps ten to fifteen per cent of the nation. This made it a comparatively broad culture, and yet it was still a minority culture in which the majority, and especially the working classes, had little or no share. And it is this exclusive bourgeois class system and culture which is today cracking up.

In retrospect some points about it are worth noting to illustrate the change. First, the system of bourgeois exclusiveness quite easily survived the political revolution of one man, one vote. It has taken a second upheaval, the present one, to shake it. Secondly, even in a country of

1. *Encounter*, June 1955.

widespread wealth, like England, the bourgeois culture was still that of a class small enough to base its social life on direct personal contacts and relations. The contacts of the head of an upper-middle-class family which mattered were nearly all direct and personal: with the fellow-members of his class, his profession, and his club; with his family solicitor, doctor, and public schoolmaster; with his tailor, his personal shopkeepers, domestic servants, and the like.

In the third place, bourgeois culture was also authoritative. It rested on a network of institutions which, particularly in England, derived authority from history and tradition: Crown and Parliament, the Law, the Church, the Armed Services, Oxford and Cambridge, *The Times* and *Guardian*, the Medical Colleges, the Learned Societies. But authority in the bourgeois society lay not only with institutions. It was also personally vested in individuals. The bearer of a title had traditional social and moral authority. So had a bishop, a judge, a senior Cabinet Minister, and a Colonial Governor. The writers of leaders in *The Times* had *their* special individual authority; so did eminent lawyers and Harley Street specialists (who may have preserved it best of all); so did all kinds of figures like public school headmasters, and England and County cricket captains; and so on and so on. Of course the whole system was buttressed by money, but not only by that – money still has its power. It was buttressed by the tradition of a whole close-knit class culture. If British policemen carried an aura of unusual authority and respect, it was because they were seen as representatives of a society sure of all fundamental belief.

The change in Britain

To understand what is happening in Britain today, one has to recognize that not only the privileges of yesterday are being swept away. The whole structure of authority of the bourgeois order has today become suddenly tenuous and is crumbling. Such traditions as public-school exclusiveness, the ponderousness of Parliamentary debate at Westminster, even the right accent – they are still all there, but have become suddenly less significant. This observation is not new, but an additional point I would make is that the disintegration of bourgeois values has gone further in England than some other countries – further than in France or than in Western Germany – and this in spite of the English retention of titles and the importance of the so-called Establishment. Or perhaps just because the traditional surface of English life is still so sedulously maintained, the real social changes beneath it appear more dramatic. On the Continent of Europe, palaces turned into museums or municipal offices have usually been devoted to this purpose for some generations, but as for the English stately home now converted into a convalescent home or approved school, people no more than middle-aged can still remember how not long ago it was filled with guests, grooms, and gardeners.

One can think of various reasons for the more rapid crack-up of English bourgeois society. There were the shocks of the First World War and its casualties, the drift of the inter-war years, the dreary years of dole queues and Stanley Baldwin, and the progressive loss of the empire. Other European countries underwent similar experiences, but I think the sharper social cleavages of English society intensified the crumbling. The genius of Lord Northcliffe also had something to do with speeding the change. The fact that the British were conditioned to read far greater numbers of popular newspapers than anybody else, did mean that they were exposed at an earlier stage to an influence destructive of the old order. The similarity of language also laid England more open to transatlantic influences. It allowed such American publicity figures as film stars and pop singers to be substituted for the traditional figures of British authority – this has also happened elsewhere in Europe, but nowhere to quite the same degree as in this country.

At any rate, historians will probably conclude that some decisive social change was set on foot in England in the bad inter-war years, some more pronounced rift, some greater loss of upper-middle-class assurance than elsewhere, which has one special result. If the post-war British affluent society is not more affluent than others, it seems to be more stridently commercial than others and more destructive of social roots.

The British affluent society

At this point it may be worth giving a rough definition of what I have been describing as 'the affluent society'.

The essence is not, as the cliché has it, mere high living standards – these are always relative. The essence of the affluent society, I think, lies in the unprecedented participation of the majority of people in its benefits and problems. As the term is here used, I would therefore say that the affluent society began to take shape when the techniques of capitalist mass production had reached such a pitch that the wheels of the economy could only be kept turning over if, in theory, all citizens of the society were turned into consumers on a full scale. I would put its starting-point in Britain at around 1950 – really the decisive take-off date when all Western Europe began to advance towards an 'Americanized' social life of cars, gadgets, and mass media.

Professor J. K. Galbraith, in talking about America, has described some of the main features of the affluent society as 'priority for consumption', 'material possessions equal status', and 'the decline of the public sector'. I would add that they also include three changes affecting family relationships, which I would put under the headings of 'Women go out to work', 'Loss of status of the father', and 'All youth is golden'.

All these trends have, I think, some influence on the relatively marginal problem of youthful delinquency, which conversely throws some light on their effects. It is therefore worth looking at them in turn.

Consumption as mainspring

Another name one could give to the affluent society would be 'the age of participation'. Because of the shape which the economy has assumed, it depends for its stability not only on uninterrupted mass consumption, but on consumption on a steadily expanding scale. Every citizen must consequently be drawn into the circle of producing and consuming at the maximum level. If the affluent society is to prosper, not merely a privileged minority but every man, woman, and child must participate in the good life of modern living.[1]

Everyone must participate. In a country like Britain, one can see this trend quite visually illustrated in the contemporary movement of the British working classes, away from their drab nineteenth-century streets, the darkened brick, the draughty passages, the worn sink, and towards the ideal of a new suburban life of small house, small garden, small car, and large television set. In the new society it is public authorities which mainly provide the new houses, but private enterprise which provides all the rest, which gives the working-class housewife her modern kitchen and appliances and the whole family its mobility and entertainment. In face of this supreme drive to create customers in the mass, the old bourgeois privilege based on exclusiveness, large houses, domestic servants, has simply crumbled. It is crumbling the faster because other influences are also pushing in the same direction.

In the affluent society it is not enough that the wants of every citizen should be met. To satisfy the capacity of the largest production interests, new wants have constantly to be created. Mr Galbraith has drawn attention to the distortions caused in American society as new wants are created and intensified by an advertising industry running at a rate of eleven billion dollars a year. The notorious example of an industry dependent upon the constant creation of new wants is, of course, the giant American motor industry, whose models have been deliberately built and stylized to become obsolescent in a few years and so to make replace-

---

1. I believe this to be the basic social trend even though I am aware of the fact that, in Britain, a substantial minority, estimated at several million people, were still living on the fringe of acute poverty, especially old-age pensioners, invalids, etc.

ment necessary. If the British economy is not yet so far advanced, it seems well on the same road. (One can, for instance, see this in television advertising in the stress on 'newness' in household appliances – some new gimmick, some new improvement, usually a minor change but presented as making the new model infinitely preferable to its predecessor.)

This creation of wants requires constant advertising. This in turn means that big financial interests must take over and enlarge the media of mass communication. The mass media must in fact become both a part of big business and themselves big business. It is worth noting that in the British affluent society the newspapers, magazines, and television programmes that carry the bulk of advertising are in actual fact already controlled by a handful of large financial interests. Indeed, in many ways the close cooperation between big newspapers, big commercial television, big advertising, and betting interests has already been perfected much further in Britain than in the United States.

The new image

This financial take-over, in turn, has an obvious result on the contents of the mass media. It involves them in the drive to create a new image of what is desirable – that of a world where through material consumption everybody is happy, wealthy, successful, and enjoying the right status. An example of this image-creation is offered (not absolutely every time but often) by the *TV Times*, among all British periodicals perhaps the cleverest expression of the ideals of British advertising. In its pages all articles seem written skilfully but indistinguishably in one single style adjusted to celebrity worship. All personalities, whether statesmen and scientists or pop singers and comedians, are brought down (or up) to the same denominator. All are presented as happy, successful, well-to-do, but at the same time as people who can smile at past failure and are essentially simple people like you or me – more than that, dear viewers, these wonderful people are only too happy to create further happiness by entertaining you; and so on, week by week, world without end.

This gigantic take-over by the advertisers has, of course, not been the only cultural trend in the affluent society. There has been a noticeable hiving off of new middle-class culture, seen, for example, in the rise in circulations of the *Observer* and *Sunday Times*; while many television programmes on any channel have also been informative, vital, and stimulating – television is, after all, only a medium. By and large, however, it is already clear that before the triumphant onrush of the new affluent mass culture, geared with the aid of highly-paid talent to the advertising of consumer goods, the significance of the historic institutions of Britain seems suddenly to have dwindled, to be no longer in the foreground of British life. It was as if a glossy wand had been waved. The affairs of the Church of England, the tribulations of the Royal Navy (or for that matter of the T.U.C.), the uninspired Parliamentary debates at Westminster, the leaders in *The Times* (trying to renew and readvertise itself), and the Left-wing views in the *New Statesman*; the attention paid to occasions like the Oxford and Cambridge Boat Race or the efforts of the Amateur Athletic Association to find a few thousand pounds – all these seemed to pale before the new foreground of the affluent society: the parade of television personalities, the arranged publicity for girl models and boy singers, the advertisements for electric mixers and Ford Consuls, the unending colour-print pages on fashions, foods, and cosmetics in the women's magazines. Through the irresistible mass attack of this new artificial culture, everything else appeared suddenly pushed into the background, reduced in size, dated. And if this social and cultural revolution has also been more pronounced in Britain than in other European countries, it was because Britain, among other things, started off with a far larger and more businesslike popular newspaper industry and a larger and more Americanized advertising industry. In these respects, other European countries are only just catching up.

The shift in social and cultural priorities has also proceeded faster because the affluent society contains a built-in economic unbalance.

The lag of the public sector

The equation which any government in a capitalist society must solve is simple. Every citizen likes to spend his income on consumption of his personal choice. All citizens equally dislike having a part of this income taken in taxation for public ends, even if as essential as schools and hospitals. The success of a government in balancing these demands against each other is a measure of its popularity. In the affluent society, however, mass advertising comes in to disturb the balance. Or to be more precise, since advertising is only an instrument, it is the fact of the giant producers having developed advertising as a scientific technique for creating and increasing the demand for their goods which has introduced a new situation, since this technique is employed only on behalf of goods produced by private enterprise, and almost never on behalf of public services rendered by the state. Professor Galbraith has shown how in the United States this one-sided concentration of 'the massed drums of modern publicity' has created a visible unbalance in the American affluent society which, if not wildly dangerous, has led already to a deplorable distortion of social priorities. He says in this well-known passage, which is still worth quoting because nothing so very much has changed:

to create the demand for new cars we must contrive elaborate and functionless changes each year and then subject the consumer to ruthless psychological pressures to persuade him of their importance. Were this process to falter or break down, the consequence would be disturbing. In the meantime there are large ready-made needs for schools, hospitals, slum clearance, and urban redevelopment, sanitation, parks, playgrounds, police, and a thousand other things. Of these needs almost no one must be persuaded. They are unavailable only because, as public officials of all kinds and ranks explain each day with practised skill, the money to provide them is unavailable. So it has come about that we get growth and increased employment along the dimensions of private goods only at the price of increasingly frantic persuasion. We exploit but poorly the opportunity along the dimension of public services. The economy is geared to the least urgent set of human wants.[1]

What of Britain? If the evidence of a similar drift was discovered only belatedly even by readers of Mr Galbraith, I think this was simply because British developments lagged some years behind those in the United States. One reason was that the post-war Labour Government gave unquestioned priority to public housing and health services. But the Labour Government went out in 1951. My concern here is not with party politics, but it has to be said that under the Conservative governments of the fifties, drifting with events towards the slogan of 'you've never had it so good', the British affluent society also began to develop an increasing unbalance. On one side there was certainly a steady rise in standards of personal consumption. Alongside this was the evident belief of the Government that the country could not *afford* to build a single new hospital – or prison: none were built during the decade. There was the lag in subsidized public housing; the inadequate provision for old-age pensioners; the relative slowness in replacing antiquated school buildings, in providing youth clubs and playing fields. Above all, the lack of social balance was illustrated by the inadequate salaries and consequent staff shortages in public services which were vital to the welfare of society, but outside the sphere of commercial advertising. There was the persistent shortage of nurses (what would have happened but for girls from overseas?) of teachers in state schools, of policemen, penal officers, midwives, youth workers (or for that matter of clergymen). Setting these shortages against the boom in all kinds of personal consumption, and in the advertising industry itself, the picture of British society in 1960 showed the characteristic distortions of an unguided affluent society which had appeared some years earlier in the United States.

1. J. K. Galbraith, *The Affluent Society*, Hamish Hamilton, 1958.

About this two comments could be made. By 1960, some of the problems arising from the decline of the public sector had already impressed themselves pretty firmly on public attention. The proposals of the Crowther Report for raising the school-leaving age to sixteen, even though postponed by the Government, and of the Albemarle Report for providing public finance for the youth services, could be seen as attempts to redress some of this unbalance within special fields. So could the setting up of an inquiry into the pay problems of the British police: clearly a point must come when an affluent society has to wake up and offer adequate pay to those who protect it. It was, however, also apparent that redressing the balance would be no easy task. There was always the one-way pressure of the daily Press with its values geared to those of advertising: any tax reduction in the Budget – cheaper beer, cheaper baccy, sixpence off income tax – was automatic front-page headline news: it was good for ads., good for business, good for circulation. On the other hand, talk about the need for more teachers' training colleges, for newer hospitals, for more probation officers – this was mere stuff for well-intentioned editorials not read by nine popular-Press readers out of ten.

The second observation – and this, after what may seem a considerable diversion brings us back to our young delinquents – is that if we take the points where the public sector has most sharply declined, it is where working-class families and epecially working-class boys and girls dependent on public services are particularly involved. It is they who have suffered from delays in rehousing; from the shortage of trained probation officers; from lack of playing-fields and sports facilities in poorer areas and niggardly public grants to youth clubs; probably most of all from the shortage of school-teachers, from overcrowded classes and the consequent lack of individual attention. Mr John Townsend in his interesting account of teaching in difficult secondary modern schools [1] has, for example, shown how the constant staff changes in such schools and the need to make do with

1. John Townsend, *The Young Devils*, Chatto & Windus, 1958.

inexperienced 'directed' student teachers and untrained Commonwealth graduates, has not only debased standards but added to the sense of insecurity of problem children:

Schools should be the one place where children from unhappy or unstable homes should find security and feel wanted ... but in face of this restlessness within the profession, and the patch-it-up policies of government and educational authorities alike, it is almost impossible to provide this; or to build and develop character in their pupils, obtain good educational standards, respect for authority, or achieve any worth-while corporate life.

In fact, if one takes just this particular social distortion – on the one side the intensified stress on money values in the message proclaimed by the affluent society to such young-sters, and on the other the visible lag in the public social services designed to help them – one can see this distortion perhaps not as a direct and measurable cause, but certainly as part of the background of rising delinquency in the fifties.

How much precise weight to give to this factor is hard to say, for the affluent society is also responsible for other great changes, particularly in family relations.

CHAPTER 10

The Family and the Affluent Society

The resilient middle class

THE changes which have recently been transforming family structure can be seen most prominently in British working-class life. But then it is on working-class life in general that the affluent society has had its most pronounced impact.

The British middle class has during the last generation changed steadily from the old bourgeoisie typified by independent businessmen and professional men into the new class of the salaried administrators and technicians of today. This has meant a lessened sense of middle-class self-assurance, perhaps also somewhere or other a loss of morale: but it is already quite clear that in a highly conservative country like Britain the upper and middle classes can coast along successfully with the new affluent society. Especially for middle-class youth, its initial impact has been distinctly positive.

It has in the first place brought a stimulating vista of expansion. The pages of advertisements of positions vacant in every daily newspaper show that the new administrative middle class of the affluent society will be considerably larger in numbers than was the old bourgeoisie. Secondly, the change has brought a very marked new spirit of competitiveness and discipline to British middle-class youth. Greater demands at schools and universities have introduced a whole new hierarchy of grades of merit. If the public schools have lost in social exclusiveness, this has been more than offset by reinforcement in middle-class numbers from the grammar schools. There are also more ladders to climb; science and technology have opened vast new avenues of employment – and how the young flock into them! Culturally, middle-class young people have been far less affected by the intensified power of the mass media than their working-class contemporaries. By contrast with pre-war philistinism, the cultural horizons of British middle-class youth have, indeed, broadened noticeably. There is far more active participation in music (including esoteric jazz), more interest in modern furniture, the modern theatre, in motoring and in international travel. In fact, as the old economic class distinctions such as having servants and being the only people to own cars have broken down, so new class differences have been reconstructed along intellectual lines; and these have, if anything, become more marked again as the controllers of the mass media directed at working-class readers have lowered their sights. Or one could put it this way: the cultural gap between a 'class' newspaper like the *Observer* and a mass newspaper like the *People* may be much as it was. But since the educated middle-class readers of the *Observer* have increased so very much in numbers, this gap has become correspondingly more significant.

In the first phase of the the affluent society British middle-class youth has benefited in many ways, but especially, I think, through the increased working discipline which has been imposed. Of course there are the problems which arise from the bigness and impersonality of the new society, and which overshadow the lives of all young people. But, against these, English class snobbery is still a powerful defence; or again, middle-class youth can find an answer to the times in earlier marriage and more pronounced retreat into purely personal relations. Across the Channel, too. discussing the new defensive outlook of French middle-class youth, Mme Françoise Giroud summed it up as follows:

Comme ils ont le cœur frileux. Vite, se marier. Vite, avoir des enfants. Vite, édifier sa niche.[1]

The lives of working-class young people have been rather differently affected in the affluent society, both positively for some and negatively for others. The positive changes are, of

1. Françoise Giroud, *La Nouvelle Vague*, Gallimard, 1958.

course, most striking. If we want to see how successfully one section of working-class youth is acquiring middle-class status, we need only look at the class background of boys and girls in grammar schools, at those who work in the laboratories and who are the members of new provincial rowing and sailing clubs, and at the classless world of jazz. As for the general benefits of the affluent society, it has, of course, brought to most working-class families an incomparably more varied life. It has brought them modern housing through the estates, and mobility through motoring; it has brought music through radio and pop records; drama through the medium of films; comment on current affairs through television; domestic science through the women's magazines; and so forth.

The negative effects of the affluent society on working-class life are certainly less obvious and less important, yet they can also be discerned. The working-classes are more immediately affected by the relative lag in public services. They are vulnerably exposed to the cultural assault of the mass media, for instance in putting across half-assimilated American values. Working-class families are also more vulnerable to the socially and psychologically harmful effects of re-housing, as expressed in a breakup of local community life. Researchers like Michael Young and Peter Willmott have shown how even well-intentioned large-scale re-housing can diminish the tradition of warm family ties and the defensive community sense of the old slum street, for which fresh air and new suburban surroundings are no substitute – at least not at first. It is hardly an accident that the largest of all London housing estates, at Dagenham, has a particularly high delinquency rate.[1] If we turn to what is called 'alienation' from work, it is the working classes who are most affected by the increasing mechanization of all

1. A local teacher put it to me like this: 'The estate was a flipping ghetto from the start. Working-class families and practically nobody else were just pushed into the place as a class and today there are a lot of angry young men on the estate. The insecurity of the parents on the estate is also passed on to the children.'

production which is turning many jobs into a meaningless ritual. (The complaint of 'boredom' at work and out of work, so widely prevalent among working-class youth, is seldom heard on a middle-class level.) Lastly, it is working-class youth which has been most intimately affected by what is perhaps the most important change in social life in the affluent society, the change in family relationships.

Married women go out to work

Yes, but should they?

This is no longer a question worth asking. The only valid question is how this revolutionary change in family life should so quickly have come about. The simplest answer is that married women are today going out to work in millions because for the first time they are able to do so. This is the initial revolution. Professor Titmuss [1] has calculated that from the mid-Victorian family of six or more the average working-class family has already fallen to an average of less than two and a half children from marriages contracted in the 1920s. In 1890 about a third of the life expectancy of a working-class woman was devoted to pregnancy and the care of small infants. Today it is only one-fourteenth of her life. By the time she has completed her cycle of birth and infant care, the present-day working-class woman has still more than half her life to live. At the same time, modern appliances have freed her progressively from household drudgery while the trend continues towards more and more state supervision of her children. Even so cautious an observer as Professor Titmuss has said that to speak of a 'revolutionary change in working-class attitudes to child-bearing' would hardly be an exaggeration.

Secondly, most married women in the affluent society go out to work because their labour is urgently required. In the current British economy this demand has already attained such proportions that by now innumerable unskilled and

1. Richard M. Titmuss, *Essays on the Welfare State*, Allen & Unwin, 1958.

semi-skilled jobs in light industry and the distributive trades could not be filled at all without the employment of married as well as unmarried women.

Thirdly, married women are going out into employment because every contemporary social force is pushing them in this direction. Advertising creates the desire for consumption goods, hire purchase the means. It is already a fairly regular pattern that the wage of the husband 'keeps' the family while that of his wife provides for the purchase of possessions like a washing-machine, television set, refrigerator, or car. Just as the advertising of consumer goods increased throughout the fifties, so did the outside employment of married women. In 1948, the estimated number of married women at work was two million, and ten years later in 1958 it was about four million, and there is no sign that the maximum has yet been reached.

Is this trend to the good or bad? Does outside work create a genuine conflict for the average working-class woman between her roles as wife and mother and as wage-earner? The fog of prejudice and platitude around the subject is not easy to pierce, but a few points seem to stand out. First of all, the affluent society has arrived; its dynamic requires married women to be both earners and spenders; and in view of the change in the size of the average family, any idea of halting the exodus of wives into employment is futile. Secondly, the material benefits flowing from the added pay packet of the average working-class wife are so tangible that they hardly need mentioning. It is largely these combined family wages which have speeded the advance towards the current *embourgeoisement* in working-class life. Thirdly, outside work is by now part of the whole process of emancipation of the working-class woman from the old drudgery at the kitchen sink. Dr Viola Klein in her survey[1] found that a large minority of wives welcomed outside work primarily because it enlarged their horizons; so did a minority of their husbands. Moreover, one can see quite a convenient pattern:

1. Viola Klein, *Working Wives*, Institute of Personnel Management, 1959.

a young married woman of today will go on working for the first years after marriage; she will then stop while she has children and they are small, and only as they reach school age and the state takes over will she go back to outside work.

However, not all women follow this pattern and everything has its price. In the unplanned way in which it took place, the mass exodus of British working-class women into outside employment has also led to a weakening of family life – at least in certain cases and on certain levels. This danger is not easily measured nor even easy to generalize about, but, I think, also not to be ignored. Certainly not in those cases where parents are already indifferent and negligent towards their children. True, as is often pointed out, working wives are numbered in millions and juvenile delinquents only in tens of thousands. Yet I think this counter-argument misses the point. The *general* exodus of married women, many of them mothers, into outside work, in itself helped to create a new social atmosphere, a new *general* way of family life, whereby 'home' for many boys and girls becomes less important in their lives, and the companionship and rules of the irresponsible gang therefore become more important. It was a picture of such general change which emerged most clearly from my conversations with penal officers, social workers, and youth leaders. In the outcome it may not be the boy or girl in the gang whose mother works the longest hours who will actually stray over the uncertain borderline into delinquency, but this is surely a detail.

There is also the argument that the mass movement of married women into outside work has led to an increase in the number of children suffering from 'maternal deprivation'; that is, of children who through lack of that security which depends on maternal love suffer from a sense of rejection; who grow up emotionally adrift, finding it hard to feel any firm ties either to their family or to society, and whose delinquency can be described as a desperate 'stealing for love' – the stereotype of such problem boys and girls is well known.

Has there been a great increase in the number of such

emotionally deprived delinquents? Well, according to the impression of penal classification officers, there has been some increase. Any causal link between this and the doubling of the number of married women at work during the last ten years is not easy to prove, yet one parallel has always been in my mind. When I have talked to middle-class married women with professional careers about their dual role, not one in my experience (and I think this is common experience) was prepared to say with certainty that her professional absence from home might not have entailed *some* psychological loss to the children and to family life. It is hard to believe that the wholesale movement of working-class wives and mothers into outside work has not resulted in a similar psychological loss in at least a minority of families – it may be quite a fair-sized minority.

Decline in the status of the father

Another change in working-class family life in the affluent society, which some would say was even more important, is the diminution in the status of the working-class father as head of the family. Here, too, we may only be at the beginning of a historic social change. It was the Industrial Revolution, breaking up the extended families of rural life, which forcibly put the industrial worker into the position of sole and vital breadwinner for his wife and children. Through this process, Professor Titmuss writes,

Women became dependent on men, not only in economic terms, but in the pattern of psychological subtleties in their relationship. Authoritarian patterns of behaviour, sanctioned in the factory, were carried into the home. The survival of the family became more dependent upon the labour power, the health and strength of the husband and father – the one who now 'earned life' for the whole unit.[1]

Well, farewell to this authoritarianism.

It was this position of being the sole economic provider which made the feared working-class father such a common

1. op. cit.

figure in English life and literature, and today it is equally clearly being broken down. Even in the household of a relatively well-paid skilled worker, the collective pay packets of his wife and, say, a teenage son and daughter may outweigh his own. In a society where respect is increasingly based on the yardstick of money, this must have a considerable effect on relationships within the family.

In addition, technical changes are today working swiftly to lower the prestige of industrial skill from which the older working man derived his status and self-respect. The men who today at the end of the shift pour in great crowds from the assembly lines of some huge works can make no special claim for the mystery of their crafts, certainly not to their adolescent sons and daughters. In the affluent society, as Professor Titmuss has also stated, the average working-class father is subjected to sharply conflicting demands. The effect of increasing mechanization in factory work is to reduce him to a passive human unit in a vast process of production in which he is required to display little initiative, if any. Yet at the same time he is asked to show greater care and forethought in planning the future of his children, because society regards each of the fewer children of today as more valuable. There is an obvious conflict between these two claims, and what is generally apparent today is that the authority of the average working-class father over his family has diminished and is exercised over his teenage children for a shorter period than formerly.

The loosening of family bonds was further accentuated in the fifties by marked changes in the relative earning power of the different generations.

All youth is golden

As the first half of this century has seen the economic emancipation of women, so its second half may see a parallel emancipation of adolescents.

If young people of today have far more money to spend than their parents ever had, the starting-point has to be seen in the changing techniques of production. In the

British census of 1931, boys still featured largely as messengers, tea-makers, errand boys, and in other dead-end jobs, while one employed young woman in three was a domestic servant. All this has been transformed. *Adolescent work is no longer menial.* Youthful workers are today drawn chiefly into new light industries (electrical engineering, home equipment, food processing) and the expanding distributive trades – that is, into the most modern sectors of the economy where many of them work as full equals with their elders. This new situation is naturally reflected in the earnings of adolescents. As between an ordinary manual worker or even, say, a ticket collector on British Railways, and his teenage daughter working in a factory or shop, the balance in earnings is shifting all the time in the latter's favour.

This is again chiefly a working-class phenomenon. Of Britain's five million young people between fifteen and twenty-one, some twenty per cent were in 1960 still receiving full-time education at school and college (or else were in the armed forces), and so played only a minor financial role as teenage purchasers. It was the remaining eighty per cent, the mostly working-class majority of three million boys and girls in this age-group, for the most part in well-paid employment, who have created the phenomenally affluent teenage market. According to the calculations of Dr Mark Abrams,[1] the average real weekly wages of young people in the fifteen to twenty-one age-group were in 1960 over fifty per cent higher than before the war. But this is only one part of the story. Because their parents were by and large also more prosperous, the new custom was for boys and girls to keep a much higher proportion of their earnings to spend upon themselves. Dr Abrams calculated that as a result the total personal expenditure of unmarried young people was in 1960 running at about £900,000,000 a year.

This assurance of easy employment, and of the money which goes with it, has helped to create the much-discussed gap in outlook between the young people of today and their

1. Mark Abrams, *The Teenage Consumer*, London Press Exchange, 1960.

parents, who in their own young days grew up under the constant threat of unemployment, something which the youth of today just cannot understand.

This new spending power of the young has also produced another phenomenon. It is only natural that whole new industries should have sprung up to supply the new market, and so we have the new commercial 'youth culture'. It is in supplying such things as records and record players, motor-cycles and scooters, soft drinks, distinctive clothes of all kinds, and cosmetics for girls, that big business since the early fifties has made soaring profits. It has also been noted that, as a result, working-class adolescents are being incessantly persuaded to spend much of their money on a comparatively narrow range of goods, mostly mass-produced. In 1960, many a youth spent a pound a week on pop records and many a girl a pound a week on cosmetics and hairdressing. The need to maintain such spending has also led to a concentrated barrage of advertising on the youth market, and to magazines, films, radio, and television shows specially angled to attract youth. In fact, the commercial youth culture (much documented) has on the basis of this spending already become an integral part of life in the affluent society, and without engaging in any sweeping criticisms there are some interesting points to be made about it.

In the lives of the individual youngsters caught up in this commercial youth culture, it represents a fairly brief interim phase, confined to their years between leaving school and marriage. From the moment they marry, set up a home, and have children, most young working-class couples have to become accustomed to entirely new spending habits, a transition for which they have usually not been well prepared.

Secondly, for all that the youth culture reflects a new affluence, it has in itself become a cause of new class distinctions. To quote Dr Abrams, 'The aesthetic of the teenage market is essentially a working-class aesthetic.' In other words, just as working-class boys and girls were in the past cut off from the social life of middle-class youth by their poverty, so today it is by their relative affluence and different spending habits.

Another point is that the youth culture flourishes mainly where it is based on commercial products which can be quickly mass-produced, such as 'pop' records, soft drinks, glossy magazines, or films and television programmes going out to audiences of millions. In contrast, even though young people have a need to congregate, in such necessarily local and small-scale efforts as the provision of coffee bars through private enterprise and of youth clubs through public effort, there has been nothing like the same progress.

The atmosphere of male dominance in the youth culture can probably also be explained in market terms. Boys in Britain today outnumber girls and also earn considerably more so that they dispose of about two-thirds of teenage spending money. This increased concentration of spending power in the hands of what are mostly unskilled or semi-skilled workers is a phenomenon which was noted in the fifties in a number of industrial countries; it helps to explain why these young men have lately been so much more in the news, whether in setting fashions or causing trouble. This masculine slant in the youth culture is also reflected in the astonishing popularity of young male singers. Apart from their talents, these can be seen as shrewdly manufactured idols of the youth culture – young men fabulously successful yet explicitly publicized as being of working-class origin, and in fact, except for their money and success, like any ordinary youngster who spends his money on pop music.

A final aspect of the teenage culture, which is especially noticeable in Britain, is its air of instability, of constant fashion changes accompanied by hectic advertising. Again this seems fairly easy to explain. Not only do growing youngsters quickly change their tastes. Over and above this, because the upper and lower age-limits of the teenage market are so narrow, the interests supplying it annually lose part of their customers as they get married, and must think of fresh ways of attracting a new generation of school-leavers. The obvious recourse is therefore to fresh advertising, new fashions, and sensations. In Britain this has also another consequence. Because the American teenage market is much larger, the interests supplying British teenagers are continuously drawing upon it and so promoting American values.

At any rate, the net result of all these trends has been a commercialized youth culture, which has admittedly led to some broadening of interests because it could not help but do so. The negative sides are that it is outwardly Americanized, though not inwardly, and always intent upon ephemeral and advertisers' values. For better or worse, it also draws young people still further away from their families and homes. And why not, one might say; young people naturally want to be by themselves. For instance, the more that they visit well-run places like the Mecca dance-halls, where they find pleasant entertainment and are taught new standards of modern comfort, the better. The answer is that many boys and girls don't go to Mecca dance-halls precisely because they are so orderly and well run. And, on a broader view, the basic fault of the youth culture remains its commercially inflated size.

The downward pull

At this point it may be possible to sum up how all these very considerable current social changes have their bearing on delinquency. The affluent society has its darker side. Briefly put, the various ways in which it has not only brought higher standards, but has exerted a 'downward pull', might be listed as follows:

1. *Weakened family ties.* Where family ties are already problematic, the new affluent materialism has made them more so: the new generation of indifferent parents and their children who roam around the streets seem alike more irresponsible and cynical.

2. *More young victims.* An outcome of this has been a notable increase in the number of disturbed and often

delinquent youngsters defiant of authority, as exemplified in the groups of aggressive young Drifters.

3. *Earlier gang life.* Also as a result of weakened family ties among a worse-off section of the population, there has been an increase in adolescent gang life, into which youngsters have been drawn at a much earlier age.

4. *The greater strain.* There is evidence that the simultaneously greater wealth and greater demands which the affluent society brings to present-day adolescents, can also prove too great a strain for those who are of weaker fibre or emotionally disturbed.

5. *Not keeping up.* With the new advertisers' insistence on money values and success, poverty is also coming to be looked on not just as a misfortune, but as a cultural disgrace. The early Teds, in fact, were protesting against the idea of being 'also-rans'. The intensified stigma of 'not keeping up' is one reason why more boys and girls will steal (and girls try out prostitution) to get extras such as clothes, cosmetics, or pop records.

6. *Social restratification.* The 1944 Education Act, with its rules for divided education after the age of eleven, may have been passed with good intentions: but in the new success-dominated climate of the affluent society, those not ascending the ladder are given a dispiriting sense of rejection by society, which educators often cannot eradicate.

7. *Increased moral confusion.* Perhaps the worst fault of the current barrage of hedonist advertising and mass entertainment lies in the ambiguity of its message: is it true or not that use of a certain shampoo will lead a girl to romance and happiness? Youngsters exposed to this ambiguity do not necessarily commit more wrongs – but must find it harder to distinguish right and wrong.

8. *Rejection within fantasy.* One view often expressed to me was that the myths of the commercial youth culture are so effective that individual disturbed youngsters can feel themselves to be failures not only in terms of their real problems, but also because they failed to measure up to their ideas of commercialized glamour.

9. *The lag of the public sector.* Since youngsters are quick to know whether they are valued on their merits or being fobbed off, the spectacle of public niggardliness in support of youth clubs, the shortage of teachers, of policemen, the low salaries of probation officers – all this must decrease both the respect of youngsters for authority and their sense of being individually valued.

10. *Uprooting.* Even social reform can be disturbing. There is much evidence that the process of large-scale re-housing in which many working-class communities have been involved has had an unsettling effect on boys and girls, especially if they have moved to new, still unfinished outer suburban estates, where they feel that no one bothers with them, and where in fact no provision has been made for any organization for them. The houses may be more attractive, but too many are inhabited by strangers; there may be more green around, but in the evening the street corners are quiet, unfamiliar, and uninviting. The first generation of teenagers living in such estates not designed for them often feels cut off from life. They only want to get out of these places where boredom reigns as fast and often as they can, to make for the nearest real town with its cinemas and pubs, or simply for the nearest main highway with its roadhouses.

These are some of the problems which their life in the affluent society had brought to certain classes of boys and girls. In the outcome, one development was by 1960 no longer in doubt. In many parts of urban England, what might be called real pockets of juvenile lawlessness had developed, against which the social agencies found it hard to make headway.

But this was not a problem peculiar to Britain.

CHAPTER II

Europe: the Bourgeois Resistance

The post-war restoration

IN different forms – and to different degrees – the Teddy-boy problem and a serious increase in youthful lawlessness have in recent years affected a large part of the world. Most Western European countries as well as Communist Eastern Europe, or, further afield, Japan, have all had their share of it, while in the United States the problem has by now assumed alarming dimensions. Clearly, there is something in the spirit of this post-war age of ours which encourages a particular kind of youthful malaise. Travelling through Europe, talking to people specially concerned with youth problems, one gains the impression of something like a near-universal trend at work, though it is also important to realize that its impact is as yet very uneven in different countries. For instance, viewed in the light of British or American experience, the countries of Continental Europe have so far been less troubled by youthful lawlessness than one might have expected.

But then the history of Western Europe since the war has altogether been unexpected. It is already no longer easy to recall the starting-point, the end of the war and its first chaotic aftermath. From the later years of the war, there is one persistent image which has remained in my own mind – a composite image of bombed, jagged ruins flanking dusty roads, along which, as we drove, one overtook groups of numbed, shocked refugees – the picture seemed to symbolize the destruction of a continent. My personal tour had begun in Southern Italy, near Naples, where in the first weeks of occupation hungry, ragged boys from the slums offered Allied soldiers their sisters (or that was the tale) and stole every movable part of a jeep left unattended for a minute. Their sheer predatoriness seemed like an echo from life of centuries ago. I can recall many troubled discussions during which we, the uneasy victors, concluded that this lawlessness would be an enduring pattern to be repeated all over Europe, and more especially in the countries which had most directly and most cruelly suffered from the war.

Not a bit of it, of course. Southern Italy, it is true, still represents a special problem. Since the war Italy has remained a state virtually divided into two separate countries with quite different standards of living. Southern Italy is still a museum piece of a region where the classic European extremes of wealth and poverty of a century ago remain disgracefully preserved. With this, not surprisingly, goes a historic tradition in youthful crime. Boys and girls from the most poverty-stricken families still grow up, as it were, in the spirit of an anti-society. A person steals or cheats simply in order to eat; the rich and powerful are always regarded as natural oppressors; if a living cannot be got by straightforward work, it will be got by other means. (Crime figures in parts of the Italian south are, in fact, *six times higher* than in the cities of the north.)

However, in the rest of Italy, especially the industrialized north, and in the other two Western European countries which had suffered the greatest losses, the most extensive dislocation and material damage during the war, France and Germany – the expected did not happen. The surprising development in these countries is not that there should have been a post-war increase in delinquency, but that it was no greater, that the problem should have remained relatively so small.

On the face of it, it would not have been surprising if France, Italy, and Western Germany had after the war been troubled by juvenile delinquency on a really large scale. All three countries were for some years catastrophically affected by war; the population of each country witnessed the shock of defeat, the collapse of a régime, occupation by foreign troops; each suffered heavy casualties; vast numbers of men were taken away as prisoners-of-war, families were disrupted, children grew up shocked, harassed, and deprived. Yet in the outcome the rise in post-war delinquency in these countries was relatively less than in Britain, less than in neutral Sweden, and considerably less than in the United States.

During the immediate period after the war, while chaos still ruled, the relative orderliness and quietism of youth was perhaps not so surprising. The very shock of defeat produced not only numbness but also a positive response. The need to overcome the enormous difficulties in the way of reconstruction, the pent-up desire for normality – these things became like an overriding purpose to which everyone in some way subscribed, and which held the fabric of society together. But there was also something else in these three countries. In all of them, I feel, traditional bourgeois culture was more deeply entrenched than elsewhere – the essentially bourgeois society of these countries was therefore not only able to recover more quickly from the ravages of war, but also to offer stronger resistance against the mass attack of the voices of the new society.

This can be seen in the special circumstances of each country – certainly in France. One might have thought that the odds would be against orderliness in everyday French life. For most of the post-war period, the country suffered from governmental instability and general cynicism in politics; the currency was repeatedly devalued; during the fifties, one unpopular colonial war was lost while another went on being waged without end. Other aspects of French life, too, might have been thought likely to cause unrest and delinquency. The difference between wealth and poverty in many parts of France remained sharp and provocative. The French housing shortage was particularly acute. By north European standards, French slums, even those bordering on the luxury districts of Paris, were appalling. Overcrowding drove French children into the street and created a peculiarly French juvenile vagrancy problem. In Paris alone, hundreds of children are still annually picked up on this charge. The problem of alcoholism, destructive of family life, was also rather larger in France than elsewhere. In addition, for a rich country, France was relatively deficient in sport and recreation facilities and in youth clubs. Considering all this, French teenagers have been astonishingly law-abiding, and this, to my mind, is due to two things. The first is the resilience of French bourgeois culture, springing from its conservatism. Under the massive impact of post-war industrialization, French life, too, has been affected by the new outlook of the affluent society which goes with mass consumption, mass advertising, glossy magazines, and television. Yet the resistance to this outlook in France has also been particularly strong. In this respect, at least, the notorious *immobilisme* of French society may have its advantages. The narrowness of French small-town life, the class antagonisms, the deep-rooted differences between Catholics and anti-clericalists, town and country, north and south, the jealously maintained local attachments, the still-living proud tradition of individual craftsmanship as well as that of uneconomic small shops and bars – all these aspects of French particularism, whatever their defects, have also helped to protect the country, and especially French youth, against that sense of rootlessness and the anonymity which emanates from a mass consumption society.

In the second place, although this is also changing, French family life is still noticeably different from that of the English-speaking countries, and so is the French education system. Both are still authoritarian, in a bourgeois sense. While French schools insist on intellectual discipline – permissive education is much less known – moral responsibility for the children remains with the parents. By comparison with their British or American counterparts, French boys and girls still live rather less among their own age-group, and are much more at home under the eye of their parents. Like certain old-fashioned touches in French school education, this traditionalism in family life may have its disadvantages, but it also seems a stabilizing influence on youth. Nor is it confined to the Catholic middle class. While the French Communist Party with its millions of adherents may no longer be a dynamic political force, it is worth noting that it remains a powerful social force. In its day, the Party created a whole framework for family and social life, and much of this still remains intact, especially in solid working-class areas. In such areas, boys and girls attend Communist clubs and go hiking in Communist groups, but in a pre-scribed way and no less under the eye of their parents than bourgeois children.

Much the same applies to Italian youth. In post-war Italy, too, one might have expected a large-scale delinquency problem to arise. The peninsula was fought over for two terrible years, refugees trudged before the Allied armies, families were disrupted, and post-war recovery came only slowly. The end of the war also saw the abject collapse of the whole Fascist view of life drilled into the young – the picture of their fathers in black shirts was suddenly ridicu-lous. The contrast between the booming industrial north and the stagnant, poverty-stricken south remained also as sharp as ever. From this contrast alone, as young southern-ers left home to seek work in the north, one might have expected a sharp rise in Italian adolescent delinquency, yet this was slow to develop. As the Rome correspondent of *The Times* reported, those young Italians imitating their wilder counterparts abroad were rather trying to keep up with the spirit of the age, than rebelling against it. 'What is generally absent is that special kind of delinquency based on a need for self-assertion and a rejection of the limits of conformity. Italian youth is still very conformist.' [1]

For most observers who have watched the excited reac-tions of the Italian authorities and Press to relatively small instances of Italian youth kicking over the traces, the reasons are fairly plain. Even in the wealthiest and most industri-alized cities of the north, Italian society is still heavily traditional in good bourgeois style. The tradition is, of course, that of centuries of Catholic social and family life, but this is not all – the tradition of Catholic religious ob-servance has proved no bar to rising delinquency in Brook-lyn or Boston. The Italian tradition is also that of a most

1. 'Young Italians Conform', *The Times*, 24 March 1959.

deep-rooted bourgeois culture; even in anti-Catholic working-class areas, no young Italian is as yet so uprooted from family, village, church, and local culture as his counterpart in London or New York. The way of life for youth is still heavily prescribed by its elders.

An even more striking example of a bourgeois society resisting change, and so resisting the new delinquency, is that of Western Germany. Even if one takes the atmosphere of continuous economic boom into account, the unexpected and dull tranquillity of recent German life has indeed been extraordinary, for quite apart from the psychologically ravaging effect of the Nazi régime and the war, actual physical German casualties were enormous. In as many as three million German families of 1957, one parent was missing, usually of course the father. In addition, very large numbers of young Germans have come over as refugees from Eastern Germany without their parents. If one were to draw a parallel with British experience, one would have thought that such wholesale disruption of families should have produced a steep rise in delinquency, yet this has not happened. Western Germany has indeed been troubled by delinquency, but not more seriously than Britain, even rather less.

The explanation, I think, lies in the enduring and highly authoritative structure of German bourgeois society. An astonishing aspect of German post-war life has been the outward restoration of this bourgeois look. Travelling through Western Germany today, one might think that the past had never happened. It is not only a matter of the extraordinary physical rebuilding. The terrible instability of German society during the inter-war years – the inflation, the mass unemployment, Nazism, the officially encouraged rebellion of children against their parents, the disruptive teachings of Hitler and Goebbels – it might all never have been. Suddenly the old traditions of Germany all seemed to be back in force: the heavy authority of German superiors, officials, judges, and industrialists; of professors, teachers, and employers; of the German ideal of industrious apprenticeship and of punctual and efficient work; perhaps even, relatively speaking, the traditional authority of the German father over his family. As observers have remarked, there has been something almost unreal about this air of West German social tranquillity. It is a bourgeois restoration that goes with not thinking about Nazi days; it has almost brought back to Germany something of the spirit of the old bourgeois days before 1933, or even before 1914. But at any rate, until very recently, German youth seemed content to fall in with this restoration of authority.

The European affluence

The extraordinary tenacity with which the historic values and hierarchies of bourgeois culture have been maintained, or restored, in countries like France, Italy, and Germany, despite the upheavals during the years of Fascism and war, is certainly an astonishing phenomenon. Yet this is only one side of the picture. There was also change in the air. True, it seemed to come peacefully. The innocent traveller in Europe some fifteen years after the war might well have received the superficial impression that an undisturbed continent had for generations known nothing except steady advance. Visually, it was an advance towards the life of an affluent society dominated by advertising and mass entertainments, cars and gadgets. As far as the young generation of Europe was concerned, it was an advance towards a youth culture reflecting that of America, a youth culture which went with the new pleasures of jive and rock, fancy clothes, the ownership of motor-cycles and scooters, and the espresso-bar life, and which was above everything international. On the level of high-brow jazz, one could walk into Humphrey Lyttelton's club in London, the Caveau de la Huchette in Paris, the Quartier du Jazz on the borders of West and East Berlin, or their Warsaw equivalents, and in each place find what seemed the same attractive-looking boys and girls, either dancing or else listening to the music with the same absorbed and serious attention. On the mass level, the popularity of James Dean in France was matched by that of

Elvis Presley in West Germany, of Tommy Steele in Scandinavia and Marlon Brando in Vienna.

All these were signs of far-reaching changes in European life. While the fabric of European bourgeois tradition had so surprisingly survived the war, the rising prosperity and the new techniques of the fifties were now initiating a social revolution. From *avant-garde* Sweden in the north to traditional Italy in the south, the basic trend was the same: the slow superimposition upon the old bourgeois class order of the less class-ridden and more fluid affluent society. With this, as in Britain and the United States, went the economic emancipation of youth on a large scale, and with this, in turn, a spread of commercial youth culture – and a rise in the delinquency figures. This latter discovery was made in the late fifties in country after country; it was also increasingly realized that a section of youth felt discontented and ill at ease, that many boys and girls spent their leisure in utterly unconstructive ways, that they had nowhere to go, that something ought to be done. In fact, while bourgeois tradition had guided young people through the post-war tribulations of the forties, in the prosperous fifties it no longer looked adequate as a guide.

The broad pattern

Looking at the state of youth in Europe as a whole some fifteen years after the war, and generalizing very broadly, two things could be said. First, the general picture of juvenile delinquency on the Continent resembled the picture in Britain, and could be linked in the same way to the pattern of social change. However, if it is dangerous to generalize too far about delinquent trends in one country, it is even more difficult to do so for a number of countries differing in historic background and in religious, cultural, and social outlook. Comparative statistics must be treated with caution. Legal definitions of what constitutes juvenile crime differ from country to country, as do definitions of the age of criminal responsibility. Figures tend to conceal demographic shifts and such changes as a tightening of police vigilance. All the same, if we take six countries like, say, Britain, Federal Germany, Austria, Norway, France, and Italy, which were all involved in the war and for which roughly comparable statistics are available (for Italy, at any rate, for the later post-war years), the delinquency figures in all these countries fall into a broad pattern showing three quite strikingly marked phases.

The first phase was immediately after the war when juvenile crime and lawlessness went up in most parts of Europe. In view of the catastrophic effect of the war, this occasioned no surprise. On the contrary, as was mentioned earlier in this chapter, in many places the increase was less than had been feared.

The next phase was that of European reconstruction. At the start of the fifties, economic expansion was already under way again in most parts of Europe, food and clothes rationing began to disappear, and everyday life returned surprisingly quickly to normal. In keeping with this, delinquency figures also declined steadily from year to year, which again was what the experts expected.

It was the third phase of a renewed rise in delinquency which was as unforeseen by observers on the Continent as in Britain. It was in 1950 that the European resurgence began to get properly under way. It was half-way through the decade that, on the Continent as in Britain, economic recovery seemed suddenly to be causing changes in society itself – the direction being a greater or lesser shift from the classic European bourgeois society to the affluent society. The change went with the new pattern of mass consumption; car ownership, for instance, increased in Germany and France even faster than it did in Britain. Television arrived as the new classless entertainment. The new material prosperity drew more married women into work and brought higher pay for juveniles. European life, in fact, was becoming 'Americanized'. The mass media came in – in Germany a gigantic glossy-magazine industry was conjured up overnight. Intensive advertising arrived, even if not quite on an American or British scale; so did the new commercial

youth culture, and so did a new wave of juvenile delinquency.

This latter phenomenon was, in fact, so marked that it
was the subject of one of the expert joint studies of the
Council of Europe.[1] This cautious document showed that in
the second half of the fifties, as unemployment went down
and the new prosperity came in, so juvenile offences went
up, notably in such countries as Western Germany, Austria,
Norway, France, and industrial northern Italy, in some
cases by fifty per cent or more. Though the absolute totals
remained, of course, small, the same countries also reported
a marked increase in youthful sex offences and crimes of
violence. The broad pattern, in fact, was similar to that in
Britain. The same was true of the wartime neutral, Sweden,
where the new affluence had arrived earlier than elsewhere
and so had the rise in the figures of juvenile crime.

The new rebels

Another sign of the unrest of European youth in the midst
of accelerating social change were the occasional mass disturbances of public order in a number of countries. Some of
the largest of these did, in fact, take place in Sweden. The
Swedish report to the Council of Europe stated :

Riots dominated by young people have occurred in Sweden,
primarily in Stockholm, at regular intervals since the war. The
most flagrant episode took place on the New Year's Eve of 1957,
when approximately 3,000 individuals, about two-thirds of them
under twenty-one, collected in the centre of Stockholm. The
demonstration was mainly aimed at the police. The policemen,
many of them mounted, were bombarded with empty tin cans
and other objects. The rioters attempted to frighten the horses
with firecrackers. They wrenched off the doors of cars, which
they forced to stop. One car was overturned and wrecked. The
material damage was relatively insignificant, and there were no
serious casualties. Of the rioters apprehended by the police,
sixty-three were under twenty-one years. The antagonism of the
crowd was clearly directed at the police, but the underlying

1. *Juvenile Delinquency in Post-War Europe*, Council of Europe,
Strasbourg, 1960.

cause is difficult to explain. Animosity towards the police has been expressed on other occasions in street riots in Stockholm. The situation appears to have improved during recent years, principally because the police are better prepared to deal with it, and partly because certain preventive measures have been introduced by the municipal authorities.

The German *Halbstarken* riots which from 1956 onwards broke out in city after city were a puzzling phenomenon. They looked like exhibitions of youthful anger and defiance that had no rhyme or reason. Thinking Germans, however, were still haunted by the memories of quite a different kind of violence a generation earlier, and, as a result, these new outbreaks caused considerable alarm and were studied and analysed in meticulous German detail. The studies showed, for example, that a starting-point of the epidemic was a much-publicized riot in Hanover in August 1956. On the day before this riot, rumours were running through the city of an arranged fight between the adolescents of two different districts (as New Yorkers would say, a 'rumble'), for which reinforcements were being mobilized on foot, mopeds, and motor-cycles. Even at this stage there was excited talk among the boys that, if they were to be 'attacked' by the highly unpopular police, they would certainly resist. In the event, the riot became much less of a fight between rival gangs than a hysterical attack upon public order. Groups of assembled youths rushed through the streets of Hanover, stopping traffic and molesting bystanders, smashing windows and hoardings and finally stoning police-cars and struggling in apparent frenzy until an appropriate number were arrested and order was restored.

Spontaneous and destructive disturbances of this type took place in 1956–8 in German cities as far apart as West Berlin, Munich, Düsseldorf, Bremen, Hamburg, etc. The evidence showed them to be much of a type. As a rule some hundreds of youths were involved in the rioting, dozens were arrested, and, if casualties were not serious, damage to property was sometimes considerable. In some cases one could fix on the starting-point of the excitement – a rock-

'n'-roll occasion in Berlin, a recital by Louis Armstrong in Hamburg; in others, the hysteria, the smashing and resistance to the police seemed to arise without any apparent cause. On the morning after, so the German records pointed out, neither the Courts nor the teenagers themselves seemed to know what it had been about. The reports also noted that the participants in the riots were predominantly working-class boys, many of them 'provocatively dressed'; that there were few girls among them; that the sensational publicity given by the German Press to one riot no doubt played its part in sparking off the next; that the youths turned up for the occasions with extraordinary home-made weapons and with a sense of emotional rancour against the police which puzzled the authorities, as did the cynical disregard of the rioters for public and personal property. In fact, the conclusion was that these *Halbstarken* riots were disturbing not so much in themselves as for the light they threw on the general increase in juvenile lawlessness and the apparent hostility of a section of German youth against any kind of public authority. What was particularly deplored was that two-thirds of this new generation of German teenagers no longer bothered to belong to any youth organization. But just as public alarm became concentrated on these *Halbstarkenkrawalle*, they faded out again, as the British Teddy-boy riots had done. Like these, they left behind rising delinquency figures, but this was another matter.

In France in July 1959, at the start of what promised, and turned out to be, a record Riviera season, a large gang of French youths armed with knives, sticks, buckled belts, and bicycle chains (bicycle chains wielded on the Riviera!) staged a pretty savage and boisterous riot on the seafront near Cannes, destroying property, molesting startled campers, and stoning the police before scattering and vanishing again. To the alarm of the French 'it can't happen here' school, similar wild riots followed in various places along the Riviera in quick succession. A culminating point was reached in a teenage fracas of quite notable dimensions when armed gangs of adolescent toughs from the port of Toulon con-

verged on Bandol, many of them motorized, annoying holi-
day-makers and noisily fighting each other and the police,
and even causing damage to a casino – this last act made
international news.

The youths who staged these disorders called themselves
by various mysterious code names, such as 'Les Gadjos'.
Because of their clothes, however, the public quickly chris-
tened them *les blousons noirs*, the blackjackets (the black
leather was usually imitation). And for a few weeks *blousons
noirs* incidents spread like a rash across France. Organized
adolescent gangs under that label appeared suddenly in
Paris. In August, one large gang staged a particularly
frenzied disturbance right in the rue Brillat-Savarin, where
passers-by were injured, property damaged, and the boys
tried to fight it out with the police. By contrast with similar
British events, many of those arrested were middle-class
boys. The Paris newspapers, which gave the disturbance
dramatic coverage, reported that some highly respectable
parents, on arriving at the police station, could hardly
believe their eyes to find their sons under arrest.

By that time, *blousons noirs* incidents had become international news, often accompanied by photographs of French
policemen vigorously swinging batons. With the biggest
tourist traffic in Europe to guard, the French police, as could
be expected, reacted with characteristic vigour. A disturbance in the Paris suburb of Drancy led to no less than a
hundred arrests. In September the Paris Prefect of Police
announced that six large gangs of *blousons noirs* were operating in Paris, but that already over 800 juveniles (!) had
been picked up for questioning. A further sign of public
alarm was a series of prominently featured articles in a
newspaper like *Le Monde*, with such headings as 'It is
Urgent to Organize the Welfare of our Morally Endangered
Youth' and demanding the provision of more youth clubs
and youth leaders. As it turned out, however, with the end
of the glorious summer holiday of 1959, the *blousons noirs*
seemed to have vanished as mysteriously as they had
emerged. They made a much-publicized fresh appearance in

the spring of 1960 – French belief in immunity from such 'Anglo-Saxon' troubles as youth riots had certainly been shaken.

Italy also, interestingly enough, experienced a relative flare-up of youthful lawlessness during the summer of 1959. By comparison with some other countries, this did not amount to very much. There were a few incidents of the Teddy-boy type in industrial cities like Milan and Turin, but on a minor scale. Still, perhaps as a variant from its preoccupation with continuous high-society scandals, the Italian Press for a time featured almost daily stories of fights and stabbings by young hooligans. One incident above all, in which a peasant girl from Bracciano stabbed to death one of a gang of seven boys who attacked her, had all the right ingredients for nation-wide publicity. It featured not only a youthful gang and an attempted sex crime, but showed virtue triumphant. At any rate, the reaction of the Italian authorities was quick and emotional. In August, the then Prime Minister, Signor Segni, requested the Italian police to proceed with utmost severity against youthful gangsters. (The Italian police, with a tradition of acting against political street demonstrations and a scope their British colleagues would envy, did in fact not hesitate. In a single *razzia* in Milan, for instance, five hundred youths were picked up for questioning, many being detained.) A rather absurd Bill put to Parliament to deprive 'socially dangerous and exhibitionist young offenders' of the right temporarily to practise their profession did not go far, but indicated the way some sections of Italian opinion were thinking. So did newspaper articles attacking the evil of pin-table machines (whose import was prohibited) and other foreign influences allegedly destructive of Italian morals. This Italian wave of alarm, too, seemed to fade with the summer, and the Press turned its attention back to other topics such as, once again, scandals in high society. Still, it had been shown that Italy, like France, was also no longer quite immune to the new mood of defiance and delinquency of a sub-section of European youth.

All in all . . .

How serious was this problem on the Continent? In summing up, one could say that Western Europe had weathered its disturbed post-war years with surprisingly little trouble from the young. By contrast, the social changes of the last few years, leading in the direction of a European affluent society, resulted in a notable and new increase in delinquency and, in a number of countries, in disturbances of the Teddy-boy pattern, and these problems have already caused growing concern in countries like Germany and Austria, Sweden and Norway, France and Italy. In these and other European countries, one also met similar and rather tentative efforts to cope with the situation. There was some public alarm over the apparent indifference of youth in general to traditional standards; it was felt that, for want of anywhere to go, adolescents were too much 'out in the streets', that purely commercialized entertainment loomed too large in the lives of many boys and girls, and that there was a need for new, modern types of youth organizations and youth clubs. (In France, a new governmental drive in this field was placed under the direction of the famous mountaineer, M. Maurice Herzog. In Vienna, where gangs of *Halbstarken* with flick knives had appeared even among the famous municipal apartment blocks, newspapers stressed that, in the design of these blocks, the adolescents had been forgotten and needed new provision. In Germany, the building programme of 'Houses of Youth', was speeded up.)

At the same time, the incidence of the problem was uneven. In spite of the rumpus created in 1959–60 by the French *blousons noirs*, and a few Italian incidents, the rise in delinquency did not seem as yet so serious in France or Italy as elsewhere. In Western Germany there was perhaps cause for more concern. While the surface of German social life looked calm, German observers themselves were disturbed by a lack of depth, a lack of confident direction beneath this surface. It was noted that the traditional German youth organizations, both Christian denominational and Socialist, had lost much of their old authority. There was, indeed, something strangely empty and purely imitative in the look of the new German commercial youth culture, which seemed completely derived from American films, pop music, and advertisements, with nothing new added. In spite of its prosperity, it was perhaps Western German society that looked most exposed to the corrosions of life in the new affluent culture.

As a generalization it could, however, also be said that the problem of juvenile delinquency loomed less large in continental Western Europe than in Britain (and much less large – see the following chapter – than in the United States). And here I come back to what, to my mind, is the reason for this difference. Even in those parts of the Continent where life outwardly seems dominated as much as it is today in Britain by such things as mass media, cars, household gadgets, mass advertising, and other attributes of the affluent society, the traditional bourgeois standards, even if they no longer have their old influence, are still preserved more strongly than in Britain. Especially in countries like France and Italy, the majority of the population has not yet been as much drawn away from these standards towards the new mass culture projected by the advertisers, as is the case in this country. But here the real contrast to continental Europe is represented not so much by Britain as by the United States.

CHAPTER 12

America: Advance from Innocence

A historic change

THE point has come to turn to a subject which I feel I have up to now almost avoided, because of its rather depressing overtones, namely the juvenile delinquency situation in the United States. This situation has in the last ten years or so had plenty of airing. It has been elevated to the rank of a major national problem, it has been publicized by stories about the formidable juvenile gang warfare in New York, in the reports of Senatorial sub-committees, and in challenging films and plays. And the problem appears in fact to have been growing steadily more serious. As Miss Virginia Held put it in the *Reporter*:[1]

There has probably never been a moment in history when adults were not shocked by what they regarded as an unprecedented wave of bad behaviour among children and adolescents. But in our time reports of gang warfare in the streets, teenage muggings, and senseless killings have turned shock to cold fear. Juvenile delinquency, particularly in the United States, has come to be considered one of the most urgent social problems of the day, and the epidemic of arrogance and crime seems to be spreading so fast that it obliterates the best efforts society can make to control it – or even to understand it.

How bad is the problem?

Viewed from Europe, the present youthful lawlessness in the United States seems both more widespread and a more intensive kind of lawlessness. For instance, the violence of the teenage street gangs in Manhattan suggests what the Teddy-boy problem might become in another twenty years, *if* the problem grew worse (and the Teds more sophisti-

1. Virginia P. Held, 'What Can We Do about J. D.?', *Reporter*, 20 August, 1959.

cated) year by year. What also strikes a European observer
is the evident inability of the New York authorities to take
really offensive action against these gangs, even though
such action was several times promised jointly by Governor
Rockefeller, Mayor Wagner, and Police Chief Kennedy. In
1959–60, after every kind of attempt to put them down, it
was estimated that 150 juvenile gangs with about 7,000 to
8,000 members were still 'operating' in New York. 'Only the
police blotters and the hospital files and the morgue records
tell the story,' indignantly wrote Mr Douglas M. Allen,
Associate Editor of *Newsweek*:[1]

And what they say is that sizable areas of the world's foremost
metropolis are splintered into feudal enclaves, run in effect by
gangs of ruthless, amoral teenagers. .... Between them, they rule
over the slums and drab housing projects of Harlem and the
Lower East Side; the Bronx, the Bedford-Stuyvesant and Navy
Yard districts of Brooklyn, and South Jamaica and Ozone Park
in Queens. They reign by terror, and strangers enter their
demesnes after nightfall at their peril. Some of the gangs are
bigger and more powerful than others, with 250 to 300 members;
some have alliances; they can field a battle order of 1,000 troops
or more.

This passage may sound somewhat dramatic – the average
New Yorker only *reads* about delinquents – but it brings
home the point that by 1959–60 adolescent gang life in New
York had developed into something well in advance of what
could be found in any other big city in America or elsewhere. The situation was that sections of New York were
dotted with organized gangs of lawless teenagers – lawless
in recognizing little authority beyond the rules of initiation
and discipline they drew up for themselves. The most recognized uniform was a black leather jacket. Each gang had
its territory, or 'turf', recognized as such by other gangs,
and which each gang was ready to defend against intrusion
by armed violence in the streets. The gangs had their colourful names, like the Chaplains, Sinners, Bishops, Cheyennes,
Demons, Imperials, Viceroys, Jokers, and so forth (unlike

1. *Newsweek*, 14 September 1959.

the London Teds who rarely rose beyond geographic appel-
lations like the Elephant Boys, the Angel Boys, the High-
bury Corner Boys, etc.). The 25,000-strong police force of
New York, which in any case had its hands full in this city
of skyscrapers and slums, of teeming immigrant quarters
and taut race relations, was quite unable to put down these
teenage gangs as a whole – as some were disrupted by the
arrests of members and some dissolved, others sprang up
again like weeds.

The enormous efforts of social agencies to 'reach' the
adolescent members of these gangs, to divert their energies
and desire for adventure into 'constructive' channels, for
instance by providing street-corner youth leaders to work
with them, also appeared to have little lasting effect. The
biggest New York Press headlines were usually accorded to
organized armed clashes or 'rumbles' between rival gangs,
of the kind glamourized in that well-known musical, *West
Side Story*, but which were really pretty ugly and blood-
thirsty affairs – the knowledge that two large adolescent
gangs in an area were feuding was enough to keep the
police detachments in that area in a state of perpetual alert.
What was probably worse, however, was that by perpetrat-
ing assaults, muggings, and robberies practically in the
manner of adult gangsters, some of the gangs were definitely
making a few areas of New York unsafe after dark as they
had not been for many years. At the same time, through
this education in delinquency, the gangs provided a steady
stream of recruits into the world of American adult crime.

Socially, most of the teenage boys in these gangs were
drawn from the lower working-class income groups of New
York, from the slums of the city or from slum families recently moved into new housing developments. They were
particularly concentrated in areas where antagonistic racial
groups overlapped. In actual fact, young Negroes and Puerto
Ricans formed a much larger proportion of young gangsters
than one would imagine from the carefully censored American official statistics on this question. The claim sometimes
made that the majority of the most violent young delin-

quents came from the one per cent of known problem families in New York (about 20,000 out of two million families) was probably roughly true. In this respect, in being big-city adolescents trying to push their way up from family life in the 'submerged tenth', the young members of the New York gangs were rather like the original London Teddy boys. But there were also notable differences between the two sets of adolescents – to compare the London Teds, or for that matter even the members of the Chicago street gangs of the thirties, with the sophisticated New York fighting gangs of today is like turning from an old-fashioned detective story to the tautly constructed American thriller of today, with the usual touch of mental illness thrown in.

There is, first, the marked difference in the degree of habitual violence. The weapons used in New York inter-gang fights consist not only of knives, clubs, torn-off car aerials, home-made zip guns, and the like, but of such savage weapons as wire whips and regular firearms; and, in fact, gangsters did not stop short of murder. The toll of one single black week of running fights between Puerto Rican and 'White' teenagers in September 1959 was four young-sters killed and fifteen in hospital with gunshot and knife wounds. Of the four killed, two were boys of sixteen, one a boy of fourteen, one a girl of fifteen shot by mistake. Casualties on this level are of course not imaginable in London. Commenting on the fact that the figures of grave acts of juvenile violence in the United States were so many times higher than in Europe – in 1957 there were 133 arrests of youngsters under eighteen for murder and non-accidental killing, an authority like Dr Melitta Schmideberg (Director of the Association for the Psychiatric Treatment of Offend-ers) has observed [1] that when all immediate causes had been discussed, there remained the conclusion that a society must expect the sort of crimes that were apparently tolerated by popular attitudes. The evident trouble was that American society did not sufficiently *abhor* the many acts of violent brutality and destruction in which youth indulged, acts

1. Quoted in the *Reporter*, 20 August 1959.

whose very thought would in many European countries be at once suppressed. In other words, at this point of violence, the aggressive fantasies of the New York teenage gangsters appeared in line with the ideas of violence given such constant expression in American popular culture.

Another difference is that the New York teenagers appear to be much more emotionally involved in their gang life. A mob of London Teds usually included a few psychopathic youths who led the others on occasional wild destructive raids. In New York, similar psychopaths are often the automatic gang leaders who rule over a whole fantasy world of violence, ruthlessly enforcing their discipline on younger and weaker boys. Again it was common for gangs of London Teds to be driven by their underlying fear or anxiety or a sense of grievance into defending 'their manor' but the attachment of the average New York gang to its 'turf' is evidently far more intense. Such a 'turf' might consist of no more than a few drab blocks of streets, a drugstore counter or two, a few back yards, a strip of parkland. However, whether the reason is that the plight of being a problem family in New York is a more dramatic one than elsewhere, so that the teenagers from such families feel more anxiety-ridden, more fiercely resentful, the fanaticism with which they will defend their 'turf', as if it were the only thing they can cling to in a hostile world, is something quite exceptional.

At the same time, the New York gang members seem also to have advanced a good way towards sophistication. It has been remarked that unlike, say, the English Teds, who are still easily cowed by the authority of the Courts, New York delinquents on arrest often reveal little sense of guilt; they will put their conviction down to the unfairness of lawyers and judges and appear to be genuinely without a sense of the wrongness of brutality and violence – what has pushed them into crime seems often not an uncontrollable impulse but simply an uncontrolled one, which brings one back to the influences of contemporary American culture which plays on the minds of these boys. Another striking feature is the early age of some of the New York gang members and delinquents. Arrests of boys of thirteen, fourteen, and fifteen after gang fights are not uncommon – there was a widely reported incident in 1957 when one young killer of fourteen calmly told New York detectives how he had stabbed another boy in the back to 'get the feeling of knife going through bone'.

As I have said before, one should not exaggerate. In the vastness of a metropolis like New York, these juvenile gangs represent only a marginal problem. American life has a tradition of turbulence, and an immigrant city like New York with its racial ghettoes has its particularly rough edges. Much juvenile violence arises from the larger problem of tense race relations, and some of the most dangerous adolescent gangs are all-Negro or all-Puerto Rican in membership. Considering the devastating psychological effects of race and colour discrimination, it is, for example, not surprising that the delinquency rate in an overcrowded Negro ghetto like Harlem should be as high as seventy-six per thousand. Even so, racial antagonisms are only a partial explanation of the gang life. For instance, while in segregated areas juvenile gangs tend to be all-white, all-Negro, or all-Puerto Rican, in the growing number of integrated neighbourhoods the gangs also tend to become mixed, which shows that geography rather than ethnic origin is most important in gang formation. Secondly, the half a million very new Puerto Rican immigrants in New York may in some ways be a fairly primitive community, yet in Puerto Rico itself delinquency rates are exceptionally low; it evidently takes several years of life at the bottom of the American social ladder to create the new resentful and delinquent outlook among Puerto Rican youth. Thirdly, as populations are cleared from the slums, some gangs break up but others simply continue their criminal activities in the new housing developments. All this indicates that while all kinds of special factors may have intensified the juvenile gang life of New York, basically it has to be regarded as a result of the general pressures of American social life today.

Extensive delinquency

If the teenage gangs of New York with their addiction to *intensive* violence provided the most sensational material for American press headlines, the 1950s also brought evidence that juvenile delinquency was growing more *extensive* in American society as a whole. The period was one of dynamic suburban growth, and in 1957–60 delinquency in the small towns and also in the new suburbia increased faster than in the big cities – the move to the quiet tree-lined avenues proved evidently no barrier. Much of it, to be sure, only consisted of petty misdemeanours, youthful drunkenness, motoring offences, the usual larceny and breaking-in. Since youth must go joy-riding and many young Americans are accustomed to have what they want, it was no surprise that juveniles under eighteen should be responsible for more than half the reported automobile thefts. It was, however, more alarming that they also accounted for twenty per cent of the known cases of rape – this was indicative of a generally growing mood of violence. In Washington, 150 cases of assault against police officers were reported during the first six months of 1959, the majority committed by teenage thugs who vanished again into the night. The new insecurity in the Federal capital was partly, but only partly, linked to the rapid increase in its coloured population. Reports in 1959 from cities like Baltimore, Detroit, San Francisco, Los Angeles, and Philadelphia brought news of special emergency measures against juvenile crime, such as strict curfew hours for young people, laws against groups assembling on the pavements after dark, or the selective arrest of known gang leaders at the first sign of trouble. In short, if in 1960 one could still say that ninety-five per cent of all young Americans grew up without *serious* trouble with the courts or the police, the lawless minority has also grown uncomfortably large – at a very rough estimate by the various indices perhaps three times larger than in Britain. One could no longer argue, as certain observers for a while tried to do, that the increase was only apparent, explained by such things as better reporting and stricter law enforcement or the increase of automobiles. Between 1950 and 1960, the number of court cases involving American juveniles went up distinctly from every year to the next, and the rise was most striking in the total number of cases of burglary and assault. Moreover, sections of American cities and even some suburban areas had been rendered unsafe after dark; the recruitment of youngsters into the world of adult crime, which by 1960 cost the United States a fantastic sum of billions of dollars a year, had been steadily increasing; and if one talked of the points where United States culture was failing in the ideological struggle against Soviet Communism, the prevalence of juvenile delinquency was one of them.

What is being done?

Plenty is being done in the United States to try to cope with delinquency and, at the same time, whatever is being done does not seem enough. A vast country like the United States is, of course, not really comparable to a small tightly-knit European state, but what strikes the European observer who looks at the American penal scene is the enormous amount of research which is continuously being produced on juvenile delinquency, and the confusing variety of American penal, social, and community agencies which in different places and different ways are all trying to deal with the problems of American wayward youth. Yet it is hard to feel that many of these efforts are directed at the basic causes of the problem, and many American experts themselves seem to share this view.

A fairly substantial proportion of delinquency [write two such reasonable authorities as Herbert A. Block and Frank T. Flynn [1]] reflects strains in the American social structure affecting families in myriad ways. Despite its roots in individual differences, delinquency as a cultural problem means that society

1. Herbert A. Block and Frank T. Flynn, *Delinquency*, Random House, 1956.

is the patient. Unfortunately the American social structure has a deceptive kind of rigidity and resistance to social change, so that anything that smacks of social planning is likely to be regarded as radical socialism.

This is surely the crux. When one looks at the huge array of American academic and practical fieldwork studies on delinquency, one feels that the required research on practically any aspect of youthful crime has already been done, much of it some time ago, and some of it research on a scale to which there is no equivalent in Britain. There seems relatively little to add to Frederic M. Thrasher's classic study of the swarming Chicago street gangs of the inter-war years, or the graphic descriptions by Clifford R. Shaw and H. D. Mackay of all the disruptive social pressures which were impelling the children of new immigrants in Chicago towards lawlessness. The problem in America today is not that not enough is known about delinquency but that remedial action presents the difficulty – which is why there is a certain unreality about even the best of such American research.

Viewed from Europe, many of the American voluntary community efforts to attack the delinquency problem seem bold and imaginative. One could say this about the 'area projects' directed by Mr Clifford Shaw and his colleagues in Chicago, in which the resources of every relevant social agency were with significant success concentrated on certain of the worst criminal areas in the city. Again, there is much to be learned from the determined efforts made under the direction of New York City Youth Board to 'reach' young delinquents through special workers who bravely and sometimes thanklessly try to contact the gangs themselves at their street corners, while simultaneously squads of other case-workers endeavour to 'reach' the families involved. Many such American efforts are admirable, but they have to be set against certain crass and continuing inadequacies in the American penal system, which may have their explanation in the special circumstances of American federal and state history, but which cannot at the present day be any longer justified. To give one illustration, American films about youth have popularized the alarming picture of frightened youngsters, arrested for stealing, or perhaps drunken driving or a sexual offence, looking terrified or defiant as they are hustled behind prison bars. The picture is not so far from the facts. Figures indicate that for want of other places of detention, between 50,000 and 100,000 juveniles are every year clapped into city or county jails, even though thinking people realize that this is a reprehensible practice.

Again, as in Britain, the penal apparatus in many parts of the United States has been administratively almost swamped by the recent juvenile crime wave. Juvenile courts in many places have been working without the regular services of probation officers. The reason given for the acute shortage of probation officers is the obvious one of inadequate pay and prospects of promotion in the profession. Seeing that probation was a penal method very much pioneered in the United States, this throws revealing light on the confusion of social priorities in the American affluent society. Or to take another point, like British approved schools, American training schools for the ten to seventeen age group vary greatly in their efficiency. Some, indeed, are very modern, but to a European observer the total number of places in American training schools seems far too small for such a vast country with so large a delinquency problem. The American penal system as a whole also lacks a national equivalent to the British Borstal system for the detention and re-training of young adult offenders in the seventeen to twenty-one age group. Though reforms have often been discussed, young offenders of this age are in many states still accommodated under demoralizing ordinary prison conditions, for the simple reason that money for anything else has not been made available, though here again thinking people know that this is wrong. These and other glaring shortcomings in the American penal system need no elaborate research in order to establish how much harm they cause. They have been continuously exposed, criticized, and written about by American authorities. Any discussion of them leads one back to the central problem – the resistance of the American social structure to certain types of effective public action, of whose benefits few individual people would need to be convinced. In fact, in the whole discussion of American delinquency and penal problems there is one basic puzzle: the *degree* of social unbalance which has already been permitted to develop in the American affluent society. That is, since this society has produced such staggering achievements in raising the general standard of living, and seeing that increasing juvenile delinquency has become a major American problem, why are American penal efforts to tackle it often so shabbily neglected or even starved of adequate finance?

The inevitable answer is that in the American affluent society, more than anywhere, it is the same social forces which have been encouraging juvenile delinquency, which are also the forces that obstruct comprehensive penal reform by determined public action.

Affluence – and its reverse

Trying to discover what precisely is going on in American society – or rather, what is going wrong – has become something of a fascinating pastime. We have in the last years been treated to sharp criticism of the current American drift from some of the most persuasive American economists, sociologists, and journalists. Because so many American trends of today are the European trends of tomorrow, their books have been read with avid interest abroad. The pastime is infectious. I myself, during an American tour some years back, found myself continuously trying to gather my confusing impressions of American society into a coherent picture of the direction in which it might be heading. There was the initial, overwhelming impression of American space and vastness, the equal impression of bounding youth and vigour, of friendliness, sociability, and easy, democratic mixing, but there were other impressions, too. In each hotel room, from coast to coast, a radio set was fitted beside my bed; I had only to press a button at random and the room would be filled with idiots' voices projecting advertising slogans or mouthing pop lyrics – how could one help wondering what would be the long-term effect of this drip, drip, drip on American life? As a result of the explosion of American cities in the automobile age, there was the depressing sense of blight and disorganization at the city centres – in Chicago, in Detroit, in down-town Los Angeles: in these places some of the essence of urban culture seemed to have been lost, and I did not feel it had been replaced in the new landscape of interchangeable suburbs, country clubs, golf courses, and filling stations into which the city dwellers were moving. The purely material concept of home ownership was no substitute for urbanity. Driving through the monotonous suburbs of a sprawling city like Detroit, in area as large as London, I thought I could sense why people there reputedly talked so much about 'roots', and at the same time were always on the move, and also why juvenile delinquency was rife.

It is important to see this restlessness as something new and contemporary – to blame American capitalism is not enough. It is not so long ago, after all, that the United States seemed an enviably easy country to grow up in. George Orwell particularly stressed this point in an essay[1] in which he discussed the enormous popularity of American nineteenth-century bestseller novels among European boys and girls of his generation. Their attraction, according to Orwell, was that they seemed to reflect the security, the confidence in the future, of an American life which was more carefree than that which European children saw around them. His own dominant childhood image of American boyhood from this reading, said Orwell, was that of

a boy sitting in a whitewashed stone schoolroom. He wears braces and has patches on his shirt, and if it is summer he is barefooted. ... The boy lives in a farmhouse also of stone and

1. George Orwell, 'Riding Down from Bangor', *Shooting an Elephant*, Secker & Warburg, 1950.

whitewashed, which has a mortgage on it. He aspires to be President, and is expected to keep the woodpile full. Somewhere in the background of the picture, but completely dominating it, is a huge Bible . . .

An image suggesting leisurely security, thought Orwell, and there was some truth in it. Nineteenth-century America was a rich, empty country which lay outside the main stream of world events, and in which the nightmares of modern man, the fears of unemployment and of state interference and the general sense of helplessness had hardly come into being. If there were plentiful social evils, together with them went a prevailing belief that there was room for everybody and if a man worked hard he was certain of a living. It was this underlying confidence which gave a buoyant and innocent look to the American view of life, as conveyed to European youth. In fact, as Orwell argued, especially if one talked about the surroundings in which children grew up, it could be said that 'the civilization of nineteenth-century America was capitalist civilization at its best'.

At the time when Orwell wrote, and this was the point he was making, this picture lay already well in the past. The phase of deterioration in simple American optimism probably began towards the end of the century, when the scale of American industrialization quickened, to become huge. Since then, change in America has been continuous; but only after the Second World War did it begin to be realized that in the American affluent society something of a new *kind* of capitalist society was being produced. By now, however, the analysis of this new society is very much the vogue. The endeavours of writers like Riesman, Warner, Galbraith, Whyte, Wright Mills, Fromm, and others to elucidate its mysteries have already been widely studied, not only in the United States but also in Europe, where it is felt that many similar social forces are today at work.

Perhaps this similarity was at times obscured. To talk of the advance from an American bourgeois society to an affluent society may sound far-fetched if 'bourgeois' is associated only with the stuffy class structure of Europe. Yet in the broader sense of the word the analogy holds. The canvas of American life of fifty years ago might have been enormously varied – that of a class-and-caste society in New England and the South, of newly-rich boisterousness in the Middle West, and beyond this of yet newer states where a frontier spirit still flourished. Yet in overall terms the United States could be described as bourgeois – as a very open bourgeois society, dominated by independent entrepreneurs and professional men and farmers, whose direct personal contacts created the tone of American life. But that is already the past. The present change appears to be that American society has already to a considerable extent been taken over by the big corporations, whose top executives have crystallized into a new social power élite, buttressed by the high barriers of exclusive clubs, colleges, and residential areas, while their employees are being graded into more rigid income groups, and at the same time a new spirit of impersonality has entered American life.

Much the same social transformation has also begun in Europe, but there are three special American developments which ultimately, I think, all have their bearing on the problem of delinquency.

First, in the United States, one is reminded much more ruthlessly that Western capitalism is not a static but a dynamic economic system, making for continuous technical and social change, and one can see more clearly that the present concentration of production in giant units is tending towards the disappearance of the older bourgeois social order as surely as country lanes are yielding to motor highways.

Secondly, it appears that once mass manufacture has reached the size attained, for example, by the American motor industry, it *does* generate a trend to divide its customers by advertising into convenient fixed market grades – a Chevrolet grade, a Buick grade, a Cadillac grade. One can also see the advantage to manufacturers of using high-powered advertising to keep customers firmly in these grades by associating them with social status – but this means that both the consumer and the consumer's goods carry a common label.

Thirdly, there is the new fact in American life of the mass manufacture by large-scale enterprise of actual homes. One can see how, once this technique of house and suburb construction has been introduced, the most profitable method for entrepreneurs – with houses as with cars – is to construct standardized one-community suburbs which are either all-white, or all-white-collar-middle-class or working-class, all-Gentile or all-Jewish. This means that Americans are increasingly divided into separate social groups not only horizontally by income and education, but vertically, according to religion or ethnic origin.

Underprivilege and delinquency

These special developments of the American affluent society have all had an effect on delinquency, both in making it more intensive and making it widespread, and in the first place among the underprivileged in this society. For example, one effect of the new class stratification imposed on the American people has been to make it appear as if the escalator along which new immigrants in the United States have for so many years been carried upwards had today been suddenly stopped, or at least badly jolted. For instance, the American Negroes have in recent years achieved some advance in employment, in the armed forces, and in integration of schools and colleges. But in the image of American life projected by advertising, such de-segregation still simply does not exist – in the image projected to sell the project, the ideal American family always appears white, Nordic, and middle class. This has always been pretty well the case, but when, as today, American advertising has become a super-industry with an inescapable impact, one can see why this impact should simultaneously set more precise cultural standards for the majority who can keep up with them, and arouse permanent feelings of rejection among the excluded. And among the young, above all, such a sense of rejection is a powerful incentive towards lawlessness. The

reaction of many young Negroes and Puerto Ricans illus-
trates this situation.

The exclusion of minorities is also being made very real by
the present American mass movement into new and vari-
ously 'restricted' suburban residential areas. Personally, I
found the picture of race segregation in, say, Chicago, a more
disturbing one and visually more depressing than that of
the cruder race conflict in the south. The latter might be
more savage, but it seemed something like a colonial problem within the United States which time might be expected
to cure. On the other hand, the residential race barriers in
Chicago, which keep the coloured population crowded into
a few mid-town areas, are discouraging precisely because
they belong to the American present. The prime cause has
become the fear of white residents that the arrival of
Negroes would cause the capital value of their houses to
fall, which was in turn due to the idea that through such
association their status would suffer – that is, race segregation had already become part of the particular mythology
of the affluent society, with its advertisers' values: no one
was wicked, but everyone followed the rules. But this very
impersonality makes the new segregation harder for those
excluded to bear, and especially for the young who need to
feel that the world is open to them – young coloured American adolescents as much as anyone else. Again, it should
cause no surprise that, as these more impersonal race barriers have in the last ten years *appeared* to harden in the
United States, so there should have been a sharp increase in
delinquency among Negro and Puerto Rican youths.

The poor of any race also seem to have become something
of a sharply defined minority in the American affluent
society. American sociological studies suggest that there has
been a significant recent change in the whole American
outlook upon poverty – it is no longer just a misfortune, as
in the past, but a kind of moral stigma, a sign of failure to
make the grade, or in the case of a young person, the failure
of the parents to make the grade. This shift in ideas is important. To be sure, in bourgeois society, too, the majority of

the urban population, especially the industrial workers, had little direct share in the dominant middle-class culture. But against this the working classes had their own class culture, with a traditional way of life that made sense, with its warmth and solidarity, and often a defensive pride in being working class – in this solidarity there was reassurance for the individual. But in the affluent society the idea is increasingly propagated that below the culture of the majority, below the material standards prescribed by the advertisers, there is no culture, just nothing – if you can't live up to these standards, you're nobody, you're out. In this sense of cultural disintegration below a certain income line one can probably see reasons why the teenage gang members in the slums of New York build up such an intense fantasy life round the possession of their 'turf', and their gang loyalty: the fantasy life, like their violent attitude against society, is a defence against the terror of having nothing. In general, it appears that in the American affluent society it is already harder than almost anywhere else for those who cannot follow the advice of the advertisers, those below the majority standards, to lead any life which is psychologically secure and dignified.

Another point must be added. As in Britain, but rather more so in the American affluent society, the existing disadvantages of being underprivileged are exacerbated by the relative decline of the public sector of society. American slums have a peculiarly dispiriting look, not only because what might be called 'lower-class culture' has been destroyed, but also through the contrast between their drab squalor and the surrounding dynamic power and affluence: the magnificently efficient modern factories, the lavishness of cars and highways, the vast consumption of handsomely packaged goods displayed in the new suburban shopping-centres. All this underlines what appears to a European an often striking neglect of American public services. As Professor Galbraith has put it,[1] this neglect is also common knowledge.

1. op. cit.

In the years following the Second World War, the papers of any major city – those of New York were an excellent example – told daily of the shortages and shortcomings in the elementary municipal and metropolitan services. The schools were old and over-crowded. The police force was under strength and underpaid. The parks and playgrounds were insufficient. Streets and empty lots were filthy, and the sanitation staff was under-equipped and in need of men. Access to the city by those who work there was uncertain and painful and becoming more so. Internal transportation was overcrowded, unhealthful and dirty. So was the air. Parking on the streets had to be prohibited, and there was no space elsewhere. These deficiencies were not in new and novel services but in old and established ones.

This social unbalance of the American affluent society affects larger issues than delinquency – such as the whole level of American education – but on the special problem of its effects on delinquency two points can be made. As in Britain, but even more so in the United States, it is the children and adolescents of the underprivileged minorities who are most acutely affected by the inadequacy of public services. In the American affluent society these groups are the majority of the coloured, the new immigrants, the poor in general: it is the boys and girls in these groups who suffer if classrooms in old schools are overcrowded, teachers lack authority, the police force is under strength, there are too few parks and playing fields, slum clearance is delayed; if there are too few probation officers and a lack of special detention facilities for adolescents. Among such young people, the inevitable sense of public neglect must both diminish their respect for society and intensify their attitude of social defiance – the outcome again is increased juvenile crime and delinquency.

As Professor Galbraith has also observed, if American society, through inadequate public services, neglects these youngsters, other and not at all public-minded interests are quick to exploit them. In a balanced community, where an efficient school was surrounded by good recreational opportunities, 'the diversionary forces operating on the modern juvenile world' would do little harm. Comics and violent modes of television, films, and advertising would have to contend with the intellectual discipline and social attraction of the school. But in a society where 'private opulence' goes with 'public squalor', the schools often cannot compete at all – not against the impact of ubiquitous television or against an output of a hundred million copies of questionable comics a month. Some recent interrogation of hardened young New York delinquents has shown how deeply they were influenced by the fantasy crime world of television, and how little by school. Again, one can see a reason for the sharp increase in juvenile crime on the lower rungs of American society.

However, as soon as one speaks of the cultural impact of the American affluent society, it has to be realized that this does not, of course, affect only the underprivileged minorities – at this point one must turn to generalizations about American youth as a whole.

The receding super-ego

To use a loose phrase, some of the cultural troubles of the American affluent society – such as the greater confusion among its adolescents – seem to me to stem from the fact that the voice of advertising has become that of a super-ego – a role which should be played by society itself.

That advertising is inadequate in this role is self-evident. Whatever may be the wording of its message about vital matters like family life, friendship, social status, and getting on in life, this is only a cover. The real aim of the images projected is always merely to sell the product. If advertising therefore looms too large in social life, all popular culture will take on a gloss of double-think, and society will advance that much further towards Huxley's brave new world.

This may appear a trite observation, but because angry American critics have inveighed so fiercely against the social havoc wrought by the morals and methods of Madison Avenue, it is surely important, even in order to see a prob-

lem like juvenile delinquency in perspective, to reiterate
that the whole advertising industry is itself only an instrument. The primary forces which shape the affluent society
arise from its economic structure. Such a primary force, to
quote the example again, is the requirement of the gargan-
tuan American motor industry that American families
should always continue to buy new cars, that American life
should always be automobile-dominated. Intensive advertising which never lets up is only the instrument by which
the automobile producers, like the other big American
producers, achieve this purpose. Yet if the instrument of
advertising is used on too large a scale, then it is true that
it acquires a life of its own, that its persuasive commands
become like those of society itself; and when this happens,
the result is likely to be a state of cultural confusion which
can be especially devastating for the young.

American sociologists have recently been busy in analys-
ing the various ways in which this is already happening.
There seem to be growing indications that one effect of
sustained mass advertising on culture is to weaken the
bonds of family life and lessen the authority of parents.
Some aspects of life in the new American suburban communities provide a good illustration of this. Leading American investigators have written pretty scathingly about what
goes on among those labour-saving little homes among the
tree-lined avenues. Where a passing European visitor may
carry away an impression of material ease, of hospitable and
sociable people, of attractive and remarkably independent
children, American researchers into Plywood Estates have
painted an almost uniformly black picture of suburban
families living in a state of social isolation – of competitiveness between neighbours, artificiality in friendship, anxiety
over status, always anxiety.

This picture may well also be overdrawn, but one thing
is probably true. There *is* something in the whole look of
the American suburban landscape which carries a suggestion of rootlessness and of a social life which is not quite
complete. The highly organized lobbies of the builders,

salesmen, and advertisers of American homes *have* succeeded in implanting the idea that the social status of a citizen is linked closely to the size and position of his house. It follows that as a man rises in his career, the voice of the advertisers is also persuading him that he must move house. (It cannot be mere native American restlessness if one suburban family in four or five is on the move each year.) But each move means tearing up roots and usually a complete change of friendships and neighbourhood attachments, both for the parents and the children. The result must be at least a measure of insecurity for the whole family, and insecure parents have less authority over the young. It has been said that some of the newer mass-produced American suburbs, where each house is scarcely distinguishable from its neighbour, are pre-eminently communities where home becomes regarded as a place where the members of different generations belonging to a family seem merely to be living together for a certain time. The result is that teenage boys and girls live much more within their own age-group, without much guidance. The result, in turn, is more of those incidents so often reported in American case-studies, newspaper articles, books, and films – of teenage boys and girls who stray through ignorance into delinquency, of cases of reckless driving, accidents, youthful drunkenness, and early sexual disorder, with parents nearly always largely unaware of what goes on in the autonomous teenagers' society. These incidents only affect a minority of American adolescents, but if it is argued that this minority is too large, that there is something unsatisfactory in the structure of American suburban life, that it lacks the sense of permanency and focused authority which young people need, and which the American small town of the bourgeois age possessed, then to see the trouble clearly one has to go back to the starting-point of the process, namely that it is enormously powerful economic interests which are today creating the American suburbia in its particular shape. And this process is not easy to change.

In recent American sociological literature one comes also

surprisingly often upon the assertion that the conflict between the generations finds sharper expression in the United States than elsewhere. Above all, older people in the United States are more noticeably hostile towards adolescents. This observation has been put forward by writers like Margaret Mead and Kingsley Davis; it corresponds with the first-hand conclusions of American teachers who have studied European schools and family relations. To the extent that this intensified American conflict between harassed adults and demanding adolescents is a fact, it is again surely no accident, but something which goes with the forced development of a separate, commercialized teenage culture. This development has been pushed further in the United States than anywhere else – by the standards of any European country, the specialized teenagers' consumption market in the United States is of staggering dimensions. And the interests of the suppliers of this market certainly run counter to ideas of parental restrictions. If American girls use cosmetics when hardly in their teens, if schoolchildren go in precociously for competitive dating, if teenagers as early as possible feel entitled to cars and expensive outfits and amusements, the overriding reason is that large commercial interests, including some of the biggest corporations, are interested in fostering these fashions of teenage consumption and the idea that American adolescence should be prolonged as much as possible. 'Don't keep them back. Don't frustrate them. Let them be buyers and consumers, just like you!' This has become the basic message conveyed by the American advertising industry, whose most advanced practitioners seem today increasingly to portray teenagers as sexually precocious pseudo-adults. (This trend is already also becoming marked in British advertising.) It is hard, and sometimes impossible, for parents to oppose these forces. But not all boys and girls are suited to this life of precocious teenage independence in lavish consumption and spending which here and there takes its toll in delinquency.

The same observation could be made about the excessively 'permissive' character of much American education, whose effect in lowering educational standards has been worrying many authorities. For this 'permissiveness', critics have blamed various influences, from the philosophy of John Dewey to Freudian precepts accepted in distorted form. Again, I think these are minor factors. Fundamentally, 'permissiveness' in schools seems a logical outcome if certain trends in the affluent society are allowed to go on unchecked. It is in the direct interest of American consumer industries that school discipline should impose no irksome restriction on the social life and the spending of teenagers. The whole impact of their advertising is implicitly directed towards projecting this idea. But again – like the economic pressure against the authority of parents – so this economic pressure against discipline at school appears to create its proportion of 'mixed-up kids' and delinquents. As has always to be said, not a large proportion. The majority of ordinary American boys and girls can cheerfully take the affluent society in their stride (as normal adolescents take anything in their stride); but still, it is a larger proportion than in a more directly disciplined society: this seems a price that has to be paid for the maintenance of a special teenage culture with high standards of consumption.

Lastly, in talking about the problem why the process of growing up in the United States has become so much more difficult than it was in the past, one comes to what is probably the most important reason of all – that young people in the affluent society are subjected to a constant and very special confusion of values all around them.

American bourgeois morality of the past was no doubt also a highly confused amalgam, composed of the traditions of bourgeois individualism, the American democratic ideal of independence, some genuine religious beliefs, mixed in with all kinds of sentimentality and hypocrisy, with class and money barriers, race prejudice, and the rest. Yet in some way all these elements added up to the genuine sentiments of bourgeois America. On the other hand, in a society dominated by mass advertising, the values imposed on the individual are not only 'other-directed' in Mr Riesman's term. What I think more important is that from their nature they represent sentimentality and not sentiment. Because the advertisers themselves are concerned with something quite different, whatever they have to say about family life, social life, social status, and the rest cannot be based on sentiment; it must be manufactured sentimentality. Obvious enough: but the danger is that when the affluent society has reached a certain stage, the advertisers' substitution of sentimentality for sentiment becomes more and more the pattern of all popular culture, especially when the bulk of mass entertainment also becomes subordinated to 'selling the product'. It encroaches on social life; it invades democratic politics – when elections become in effect campaigns waged by business interests through advertising agencies and advertising methods, politics are no longer the same. And at this stage, society also ceases to be adequate in its role of collective super-ego, as far as the outlook of the young is concerned.

There are various indications from the United States how this contradiction between accepted sentimental precepts and the realities of life makes it harder for young people to know what they should think. American sociologists have pointed out how advertising is constantly urging people to upgrade themselves socially through increased consumption just when a certain hardening of class barriers actually makes such upgrading more difficult. Critics have recently stressed another point where the realities of the affluent society clash with its precepts. It has been the long-accepted ideal of the American boy to tinker with machinery. Only a short time ago, the ambition of an individual boy might have been to become a motor mechanic working in a garage – to take pleasure in dismantling, reassembling, repairing the engines of cars. Today such a boy soon learns that this ambition, too, has been relegated to the realm of sentimentality: the last thing the big manufacturers want is that any but the most superficial repairs should be effected on their cars – for some models, indeed, no spare parts are issued after five years – and that the minimum service or even shoddy service does as well as craftsmanship. Naturally he soon falls into line; but, with craftsmanship, another set of once traditional values has disappeared. (Probably one should make this observation with caution. Although American writers have written much about the current 'alienation' of Americans from meaningful work, European missions of trade unionists still find that many ordinary Americans still take greater pleasure in the sheer efficiency of their work than their European counterparts. But the significant word here is 'still'.)

To turn to another contradiction – since the stern old days of the woodpile and the Bible, American religious observance has also undergone a transformation. In the new suburbs one meets with a surprising amount of regular church-going (far more than, say, in England), but from all accounts this serves a mainly social need. The manifest aim is to turn the suburban church (or synagogue) into a new focus of social life. There is nothing wrong with this aim, which corresponds to the spiritual hunger of people genuinely anxious for roots, but the point is that a young American must soon see that this increased church-going (or synagogue-going) has apparently little link with the other sides of American social life. For example, the bulk of American mass entertainment (always with laudable exceptions) seems devoted more than ever before to the cult of violence. As Block and Flynn put it,[1] 'it is likely, though not proved, that a demoralization of our youth, seen in its broadest terms, results from the continuous exposure to the spectacle of untrammelled sex and violence in our recreational media'. Or again, what should young Americans think about the comics industry, the worst of whose productions, in the words of a Senate report, offer short courses in murder, robbery, carnage, sadism, etc.? Well, American educational authorities (like those of other countries) are divided about the direct effects of horror comics on young readers. One need not, perhaps, worry too much about their effects on

1. Herbert A. Block and Frank T. Flynn, *Delinquency*, Random House, 1956.

normal, balanced children. But there is some good evidence to think that to the disturbed, the delinquency-prone and suggestible child they can provide both stimulus and documentation for delinquency. Even so, I think this direct effect is relatively only a detail. The real trouble and cause for alarm is that in a society which places such stress on increased church attendance, this flood of horror comics should even exist, just as it is cause for alarm that the juvenile gangs of New York should even exist. The real trouble, in fact, is the constant confusion of values which goes with the affluent society. In this context, the case of the large number of young American prisoners-of-war in Korea, who put up only weak resistance against Chinese brainwashing – something which came as a shock to American public opinion – was, I think, not only significant but also understandable. Such over-exposure to the advertisers' message, which is never what it seems, has to cause a confusion in the minds of young people, in which the ideas of democracy and freedom become hardly distinguishable from the slogans in car and toothpaste advertisements, and can therefore be as readily discarded. Much more than anything else, this constant confusion between moral values and advertisers' values is surely the reason why in 1960 about two million American boys and girls were involved with the police or the juvenile courts for petty or more serious acts of delinquency. These figures must of course also be seen in proportion. Within the vast scale of American life, even such high rates of youthful delinquency are only a marginal problem : but they do show disturbingly how all is not well with this life. To put it in a simplified way, one feels that the voice of the American affluent society, as it is heard by adolescents, is no longer adequately that of the collective super-ego. And this thought brings one to the current American situation, and to President Kennedy, who already in his first spirited year in office set himself to attack some of these inadequacies. . . .

If this analysis is correct, as I believe it to be, it is all the more surprising that so different a type of society as the

Soviet Union (and other Communist countries) suffers from apparently similar problems of youthful unrest and youthful rebellion. Yet this is undoubtedly happening, even though in the case of these countries, we have, partly at least, to look for very different causes.

CHAPTER 13

Moscow: Youth under Authority

What can we learn from the Russians?

LIKE the West, the Communist countries behind the Iron Curtain have been affected by the wave of youthful unrest which started in the fifties.

This coincidence in time is, I think, not accidental. For instance, it is interesting and significant that, on this and the other side of the Iron Curtain, the cult of jazz should have become a symbol of youthful revolt. At the same time, we should also recognize some basic differences in the two movements. In the West, sections of the young have rebelled against moral confusion, too little guidance: they have reacted against having too much easy money and not enough money for special purposes. In Eastern Europe the young rebelled against drabness, against regimentation, against political unfreedom and oppression: this was a revolt on quite a different intellectual level from any movement in the West. In the satellite states, and especially in Poland and Hungary, this revolt expressed itself in a remarkable mass repudiation of Communism by the young people living under it – one might almost call it a teenage counter-revolution. This passionate defiance of Communism by Polish and Hungarian youth was one of the astonishing phenomena of the mid-century, about which not enough has yet been written. It not only created its heroic legend in the Warsaw and Budapest risings of October 1956 – it probably decisively influenced the trend of Communist rule in Europe.

Because of their special political circumstances, these Hungarian–Polish events are outside the scope of this book. However, in its own way, Soviet Russian youth has also not remained untouched by the unrest of our age. Even Moscow, with its *stilyagi* in Gorki Street and gangs of young hooligans in the workers' suburbs, has its rebels without cause. And, on another level, its fairly angry young writers: the serious disenchantment of young Russians with the inequalities, the self-seeking and the continuing hardships of Soviet life has been reflected in novels like Dudintsev's *Not by Bread Alone*, Aksenov's Soviet Teddy-boy tale *The Way to the Stars*, or in Yevtushenko's critical poetry. How far this disenchantment has already had a political effect in a country under Communist dictatorial rule is hard to say. To speculate on this would lead me beyond my theme, but I think that the state of mind of youth which the Soviet system has produced is an interesting subject in itself. For obvious reasons, one can here only deal in very general impressions. But it might be useful to start with the top Soviet achievement.

All problems solved?

A visit to a top-grade Soviet school is usually a rather startling experience which an English or American writer especially finds hard to reconcile with preconceived ideas. The picture has been made familiar to us by a host of Anglo-American correspondents, from Mr John Gunther downwards. Our correspondent would be taken to visit Moscow public school No. 315 or perhaps No. 151 (to judge from the published stories, No. 315 is a favourite showplace), and if he is an intelligent middle-aged observer, he would feel at once alarmed by the standard in education achieved and puzzled by something nostalgic in the whole atmosphere of the school.

From the entrance hall onwards, our observer would notice on all walls large, patriotic portraits of Tolstoy, Lenin, and Gorki, of Marshal Suvorov and other Russian military heroes, and might ponder about this touch of old-fashioned authority. Starting his tour with the younger pupils, he would find himself in a classroom full of surprisingly attractive children ('The children were entrancing, bright as fireworks' – John Gunther) sitting at old-fashioned double desks with inkwells; they would be neatly and uniformly dressed, the girls in black or brown pinafores with their blonde hair in plaits, the boys in their little semi-military belted uniform (rather like German or Scandinavian schoolboys of 1910). Boys and girls who were in the Pioneers, the Communist equivalent of the Scouts, would be wearing bright red kerchiefs round their necks. All the children would seem responsive, spontaneously natural and yet polite, with that impressive look of bright eagerness which a sense of purpose together with tight discipline can give to youngsters. (I myself noticed this with a shock in the *Hitlerjugend* in Berlin in the summer of 1939.)

Proceeding to the classes for older boys and girls, our writer might well feel that the curriculum in this Moscow school for *all* children appeared to be equal to that of the best Central European schools for selected upper-middle class boys and girls. A British journalist, if imaginative, would note with, one hopes, a certain shock, that the Soviet school system was managed without any 11-plus test. The basic theoretical arrangement was for *all* Soviet children to receive ten years of strenuous, purposeful academic education. There was nothing like the British idea of segregating a middle-class minority of children who received a similar education from the working-class majority who did not; nor any hint of the resistance to middle-class culture often found in British secondary modern schools. This difference between British and Soviet schools in the matter of class outlook would alone be enough to make a British visitor feel thoughtful.

Again, an American visitor comparing the schools of Moscow and New York would be struck by the apparent total absence in Moscow of any distracting commercial youth culture: he would find no twelve-year-old girls prematurely occupied with dating and cosmetics, no exaggerated cult of athletics, no commercial television, no horror comics. Above all, among all these serious and attractive Soviet children he would be impressed by the unquestioned authority of the teachers and the respect accorded them. (He would be told that there was no shortage of teachers; at an average salary of 800 roubles a month, they were relatively well paid by Soviet standards.) In this respect, our American might feel uneasily, a Soviet school of today was rather like the ideal of an American school of the bourgeois past, before big advertising and the teenage market had been invented. ... Yet the Soviet school system appeared simultaneously to provide a purposeful preparation for the scientific world of tomorrow. Every child took four years of chemistry, five of physics, and six of biology. The average Russian boy or girl, Mr John Gunther reported, got more than five times the amount of science and mathematics stipulated for entrance even to such a specialized American institution as Massachusetts Institute of Technology.[1]

Moreover, according to what our visitors were told, there would seem to be little difficulty in pushing all ordinary boys and girls through this curriculum. If our visitors asked the headmistress of such a Moscow school whether, as they had been told, some pupils did indeed leave at the age of fourteen or fifteen, the answer would usually be that a certain number did go, but only to receive the practical, specialized technological training of which the continuously expanding Soviet economy was in such need. And, as compared to this drive for scientific and technical knowledge, problems of occasional indiscipline at school caused evidently only very minor worries. The headmistress would clearly not be very interested in this question; or she would reply that the children had naturally already acquired the habits of spontaneous discipline and the desire to learn at one of Moscow's 2,000 kindergartens. Our visitors would meet the same atmosphere of youthful zest and discipline when they went to a Pioneer institution, say the Central House of the Pioneers in Moscow. Here, in a vast club-house with a wealth of wonderful equipment, they would meet boys and girls every one of them absorbed in 'constructive leisure': spending their free time being taught crafts and hobbies; studying literature, dramatics, the arts (the latter in a good bourgeois way – girls would be embroidering, painting water-colours,

1. John Gunther, *Inside Russia Today*, Hamish Hamilton, 1958.

playing piano *études*, as schoolgirls in the West did a generation ago). And if our visitors in their tour of Soviet education passed on to, say, Moscow's skyscraper Lomonosov University with its 2,000 laboratories and 5,000 rooms (costing five times as much as Chicago University), if they were overwhelmed, as they usually would be, with Soviet educational statistics and watched the serious, mature-looking students swarm in and out, they might be pardoned for feeling a little dizzy. Since most visitors would be unaware that this stress on more and more education had been maintained even during the worst severities of the Stalinist days, they would feel themselves faced with puzzling contradictions in the Soviet system. An American visitor, particularly, might by reaction feel that the Soviet leaders had solved one of the great problems troubling America; that, however repellent their political system might be, they had somehow inculcated such a drive for knowledge and culture among Soviet youth that questions of indiscipline, youthful disaffection, and delinquency simply solved themselves. . . .

One could put it another way. I have earlier mentioned George Orwell's picture of the American nineteenth-century romantic ideal: of a barefoot boy sitting in a whitewashed schoolroom dominated by a big black Bible, who aspired to become President, but had first to attend to the woodpile. After a tour of a showplace Moscow school, our American observer might imagine that Soviet education had simply progressed from this same ideal. The authority of the black Bible – in its place one had that of Marxist-Leninist teaching. The woodpile – from the start, the notion of social duties was drummed into the head of every Soviet child. And the dream of becoming President – this was embodied in the enormous opportunities for young Russians of today to lead cultured lives their parents had never dreamed of. In fact, it might seem as if the Russians had done a very simple thing: maintained the ideals of the bourgeois age, broadened them to include every social class, and carried them forward into the scientific age: how unlike the West.

Appearance and reality

This, roughly, is the rather alarmed impression of Soviet education one can gather from the accounts of a number of British and American visitors, usually short-term visitors, and especially from American visitors arriving in the Soviet Union with superficial preconceived ideas and with worries about American commercialized culture back home. But just because this idealized picture of Soviet youth is in some ways valid, it is equally important to know where it does not tally at all with Soviet realities.

To give just a few points: *Item:* It is British and American observers who are most startled by the educational standards of picked Soviet State schools. Visitors from Germany or Scandinavia, where the school system is not very different, would be much less surprised. *Item:* Soviet higher education is not free from the disorders troubling the West. The competitive rat-race to get into universities is so fierce that a recent Soviet inquiry found that a large number of seventeen- and eighteen-year-olds were working themselves into a state of nervous and physical illness. *Item:* As almost all foreigners find out, most Soviet young people are enormously attracted by the Western youth culture which is officially attacked and derided by their propaganda. Students make and trade 'black tapes' of Western jazz, recorded from foreign broadcasts. After an international youth congress, fortunate Russian girls eagerly display acquired Western clothes. *Item:* Boys and girls who do not pass their examinations into higher education suffer from an acute sense of social failure, of not getting into the superior social class. They are, indeed, often impelled very ruthlessly into jobs in factories, mines, in agriculture or clerical work, wherever the Soviet economy needs them and whether they like it or not – hence, the noticeable cynicism of many Soviet adolescents who have left school. *Item:* The universal ten-year education is still only a theoretical ideal. In 1958, Khrushchev admitted that only eighty per cent of children in the Russian Soviet Republic (and certainly less in the outer republics) completed even the full seven-year school. *Item:* The Soviet Union has a hooligan and delinquent problem large enough to feature in the national Press. Some districts of Soviet towns are also not safe at night. In cities like Moscow, Leningrad, and Kiev, squads of young Communists have been detailed to help the militia patrol parks and streets as guard against youthful gangs. *Item:* With the arrival of the first Soviet affluence, with such things as TV-sets, brighter clothes, and even some private cars, the Soviet penal code towards young offenders has become not milder but in some ways has regressed towards severity. Innocents in the West, who imagine that anyone who is 'Left', like a Communist, must also be an enlightened penal reformer, can be sorely disillusioned from the Soviet Press. In summer 1958, as a reaction against Stalinism, the Supreme Soviet passed a first penal reform act, gradually reducing penalties. But this trend was again swiftly reversed. Hardly was the act passed when the Soviet youth journal, *Komsomol Pravda*, started a campaign calling for the death penalty for killings resulting from so-called 'acts of youthful hooliganism', not only for the actual assailant but for any member of the gang found with weapons. Similar demands for increased penalties could be found in the Soviet Press throughout 1959–60, and the new penal act of May 1961, which introduced the death penalty for civil offences like embezzlement, theft of state property, and counterfeiting, once again made the Soviet penal code towards juveniles incomparably harsher than any in the West. For instance, for offences including some coming under the heading of 'parasitism', young people could be sent to labour colonies for up to five years.

On a closer look, therefore, these are some of the real contradictions of the present Soviet social scene: on the one hand, an intense educational effort, in which the young are kept under tightest authority, side by side with a widespread feeling among many young people of being 'also-rans', plus quite a large delinquency problem, possibly larger than in many countries of the West.

Education as priority

How have these contradictions come about? I am aware
of the difficulty of writing about any single aspect of the
Soviet system in isolation, and in oversimplified terms. Still,
it is instructive to keep one's eye on one factor, namely the
continuous development of the Soviet education system,
starting from the original aim in the minds of Lenin and his
colleagues that every Soviet citizen should be educated up to
a level previously thought appropriate, in the Western
world, only to the middle class, or even the upper-middle
class.

In forty-five years of practice, this aim has not been anything like fully achieved. Even so, it holds vital lessons for
the West as to *the quantitive scale of education* which an
affluent society can well afford. At the same time, to understand the defects of Soviet society and culture one must see
this educational drive in context and perspective.

A first point to bear in mind is that already long ago –
long before 1917 – education in Russia had that special
social prestige it often has in underdeveloped countries – the
technical know-how of Germany in particular exerted an
enormous attraction on the Russians. The Tsarist Russian
education system was, in fact, closely modelled on that of
Imperial Germany, from state primary school up to *Gym-
nasium* and *Realschule*, with good bourgeois stress on discipline, hard work, and learning. Proceeding from this
starting-point, the Russian intelligentsia had in its revolutionary struggles steadily developed the theme that the
spread of education was *the* key to the new society. The
Populists had hoped to achieve such inspired universal education from below. The Communists after their seizure of
power were, on the contrary, determined to impose it by
decree from above. In the flush of revolutionary enthusiasm
the Communist Party programme of 1919 laid down that
every Soviet child should have ten years at school. This, of
course, proved for a long time impossible; the target was for
many years reduced to a minimum of seven years. Even so,

even if the overriding motive of the Communists was simply to make the Soviet state powerful, this educational drive, consistently pursued, has been the one aspect of the Revolution to draw a consistent and powerful response from the Russian people.

This is a first point to bear in mind; a second is to see in what different ways this educational drive has been pursued. The political purpose of the Communist leaders was ruthlessly clear: to destroy the old order and build a new one on its ruins. One means to this end was to harness the enthusiasm and loyalties of the young completely to the purposes of the Soviet state. (Lenin had already preached such regimentation in 1905.) The Communist leaders also had another impelling motive for seeking total control over the minds of the young. Ruling as a minority by dictatorship, they felt they could not trust the older intelligentsia. Their explicit aim was therefore to train a new generation of 'their own flesh and blood' as loyal to the State. This indoctrination was to be achieved not only through the school. It was to be driven home by organizing the out-of-school activities of children through the controlled Pioneer organization, while older boys and girls were to be shepherded or forced in the right direction by the dedicated revolutionary 'vanguard' of the Young Communists, or Komsomols.

For over a decade, therefore, Soviet boys and girls were deliberately educated to a wholesale rejection of the past – this often meant a rejection of all that their parents stood for and often of the actual parents themselves. This was the phase of the great flush of Soviet experiment in literature and the arts, in such things as easy divorce and abortion, and the Soviet education system in this stage also tended to be strikingly *avant-garde*: the Dalton plan, the Montessori plan, children's self-government in schools – it included the lot. This phase in the twenties was also the time when Western observers talked most of what could be learned from Soviet education. It is therefore important to note that this experiment of teaching boys and girls to reject their parents and tradition, but without putting them under an equivalent alternative authority, ended in failure. The authority of the Russian family was broken by the Revolution – but one outcome was disorder. Indeed, as one could read from admissions in the Soviet Press, one result of the Revolutionary vision of youthful emancipation was widespread inefficiency, delinquency, promiscuity, and a sharp fall in the birth-rate, or, as the Soviet leaders saw it, 'a loss of cadres'.

As a result (for other reasons as well, of course!) Stalin went heavily into reverse to clamp down on youthful freedom. The formal traditions of family life were restored and puritanism swept back; out went easy divorce, grants for unmarried mothers were abolished, abortion became illegal. The new concept was called 'Communist morality', but it looked remarkably like Victorian morality. In schools, the return was to Tsarist discipline, and it went all the way; out went co-education, uniforms came back, children stood up when an adult entered the class, there was no more nonsense about children's self-government. Out of school, puritanical standards were by order of the Government, i.e. of the Communist Party leadership, imposed through the Pioneers and the Komsomols, based on collective responsibility of children for each other – a system of collective informing and shaming, with harsh penalties. It looked as if the clock had suddenly been turned back. This was the time when, in surprised disillusion, Western intellectuals stopped asking what could be learned from Soviet education, for in undergoing her industrial revolution Soviet Russia seemed to have turned back to the puritanical morals of the nineteenth century. The very appearance of the new Soviet art and architecture and life had suddenly a Victorian air.

Yet I think this loss of interest was a pity. True, Stalin's counter-revolution was directed sweepingly against the whole message of emancipation of the Revolution, especially the emancipation of youth: brutal authority and not freedom was now the watchword. But behind the 'Victorian' façade, it was not the authority of parents, of the bourgeois past, which was restored. On the contrary, the authority now reimposed on the young as well as on their parents was completely that of the State, represented by the Communist Party, which, whatever its words, in reality spoke not of freedom but of work, of duty, of submission to the demands of State authority. Here, in this counter-revolution, we have the start of the problem of how far a young person's life can be influenced by, respectively, his own wishes, those of his family, and those of the State, a problem which is still completely unsolved in the Soviet Union of today, and is certainly a cause of large-scale youthful malaise.

For a time, however, this reality behind the Soviet 'Victorian' look was hidden by Stalin's rule of terror which for some years reached such a pitch (with greater oppression as the Soviet Union grew stronger and with millions of people done away with) that the whole of Soviet life was shrouded in impenetrable mist. During these years, face-to-face groups were afraid to talk; under the terror, society seemed atomized. Yet it was striking that during these same years the Soviet education system went on expanding steadily – the drive went on and on.

In retrospect one can see reasons. The overriding aim of the Communist leaders was to make the U.S.S.R. economically and militarily strong, which meant promoting technical know-how and mass literacy – during all their political phases the Communist leadership never wavered from this aim. But there were also other reasons for the uninterrupted expansion of education. Because planted in receptive soil, the idea of social betterment through universal education remained the one concept of the Revolution eagerly accepted by the Russian people. Moreover, as the early Bolshevik leaders had done, so Stalin now aimed to create a new indoctrinated generation of intellectuals and technicians entirely loyal to himself, and so, even during the harshest days of his rule, technical education was given priority in resources. Again, amidst the austerity of Soviet Russian life under Stalin, education stood out as the one supreme avenue through which young people could better themselves and achieve social advance, all the more so as the alternative avenue, that of becoming a member of the Communist Party aristocracy, had now become highly dangerous.

For all these reasons, schools and colleges in Soviet Russia continued to be given first priority. And something else happened, too. In the West, the bourgeois educational ideals of fifty years ago, with their stress on discipline, on formal good manners and the notion of the good apprentice, have been very much changed by all the influences of our commercialized culture, with its advertised hedonism. But in Soviet Russia, where for years there was no such consumers' culture, the pattern of this bourgeois education of fifty years ago has been curiously preserved, right to the present day. The more I read about the atmosphere and appearance of Soviet schools of today, the more it reminds me of that sound Swiss–German school which I myself attended many years ago.

However, life for ardent youth does not consist of school discipline alone. What was also preserved in Stalin's society without commercial youth culture was the utter boredom of the young within the Komsomol organization and a life of squalid pubs where young rebels drank adulterated vodka. Under Stalin's police rule, all this could be maintained, but since his death the Soviet rulers have had to give ground to the normal demand of youth for spontaneity. But how slowly! Early in 1962, two 'youth cafés' with modern décor were opened in Moscow, where young people can meet over coffee or soft drinks, wearing Western-style clothes and listening to American jazz. But as Moscow *Pravda* itself said (March 1962), only two such cafés to keep the young off the streets in a city of millions! And it has taken nine years since Stalin's death for the Soviet rulers to get to this present point, and along their road of slow retreat they have certainly been beset by delinquency problems.

Guesses about Russian youth

And so to this present day, with Russia more accessible but still such a closed society that one can only indicate the evident trends among youth. Most Soviet Russians over thirty or thirty-five appear agreed that, whatever present difficulties, by comparison with the days of Stalin's terror and those of the war they have emerged from the shadows. Recent years have at least seen an advance towards greater amenities in Soviet city life: new apartments, more television, an enormous boom in every single kind of sport. The promise no longer sounds so unreal that there will soon be far better and brighter goods in Soviet shops and that, just as in the West, such possessions as cars, washing-machines, and refrigerators will be available on hire-purchase terms in real quantity supplies. For the overwhelming majority of ordinary Russians, these material benefits, and not politics, are the things that really occupy their minds. Angry young Soviet novelists have already written scathingly about the evidently pretty ugly scramble for jobs, possessions, and status which this new material advance has unloosed – stressing that all the old Communist romanticism has vanished. However, for the young, this post-Stalinist Soviet world of rising living standards, ruthless competition, and vanishing ideals is the only reality they know. From the reactions of Soviet young people we now also know more about their worries. At the first glance, American and Soviet society seem like precise opposites in their youth problems. American complaints are about lack of drive in schools, insufficient authority over adolescents, and an overdose of commercial youth culture. By contrast, Soviet education is tight and disciplined, but out of school youngsters feel repressed by rigid authority, while the lack of spontaneous teenage culture is a major social problem.

If one talks about youth in the Soviet Union, one still has to begin by talking about the Soviet State education system. The historic message transmitted from the revolutionary intelligentsia to the Russian masses, that learning can give a social status higher than anything else, still evokes a passionate response. But in the changing Soviet society of today, the drive for education has already also come up against new limits and produced some social problems familiar to us. For instance, in keeping with the Party programme of 1919, the Soviet leaders in 1950 decided to raise the length of school attendance for all children from seven years to ten years, the change to be effected by stages by 1960. In this form, however, the scheme was abandoned half-way. If one takes the figures both for the towns and the schools in the countryside, it had in actual practice been nothing like fulfilled. Even so, in urban areas, this extension of secondary education created new troubles because it touched on a sore spot in Soviet life – the gap in status between those who passed via school and higher education into the new class of Soviet administrators and technicians, and those who did not and were consequently relegated, perhaps to manual work. For many secondary school pupils this was a sufficiently frightening prospect to make them feel social failures, 'also rans'. The result of the new policy was to create a whole class of adolescents who, on failing university entrance, did not go into jobs but tried despairingly to take the examination again and again.

That is, Soviet society had very much become what is called a 'meritocracy', and whatever Communist dogma might state there was very little tendency among the sceptical young themselves to agree that being relegated to boring manual work was the same as an administrative career. This was made clear by the official reaction. The first response of the Soviet leadership was strong-arm pressure to compel dissatisfied youngsters to take ordinary manual jobs in industry and on collective farms, or to go out as pioneers into the virgin lands to the east; as especially Mr Khrushchev demanded in his orations. The pressure was accompanied by rather strident propaganda against *beloruchki* – literally, those with 'white hands' – that is, adolescents who did not care to go into manual work and so, in Soviet parlance, were shirkers who refused their patriotic duty. However, as these methods of persuasion proved inadequate, the Soviet leaders – and this is interesting – in the late fifties put their whole education policy into reverse. The first measure was to introduce a sharper division, usually made at the age of fourteen, between those secondary school pupils who were to continue with academic education and others who were to proceed straight into some form of practical and technical training – a kind of British 11-plus test, if at a later and more suitable age. The next step, proclaimed in detail at the 20th Party Congress in 1956, was a call for the 'polytechnization' of the entire Soviet secondary education system. All secondary school education was now to include some periods of practical training in industry and agriculture. A third innovation was the introduction of boarding schools for boys and girls, of which a considerable number have already been set up. Their slant as compared with day schools is still uncertain, but one thing is clear: one main purpose of introducing boarding schools is to give the authorities – that is, the Communist Party leadership – greater physical control over Soviet adolescents.

I have mentioned these innovations in Soviet educational policy because I think they throw some light on the state of mind of a section of Soviet youth, on that evident mood of apathy and cynicism held by a good many young people, in spite of the education which they have received, against which the Soviet Press constantly inveighs. The problem which the Soviet authorities now face in trying to combat this mood is a very real one, real in the West, too. What sort of education shall we give in our affluent society to those who must necessarily perform jobs that are monotonous and of no distinction, and what sort of social life can such young people demand?

From the nature of Communist society, this question remains very much unsolved in the Soviet Union. It is true that Soviet education is technically excellent. The old target of academic education for everybody has been dropped, but the official policy still aims at providing some kind of full-time education for *all* children up to the age of seventeen – an aim which could well be emulated in a country like Britain. The current Soviet programme for the polytechnization of secondary schools probably also contains valuable ideas for training boys and girls to face our technological age. But it is *after* school, after the competitive examinations, that the real competition for a much smaller number of prizes begins for Soviet teenagers – and deep disappointment often sets in.

There is, first, the sharp disillusion in store for those who do not make the grade. About seventy per cent of the students of Moscow University at the present day are themselves the sons and daughters of the intelligentsia. If, as is common knowledge, they are often scared by their parents with the phrase 'If you don't work hard, you'll become a simple worker', this throws light on the plight of those who are condemned to precisely that. For in the Soviet Union, as much as in the United States, failure to rise does not merely mean less pay and status. It is also like an offence against the national myth. 'I was a shepherd, a shepherd's son, and now I am a cultured man.' Such personal advance has for long been a constant theme of Soviet literature and propaganda. Mr Khrushchev himself has liked to stress it again and again, citing himself personally as an example. But in the more developed Soviet society of today, where ruthless competition forces many an adolescent to feel 'I have been through school, but I have not risen socially, I'm an also-ran', it appears that Mr Khrushchev may soon be untypical. At any rate, the failure of many youngsters to achieve that particular social status to which constant propaganda had made them feel entitled is certainly a cause of youthful disaffection, especially as Soviet life offers so few other social and cultural compensations for those who do not rise. It is this mood of pervasive disillusion among a large section of Soviet youth which Mr Khrushchev has sought to counter by his tirades against idle intellectuals, by his sponsored schemes for pushing the young into raw new territories, by trying in general to revive the idea that all work for the Soviet Union which is economically useful is thereby noble – 'therefore be happy, though frustrated'. The new boarding schools are probably conceived as instruments for inculcating this patriotism.

The missing teenage culture

Can this be done? We come now to the most dramatic recent development in Soviet life, the public denunciation and dethronement of Stalin at the 22nd Communist Party Congress. The manner in which this was carried out also throws light on the way in which the Soviet leaders envisage their task of controlling the young generation.

By and large, the slogan under which Mr Khrushchev and his colleagues have retained the threads of power in their hands has been one of 'Back to Leninism'. Times may be changing, but there is to be no yielding over the question of totalitarian rule over the whole country by the Communist Party apparatus and its top leadership. As far as the young are concerned, it is still the official policy that the whole sacred apparatus of Leninist regimentation must be kept intact. Indeed, in his speeches Mr Khrushchev has stressed his intention to raise the new Soviet generation in the spirit of some sort of revived militancy.

But will this be possible? To my mind, this is highly doubtful. Today, Soviet society has clearly reached a stage where it can do without this coercion. The managerial and technical know-how, the industrial power, for whose attainment the Soviet people suffered for so long, are today all there. If mere affluence is now the goal, as announced in the new Party programme, revolutionary militancy and discipline are simply no longer necessary. And Soviet young people have also changed. Since the shock of hearing of Stalin's gigantic misdeeds, they can no longer be stopped from asking whether they are really living in the best of all possible societies. And one of the difficulties in reconciling those who have to perform lesser jobs to their fate is the lack of teenage culture which the system offers. Here, indeed, lies a crucial weakness of this system.

One simple reason for this lack is that outside the centres of the main cities, Soviet life is, by any reasonable Western standards, still outstandingly drab, with some exceptions: for instance, in recent years increasing facilities have been provided for sport. But, speaking generally, the demand of the young generation for bright clothes, a more relaxed social life, for such an innocent pastime as listening to jazz (which holds an enormous attraction) has simply not yet been met, and Soviet young people of all classes seem aware of this deficiency. Miss Sally Belfrage related in her entertaining account of life among young people in Moscow[1] how Soviet students talked with no hesitation about the limitations which the housing shortage imposed on their sex life, the tiresome stratagems it made necessary. Lower down the social scale, it is this same general drabness of life which evidently drives so many adolescents to the one main outlet of Soviet life – getting well and properly drunk. Mr Khrushchev himself took up the problem in his speech to the last Komsomol Congress, saying: 'It is necessary to combat the *intolerable* phenomenon of drunkenness among young people.'[2] Western Prime Ministers have not yet had to make such an exhortation.

The absence of a real youth culture, by which I mean the chance for Soviet young people to have some independent social life and entertainment, has also become a more urgent problem in Soviet life because one gets the feeling that by today the Communist system of organizing and regimenting all young people within centralized State youth organizations has very much seen its day, at least as far as adolescents from the age of fourteen or fifteen upwards are concerned. It is at this age-level that the Soviet system has been failing. For example, it is noteworthy that while the official children's literature is generally well edited and often brilliantly imaginative, for years the books and journals produced for adolescents have been unbearably empty and dull. Perhaps this is not surprising. Children recognize and respond to authority. But it is difficult to stimulate the imagination of adolescents while at the same time ordering them to remain rigidly conformist, in line with the ideas of a past generation.

1. Sally Belfrage, *A Room in Moscow*, André Deutsch, 1958.
2. *Pravda*, 15 April 1958.

This dilemma is today met above all inside the official Soviet State youth organizations, through which out-of-school, holiday, and free-time activities are organized. The Pioneer Movement probably still works well enough, though there is evidence that even young children get bored with having their holidays and play activities always organized from above, instead of being able to arrange some of them for themselves. However, of more significance for the future of Soviet life is the fact that the Komsomol, the official young Communist organization and the régime's principal instrument for controlling the activities of *adolescents*, has by general admission lost its drive and its appeal to youth. Again, this is not surprising. The Komsomol organization was created during the revolutionary days to function as a small voluntary body of young Communist enthusiasts. Today, with practically the entire adolescent age-group enrolled, the Komsomol has become something utterly different: a rigid, centralized, State youth organization, in which social life is linked with sluggish political indoctrination, but in which the Soviet young people of today feel, above all, profoundly bored. At any rate, complaints that modern Soviet youth in the Komsomol is apathetic, that the young show no altruism, are unwilling to engage in political duties and find political discussions a bore, form a constant refrain in the Soviet Press. In his preparatory report to the 22nd Party Congress, the Komsomol Secretary, S. P. Pavlov, even made this situation a point of attack, declaring that entire regional organizations of the Komsomol in fact did nothing but collect membership dues. For this apathy, since this was the melodramatic theme of the Congress, Pavlov blamed the purges and the idolatry of the Stalin era, as well as those former Party leaders who were now declared responsible for it:

We can now see particularly clearly what terrible damage the cult of the individual did to the Komsomol. . . . It is particularly painful and bitter to remember the fabricated trials which tore so many of our best workers from our ranks. As we know, the atmosphere of those years was soaked in mistrust, suspicion, and red tape. The soulless extolling of a single personality produced social passivity among youth.

At the Party Congress, Khrushchev himself, and other speakers, demanded that the Komsomol had now to be revitalized. Yet does this look possible? To hazard a forecast, it seems far more likely that in the changing Soviet society of today this whole system of politically controlled State youth, with instructions always passed from top to bottom, has outlived its usefulness, and is certainly no barrier against infectious cynicism and a good measure of delinquency among a large section of the young. There are at least signs of implicit admission by the Soviet authorities that the opposition of the new Soviet youth to regimentation is genuine. For example, it is interesting that the Komsomol book and magazine publishers have, in the last two or three years, taken some hesitant but probably significant steps to give ordinary adolescents a chance to express their genuine individual views on 'human interest' topics. Usually this is done by getting a letter-writer to raise a problem and to invite comment from readers. The story is as a rule a simple one, in the style of 'true confessions'. For instance, a girl, who is a good Communist, may have been going out with a boy who is the son of some local high official, who rides in his father's car, who looks down on her poor but honest parents, and whose only interest is in dancing and flirting. Though it made her unhappy, was she right to break off the relationship? In spite of their careful selection, the young readers' comments on such questions seem to reveal one thing: a powerful, underlying desire by Soviet adolescents to argue out their own views on 'human interest' questions, to arrive at their own decisions – to have their own youth culture.

It is also significant that since the turning-point of de-Stalinization, this trend to meet the ideas of the young has been accelerated. For instance, questionnaires have been sent out to find out what Soviet young people were really thinking about the world around them – by the summer of

1962 there had been five such fairly extensive investigations. The selected results published in *Komsomol Pravda* showed that what troubled Soviet boys and girls was nothing very unexpected: they worried above all about finding a *meaning* to their lives. Or again, there has been the publication of W. Aksenov's novel *The Way to the Stars*, which without much heavy critique described the lives of a particular group of rebellious Soviet adolescents who were described as profoundly sceptical, living as hedonists on the impulse of the moment, uninterested in Soviet society and, for that matter, ready to break its laws. It is true that Aksenov was attacked from the usual old-Stalinist quarters for his objectivity, but he was equally allowed to defend his young 'anti-heroes' in print as not villains but victims of their circumstances. Or, as mentioned before, there has been the opening of the two Moscow youth cafés, with their permitted American jazz and unsupervised informal mingling of young people. True, by the summer of 1962 there were only two such cafés in existence, and only for young Moscow sophisticates; but they can hardly fail to become a model.

What results these stirrings can have in the strait-jacketed, censored Soviet society in creating a more spontaneous youth culture is hard to say. But there is another aspect of this issue on which we should keep our attention. In the few contacts between West and East which the Soviet leadership has not been able to avoid, it is always Western youth culture which has exerted the fascination: it is always Soviet adolescents who are fascinated by Western art, by nylons, jeans, and jazz, by free Western ways – the attraction never works vice versa. In other words, the Soviet education system may be exemplary in its technical standards, but in almost all other sides of life which interest young people it is the doctrinaire Soviet leaders who are trying to hold back the international *Zeitgeist*, who are out of step with the questing outlook of youth of today.

Not that Soviet leaders like Mr Khrushchev show any sign of giving way. One can only guess how they will manoeuvre to meet the general dissatisfaction of Soviet youth with its too narrowly limited life. Among the majority of Soviet young people, this general dissatisfaction is probably still no more than a vague emotion, but in the meantime some actual groups of young rebels against Soviet authority have become more defined.

Who are the rebels?

They can be divided into four groups. Starting at the top, there are the students who are *politically* openly dissatisfied with Soviet censorship, with the lack of free expression and the dreary rigidity of Marxist-Leninist dogma; students of the type of the small groups who at the time of the Hungarian revolution formed private discussion circles. Today, in an already easier climate, their aim is to build closer contacts with Western thought and literature. These young dissidents certainly exist. In 1962 they have been prominent among the listeners to the poetry-readings of young writers like Yevtushenko, who on the basis of unchallenged Soviet patriotism have been boldly and rather skilfully asking for greater freedom. One can only wish this vanguard well for the future.

Below these are what journalists have called the 'jet-set'; the members of this set, as Mr Edward Crankshaw has said, are what the name conveys,

the sons and daughters of the very rich and very privileged, who have no intention of working, believe in nothing at all (not even in revolt), and do their best to turn their fathers' Sochi villas into imitations of Palm Beach. They dress in imported European clothes; they drink themselves silly; they philander and fornicate; they gamble and dance. Regarding the mass of the people as cattle and the intelligentsia as prigs and bores, they live almost entirely to themselves, in and out of each other's houses, and are thus rarely seen.[1]

The 'jet-set' are only a minority phenomenon. So, though more numerous, are the next group below them, the *stilyagi*, or 'style-boys'. These bright young rebels of the Soviet big cities have perhaps been given more publicity than their

1. Edward Crankshaw, *Khrushchev's Russia*, Penguin Books, 1959.

numbers merit. Their speciality was that they faithfully copied the flashy clothes, the haircuts, the mannerisms of British Teddy boys and American zoot suiters; they evidently managed to do this through glimpses of Western films and magazines – and through all kinds of other strange loopholes in the Iron Curtain. They were intent, above all, as an act of deliberate adolescent rebellion, to copy everything they thought Western; their dominant craze was for jazz, rock, and jive; they eagerly created a black market in smuggled jazz records, often home-made and copied from foreign broadcasts. The *stilyagi* were jeered at by the Soviet Press, and written up with some excitement in the Western Press. The main interest of the *stilyagi* phenomenon was in showing that such a rebellious fashion could burst out in the Soviet Union at all. In a way, the *stilyagi* movement displayed a course curiously parallel to that of the Teddy boys. The vogue seemed to have passed its peak in 1960, but it had had its effect. The Soviet authorities had been forced to accept jazz and jeans as fairly normal – at least for Moscow youth.

None of these groups was numerically large. They were all minority phenomena of the new Soviet middle class, and the great majority of young people in this class, like their counterparts in the West, are today too preoccupied with the expanding professional opportunities before them to stray far from the conformist path.

A much more serious and persistent problem is posed by the 'young hooligans', as they are always called in the Soviet Press, lawless youths mostly belonging well down the social scale, some of them moving about in defiant gangs, who are found in most parts of the Soviet Union. In the immediate post-war period, this hooliganism was largely linked with the poverty and disruption which the war had brought to Soviet Russia. It is interesting, however, that such gangs of 'hooligans' have been produced in apparently undiminished numbers during the recent, more settled period of Soviet life. There does seem to be something international here, some basic trend of our age. For, in fact, most Soviet accounts of the 'hooligans' reveal them as very ordinary young criminals, as juvenile delinquents, or simply as cynical young members of mutinous gangs, numerous enough to form a recognizable stereotype in Soviet life.

Individually, they seem to have drifted into this life for the usual reasons, such as an inadequate home background. What is interesting is that Soviet society, in spite of the disciplined school system, the Pioneers and the Komsomol, and in spite of the general passion for education, should have produced these young delinquents in such numbers that their gang activities have rendered districts of Soviet towns and cities unsafe. Exactly how large the problem is cannot be stated – comprehensive crime statistics are not published in the Soviet Union, which is probably significant. However, according to the Leningrad *Pravda* (14 March 1959), 'until recently, about 62·5 per cent of all disturbance of the peace in Leningrad were committed by young persons below twenty-five years of age.' That the problem is, however, pretty large can be gathered by the usual signs – the frequency of solemn newspaper editorials treating 'hooliganism' as an urgent public problem, and the formation of special youthful shock brigades to aid the militia in coping with it and in patrolling the streets and parks.

The likely reasons for the wide spread of hooliganism are the deficiencies of Soviet society mentioned earlier. There is the general drabness and the lack of teenage culture. There is the resentment of the 'also-rans' in a society where, as in the United States, the official myth has it that everyone must rise. 'Hooliganism' also seems a straight reaction against the regimentation in Soviet life. The answer of at least a section of Soviet youth to constant, arid indoctrination lies evidently in pretty complete cynicism.

To sum up, therefore, as far as one can do so in the remarkable flux of Soviet life after de-Stalinization, one could make three points. First, the officially fostered conformism of the new Soviet generation is evident enough, but it seems accompanied by much youthful demoralization and delinquency. Secondly, the West can learn much from the scale and drive of the Soviet school system, where the bourgeois ideals have been developed without intervention from the siren voices of commercialized culture. But from the Soviet system of regimenting adolescents in state youth organizations like the Komsomol, the West has little or nothing to learn. Quite the reverse. Wherever Western personal freedom and Communist regimentation have been in competition, the West has won hands down. The greater changes in the life of the young are likely to come on the Communist side of the Iron Curtain.

PART THREE

WHERE DO WE GO FROM HERE?

CHAPTER 14

Some Penal Impressions

The problem of re-training

BACK to Britain – to these small and crowded islands, to the British affluent society, which is, however, also a Welfare State society where the problems of youth, delinquency, and education should like other social problems be of manageable proportions.

In principle, what should one do to stop a juvenile crime wave – educate the young offenders out of the error of their ways, or use tougher methods to teach them a different lesson? Whatever alternative is chosen – and the choice is fairly obvious – the methods cannot be easy. As must have appeared from the thesis of the preceding chapters, no miracles can be expected from the mere apparatus of the penal system.

For example, regarded in the light of British life in 1960, the general British penal system had the look of a 'semi-converted' British house, like so much else in Britain. In its structure one could still detect the traces of several periods: of the brutality of the early nineteenth century, when the British rulers felt that they had to fight Jacobinism through savage legal penalties; of the sentimental ideas of the Victorians, who thought that wrongdoers could best meditate on their sins and so be reformed within the vast, dank, and claustrophobic prisons which they built; and of the succeeding phase of twentieth-century enlightenment when it was hoped that crime might disappear with poverty and slums. The defect of this creaking system, when finally the affluent society produced its crime wave, was that it was long neglected (no new English security prison had been built in the twentieth century!) and like other public services suddenly discovered to be old-fashioned in its apparatus, and under-staffed and under-financed.

However, this did not apply in the same degree to the relatively more modern British *juvenile* penal system. In spite of archaic survivals (such as that children were deemed criminally responsible before juvenile courts from the tender age of eight upwards) it could be said that, from the end of the First World War, the British treatment of young offenders was by international standards quite reasonably progressive, humane, and responsible. For example, Britain had been in the lead in pioneering a juvenile probation service. The imitative public school pattern of the Borstals, to be sure, had begun to look odd in the society of the fifties; but historically viewed as residential institutions for young adult offenders of seventeen to twenty-one the Borstals could display several achievements. Through the very fact of their public school imitation, they had in the British class context attracted able and public-spirited men into their service. By 1960, more training Borstals were 'open' than 'closed', which meant that the majority of young adult offenders aged seventeen to twenty in Britain were being re-trained without bolts or bars. Thirdly, the fact that Borstal officers and their families, from the Governor downwards, lived on the actual premises helped to give open Borstals a certain community spirit often praised by experts from abroad.

In the case of the younger offenders aged seventeen or under, the approved schools dotted about the country, also with their English boarding-school airs and their mixed voluntary or local authority managements, were certainly varied in quality, but the best were responsibly run – the problems were of shortage of money and trained staff rather than of ideas. Experimental additions to the system during the fifties were the detention centres, where it was hoped to give certain adolescents a 'short, sharp shock' by keeping them on the run, and the milder attendance centres, where shirtsleeved policemen played schoolmaster on Saturday afternoons. During the same period, the British juvenile penal system also progressed notably in the classification of offenders, and in providing rather more, and more expert, psychiatric treatment for the maladjusted as a further shift from the older concept of punishment to the newer ideas of re-education. Some critics thought the system too soft, others still too restrictive. However, given the limited resources and aims of the British juvenile penal system, all in all (and this is borne out by foreign observers) its structure was reasonable and sound.

The changing framework

In the new circumstances of British post-war life, the increased stress on re-education rather than punishment also seemed justified. True, in this period the *coups* of more efficient adult lawbreakers hit the sensational headlines, but, if one generalization can be made, it is that numerically crime in the affluent society has become largely a problem of male adolescence. As the figures show, law-breaking has become a preoccupation of boys and youths in the fourteen to seventeen and seventeen to twenty-one age-groups. After twenty-one the incidence of criminality declines significantly, to dwindle rapidly after the age of thirty. It could therefore broadly be assumed that a good many boys committed offences only during the erratic years of their adolescence, but got over this as they reached maturity – the obvious penal aim was therefore to see to it that as few young offenders as possible should proceed into the far more dangerous world of adult crime. To keep such youngsters under safe supervision during their difficult phase, to watch over them through probation or to keep them for a spell out of harm's way in a disciplinary training institution – all this seemed no more than penal common sense.

The arguments are still valid, yet it is this same reasonably thought-out British juvenile penal system which since 1955 has been plunged into a crisis. The crisis is real enough. First, quantitatively: by 1960, admissions to residential penal institutions had risen to record heights; the sheer numerical growth of juvenile criminality threatened to swamp the whole classification machine and angry magistrates complained that it was as hard to find a place for a boy in a Detention Centre or closed Borstal as at an exclusive public school. Mr Butler's 1959 White Paper, *Penal Practice in a Changing Society*, which confirmed the Home Office faith in progressive penal methods, had therefore to be accompanied by the announcement of an unprecedented programme for building new juvenile penal institutions. But numbers were not all that had changed. Penal officers complained that earlier maturing, combined with the Teddy-boy outlook, made a section of the new offenders harder to deal with. It was also noted that a higher proportion of this new generation, the boys above all, required treatment for the maladjusted and neurotic. Most disturbing was the drop in the institutional penal 'success rate', a 'success' being counted as a boy or girl who for three years after discharge committed no further serious offence. After having stood at around sixty per cent for boys (and a much higher figure for girls) this 'success rate' began to drop steadily from about 1953 onwards, suggesting that new social influences were at work.

This very real penal crisis was reflected in the fact that the Home Office in 1960 listed as many as thirty-two official research projects into juvenile crime and penal methods as being under way at the universities and elsewhere. The crisis also found its reflection in public argument and in the clamour for corporal punishment and other strict methods, to which Mr Butler and the Home Office were periodically subjected. With the details of all this debate I am here not concerned, except for one fundamental issue which is surely the main problem for penal theory of today. If it is accepted that the new juvenile crime wave is a sociological phenomenon, then one can also see where the new social pressures on the juvenile penal system lie. As this British system has developed, the basic method of re-education is that each penal institution should be fashioned into a little autonomous society, to which the young offender can feel that he or she belongs, in order to learn to live in the greater society outside. Now the question is – what should such a society be like? How far should it reflect not only the theoretical but the *actual* values of the outside world, when these are changing rapidly? This is not a new problem – there has always been a debate about how far young offenders can be trained under security conditions for a life of freedom – but one has only to talk to staff members of penal institutions to see how this question has today become more complicated.

There is, for instance, the basic change in the moral climate of today. The early Borstals of a generation or two ago still functioned within the framework of a generally accepted morality. To the middle-class mind, at least, this still seemed a fixed morality, based on religious observance, patriotism, respect for the law, respect of the person and property, the ideal of honest work, and so on. Today this morality has become less assured. Not only because of wars, the Bomb, and the arrival of psycho-analysis. Disintegration of values has come nearer home: what should an approved school housemaster say to his charges about the values of popular Press front-page headlines?

There are also changes in the whole class structure to be taken into account. As was said earlier, the whole Borstal system was designed very much on the lines of English upper-middle-class ideas. It is true that of its message of public-school virtues, a good deal probably passed over the heads of most working-class Borstal boys, who took it simply as part of the peculiar moral lecture, which, while sweating out their time, they had to endure from 'them', their social betters, because they themselves had broken the law and been silly enough to get caught. But at least such boys accepted the unchanging existence of this morality imposed on them from above. 'They', their social betters, were always there; and so was their authority.

Today this is already much less the case. An approved school housemaster who tries to set the right tone, to talk about a steady job and the virtues of saving, has today to compete with the appeal of the young pop singer whom an incessant publicity portrays as leading a glittering life of fabulous wealth, with no mention of thrift whatever. A boy who is obliged to attend religious service knows that after his discharge it will not be chapel that is waiting for him but the cinema, the dance-hall, and the record shop.

It is also no accident but a reflection of social priorities that the representatives of penal authority have suddenly been allowed to become relatively poor. Since probation officers have been featured on television as heroes of the new affluent society, the problem of the grotesque underpayment of members of the penal service has had a good airing. The additional point to make here is that at a time of full employment, such underpayment is like counter-propaganda: in the eyes of boys fully aware how much money their friends outside are spending, the cramped life imposed on an approved school housemaster and his family inevitably diminishes his personal authority. No doubt this anomaly, which has already led to severe staff shortages, is something which can be corrected. As *The Times* pointed out editorially, 'less derisory salary scales' would be at least one way of attracting professionally qualified social workers into the juvenile penal service. This would be of some help, but at the same time I feel that the crisis goes further. The task of adapting life in penal institutions to a changing society is a very long-term one – this was my impression during visits to such institutions.

Classification Centre

A mile or so west of the sleaziness of Shepherd's Bush, hidden away among quiet Victorian stucco terraces, lies Stamford House, the London County Council Remand Home for boys. Here the telephone rings day and night as the police are at the other end of the line and boys are brought in. Boys arrested for an offence; boys who had run away from home or an institution; boys whose parents could not be found to bail them out – the parents often seem to be in Ireland. From their particular viewpoint, the officers at Stamford House were given constant insight into the ragged edges of London life. In the opinion of one experienced officer, the instability had lately been increasing – it was the usual tale:

The raising of material standards has meant an increase in selfishness. Mother is financially independent of father – the mother is working in ninety per cent of the cases we get here. You get a boy of fifteen brought here with £5 in his pocket. The parents are often not in need : the kids are left with a high proportion of what they earn, and no sense of responsibility in spending it. ... The parents don't supervise leisure time. You ask what was Tony doing last week, and they haven't the vaguest idea. He was knocking about in some other part of London, in dives or caffs – they didn't even know.

Apart from being a Remand Home, Stamford House serves a second function, namely as Classification Centre for boys from eight to seventeen whom a juvenile court had thought fit for Approved School. Such boys are observed for four weeks. They are submitted to the battery of standardized modern educational and psychological tests; their behaviour is observed by housemasters and supervisors and, if need be, by consultant psychiatrists; while this goes on, social workers investigate the family background. Finally, working from elaborate dossiers, a classification conference of experts tries to allot each boy to the type of approved school most suited to his need (provided that there is a vacancy). This is by now already recognized routine. What I found particularly instructive was the special life, the special little society created at Stamford House.

The picture I had carried away from a visit to a remand home just after the war had been of silence, of boys slumped apathetically at tables, of supervisors looking on sternly. Now, by contrast, the first glimpse of the main hall at Stamford House was a bewildering one of boys of all sizes in khaki shirts and either flannel trousers or shorts, milling about in what seemed like market-place activity. The central hall looked bright, colourful, airy. The walls were decorated with colour prints – Cézanne, van Gogh, Breughel. Some boys were playing ping-pong; others crouched over draughts-boards; some, beyond an open door, were watching television, others were just standing about; most of them appeared noisy and unrestrained; the supervisory adults

present looked informally at ease. The hall also contained
four aquariums, a cage of budgerigars, and a parrot; a dog
was dashing about and barking.

Intent on their games, the boys took little note of the
entry of a stranger like myself. On closer sight, I thought
that they had perhaps a trace of the approved-school look,
shown in a certain slouch, a crudeness in expression. Yet
there was no doubt that they looked both eager and at ease.
My attention was caught by a boy who was six foot tall,
incongruously still wearing a guardsman's uniform. I was
told he had been brought in only a couple of hours before,
picked up at a railway station. A few weeks earlier he had
given a false age when enlisting. Overgrown and clumsy,
he was now eagerly retrieving ping-pong balls for boys half
his size, trying to please. He noticed me and for a moment
I saw him staring at me with bewildered blue eyes.

Upstairs in the dormitories, where sleeping-clothes lay in
neat baskets at the end of each bed, one of the younger
officers gave me a summary of the method employed. The
informality I had witnessed was no accident. A boy arrived
with a record; he had broken the law, charges had been laid
against him, but this was only one side of the case. At
Stamford House the job was 'to eliminate biased reports by
biased observers and get down to scientific objectivity'. This
could not be done under a repressive régime. Boys anyhow
became test-conscious too quickly. 'A proper classification
job, as we see it, requires not only the usual tests but getting
beyond a boy's glibness, always seeing how he moves with
other boys and with adults.' For this reason the discipline
was deliberately kept light, with little standing to attention.
While this light touch was a means to an end, to put the
boys at ease while they took the tests, my informant said, it
was remarkable how quickly almost all the boys responded
to it. 'A new boy of today is already the old boy of tomorrow,
telling the others the ropes.' For many a boy, indeed, this
easy informality was his first sensible contact with adults
for years. In the second place, however, the boys also had to
follow a strict timetable of work, tests, and play, of cooked

meals whether they liked it or not, and regular showers (the physical side was important). And to this sense of order they also responded.

Basically, all boys want to know what the rules are. If they approve of them and find you're not talking down, they are usually law-abiding. Very often the time that a boy is with us is the first time he has known real security, in the sense of knowing what the next day will bring. There's a remarkable change to be observed in such boys – as a rule it happens already in the first days.

I felt that what I saw confirmed this. When I returned to the hall downstairs, a bell had just rung. The boys came crowding from every direction in the untidy manner of schoolboys. They were called up to take their evening snack under supervisory eye, yet informally. The boys looked well fed, good physical specimens. Above all, there was an eagerness about them which I remembered from my own school days: those extra quick movements, the raised voices, the look of keen group interest, in fact that air of market-place activity I had noticed at my first entrance. It was hard to think that these were a scattered collection of problem boys who not long before had been brought in by the police or removed from home for their own protection.

Later I was shown the room where the outfits were kept which the boys had been wearing when picked up by the police. It was as if the suits had their own life. Row by row, there they hung, grotesque and expensive, the tenth-rate imitations of advertised ideals, the suit in Ted style, in pop-singer style, in the imitation of the Californian thug. It seemed hard to believe that they had been worn by the same boys I had just seen in open shirts, shorts, and flannels. The young supervisor at my side laughed – he said the room always made him laugh, like some of the boys when they first arrived:

You would hardly believe it – they turn up in tight jeans, with fancy haircuts, suede sandboots, irridescent shirts and linings. ... They are given the khaki and flannel clothes and told to change into them. With this change it's hard for them to keep up the pretence. As they get into normal clothing, they drop the façade.

Some of them at first are rather shocked – they feel they are committed to school again – but in a couple of hours they usually come round and join the other boys. Some resist – they say 'no bloody shorts' – but we don't have to use coercion. We just say they can't join in, and leave them sitting in another room. Pretty soon they are laughing at themselves and let us pull their legs.

Or more or less like this. The contrast seemed to illustrate at least one half of the delinquency problem.

On the one hand, Stamford House indicated the sort of life these boys ought to be living, namely quite simply as *boys*: to dress like boys, to play and to learn like boys, to be guided by adults as boys should be. (It was true that to maintain the society in a Remand Home was a subtle and expensive business which for a population of a hundred boys demanded the service of fifty trained adults. But this did not alter the case.) On the other hand, the suits in the cloakroom stood for those influences of an acquisitive society, a society dominated by grasping mass entertainment, which had forced these boys into a false maturity, a moneyed life long before they were ready for it, a pseudo-adult life which for many of them had proved far too great a strain.

Of course, this was not all. As I saw at a final classification conference, each of these boys was a 'problem youngster'. It might be because of a broken or hostile home, a history of truancy, failure at school, repeated convictions for dishonesty – the cumulative picture was depressing. At this round-table conference, which was also attended by an eminent psychiatrist, one could not but be impressed by the care taken to agree on the special handicap of each boy, whether it was lack of affection at home, emotional immaturity, neurosis or a learning disturbance, and to compensate for this by sending him to the most suitable approved school, strict or permissive, for the well or the maladjusted, emphasizing ordinary teaching or manual crafts. (Once again, if there was an available place at such a school.) All this was efficiently done. But the impression in my mind, as I left, was still of what seemed to me the primary contrast between the boys, dressed and behaving as I had seen them, and the pseudo-adult suits in which they had arrived, standing for the pressures of society which had helped to make them delinquents. Here was a destructive element that lay outside psychiatric control.

Green Mansion

I felt conscious of the same contradiction during a visit to one particular senior approved school for backward boys – let me for anonymity call it Green Mansion.

Already the approach to Green Mansion made it hard for me to feel that I was going to a penal institution. For the last few miles I was driving along winding lanes through a stretch of secluded, peaceful countryside. The school was housed in a Victorian stately home, standing in green and spacious parkland. The curriculum included both building work and horticulture. Every day squads of backward boys worked on the mansion and in the grounds so that at the first approach, and in the sunshine, they looked almost improbably spick-and-span.

Indoors, the high-ceilinged Victorian reception rooms with parquet flooring, through which I walked with the headmaster, were now the common rooms for the 'Houses' into which the boys were divided. I caught a glimpse of bright, modern wallpaper; the usual colour prints were well framed; the television sets and record players in the corners looked new. A few boys were indoors – they were really youths of fifteen to nineteen, wearing open-necked shirts and blue overalls. They greeted us with institutional politeness. Out of doors we met more youths who were marching heavily-booted to working sites, carrying their tools. They had an emphatically proletarian and awkward look. To see them against the setting of this house and park was somewhat like a scene from a Russian film, in which the workers had taken over the former aristocratic mansion – only these young proletarians were here by compulsion.

After lunch I walked through the grounds with the headmaster, who talked to me about plans for the future. He conformed to a type I had been meeting in the penal service, one of the enthusiasts, who, once caught by the spell, would not think of other work. Tall, strongly built, with a firm handgrip and quickly mustering eyes, he looked eminently like a man who from experience knew how to handle boys, how to set the right tone, to deal with awkward sex problems, to take both cricket net-practice and prayers. Only now he was talking to me in the technical terms of modern psychotherapy.

He had just returned from a week's conference with colleagues in the service. As we walked in the grounds past landscaped trees and an ornamental lake (I had guessed from hints that the school was a show-place and the headmaster an exemplary guide), he talked about new ideas. It seemed to me that his plans for progress all concerned improved psychotherapy, while his problems derived from greater *social* disorder.

Plans for progress. Green Mansion took in some eighty boys of three related categories. The first was boys classified as immature, which meant a negative selection: one could not mix lost little boys with sophisticated back-street toughs. Secondly there were boys without a normal home, through circumstance, who had become over-institutionalized. Thirdly, boys from particularly bad homes who had suffered from cruel or neglectful parents or an emotional problem like illegitimacy or a hostile step-parent. In other words, all were boys who lacked some element of a normal background. True, they had also all done some wrong, committed some offence which could not always be traced directly to their circumstances. Still, a defective family life was the most recognizable common factor in their delinquency. This meant that the education at Green Mansion must have a social slant. As he himself saw it, said the headmaster in a telling phrase, 'here are eighty-odd personal lives which have become unravelled, and have to be knitted up again into a sensible pattern.'

Green Mansion had already a successful tradition of teaching boys good manners, self-respect, and how to work. Now, said the headmaster, this was to be backed up by more specialized forms of treatment. Green Mansion was already being visited regularly by a consultant phychiatrist. He had also asked for the addition to his staff of a full-time psychologist to deal with the harder cases, and of a full-time social worker who would concentrate on those instances where there had been a complete breakdown in a boy's family relationship. He had also reorganized the functions of his teaching staff. In the old days the teachers simply gave their scheduled hours of instruction and then knocked off. Under his re-arrangement, each teacher also saw some individual boys in the evenings and at week-ends; he might take them swimming or canoeing; he would encourage them to talk about their worries – in fact, participate actively in casework.

The purpose of all these changes, said the headmaster, was to help his housemasters, the key figures at Green Mansion, whose task it was to know about the problems of every boy in their charge, to build up his confidence, to keep in touch with his family and his after-care representative. Relieved of other duties, each housemaster would now be able to concentrate on this role of being a real substitute father or mother figure to every boy in his charge, which was what these particular boys needed most.

As we retraced our steps from the furthest extent of the park, I asked the headmaster about his own worries. Here we were immediately back in the world of current and increasing social problems.

There was the question of inadequate pay and consequent staff shortage, about which I had already heard enough. There was the ignorance of certain parents. If some appreciated what educational advantages Green Mansion offered their sons, at a weekly cost of £10 per boy, others remained dull-wittedly antagonistic and indifferent. No wonder that, whatever one did, many boys still thought of their time at approved school as 'doing a stretch'. The approved schools were still in need of more psychiatric facilities – this might surprise me but he would give me a typical case:

He's one of our lads – I'll call him John Smith. His mother was a prostitute who abandoned him in a gents' lavatory in the West End of London. He was taken over by the L.C.C. and has never known what it means to have a proper home. He has known plenty of care, but it's always been a life of dormitories, a row of beds, bells ringing. Sometimes this doesn't work. In this particular lad's case it's no wonder that his attitude became completely anti-social. When he got here at the age of sixteen there were fifteen different addresses in his file.

By this time we had completed the tour of the grounds and were back on the terrace of Green Mansion. On the way I had seen boys working as carpenters, in the tailoring shop, the greenhouses, and on the building site. A group of the latter, led by a fair-haired Cockney youth, trudged past us. 'Hello, Norman, I'm glad to see that you've finished that wall,' called the headmaster, and then to me: 'That particular lot are working without supervision. That's another line we are pursuing.'

He seemed able and confident. Everything in *his* school was under control. Yet as I stood looking out across the parkland – there were boys at cricket practice and I could see a shimmer of water – I felt that I could see the flaw in this whole penal work. To catch John Smith and to prevent his start in life in the gents' lavatory from leading him into an anti-social career of crime, Green Mansion was being turned into a more and more efficient instrument for psychotherapy. But if society produced more John Smiths, and if this evil was not attacked at the source, would there not be need for more and more rural retreats like Green Mansion to cure them?

Pollington

Another interesting experiment in teaching young offenders how to adjust, by creating a special society for this purpose, was something I saw during a visit to Pollington Camp. This is an experimental open Borstal, housing selected boys, who according to the Mannheim–Wilkins prediction test are by and large not expected to commit any further offence. At Pollington they are given a short, intensive education in self-discipline.

Pollington stands without fence or gate right beside a busy highway in Yorkshire. In appearance, it is like an encampment of army huts round a parade ground which had just been spruced up and polished for a general's inspection. The impression on the morning of my visit was of bustling work on every side. Cheerful-looking youths in overalls were getting down to their tasks. I met them in the carpenter's shop, in the kitchens; some were scrubbing floors or polishing windows in the dormitory huts; another lot were piling into a lorry to be taken into the fields. In the background, among the prefab houses with small gardens where the staff live, I could see children playing and could faintly hear their voices. Something in the look of the place reminded me distantly of an Israeli communal settlement. I could tell from the firm posture and relaxed expressions of the boys that they were not the usual Borstal boys but the pick of them.

This was confirmed by Johnnie, a tall boy picked out at random to show my companion and myself over the institution with explicit freedom to comment. He took us through the dormitories, explaining relative points of spit and polish and neatness that gained or lost marks – Johnnie laughed at this. Six foot two, tousle-haired, he was engagingly frank. In his present institutional situation he had no inhibitions. He had the look, I kept thinking, of a confident young man who back in his home town would go far, who would presently be a solid citizen, perhaps a works foreman, driving his new Austin, with his children perhaps going to grammar school.

As we stood at the edge of the road I suggested that it would not be difficult to get away from Pollington. Johnnie agreed; all one had to do was to thumb a ride on a lorry.

But where would that get him? Only back to the punishment Borstal at Reading.

'So you wouldn't do it?'

'I'd be silly, wouldn't I?' said Johnnie. 'Today I *think*. I'm supposed to be learning self-discipline. That's why I'm here – because I didn't know how to think.'

He came from a small town in East Anglia. There was an American air base in the neighbourhood and an R.A.F. depot not far off. The town had coffee-bars and pubs with bands; it was a place of many fights; there were rough places, a lot of Teddy boys about. His father kept a small shop there. He himself was the only son.

I asked how he had managed to get himself sent to Borstal. 'Just for a laugh. It's a fact.' There had been trouble in the family, father and mother at it every evening, then finally mother walked out. For a while his father made him help in the house. 'It was enough to get you down.' Going out nights to get away from home, he had got in with a rough mob. His mate at the café said to him: 'Do you want a laugh tonight?' He found it meant breaking and entering – well, it meant breaking into a television shop, but the way he was feeling about things, it would have been chicken to refuse. And in any case, 'I just didn't *think*. It's a fact. I'd know different today.'

Johnnie had two more months to go before his discharge. On the face of it, if he had learned nothing else, he gave every sign of having learned to think cautiously about looking after number one.

At Pollington the training spell in self-discipline, in learning how to think, is short, on the average only ten months, but intensive. The boys rise through four grades of increasing privileges, provided they obtain a minimum of points which are allotted each day for conscientious work. Loss of points can mean additional days' stay. The self-education extends further than this. The camp has a number of elected committees; a kitchen committee with some scope for varying menus; committees for running entertainments and sports; most important, a disciplinary committee, with one member drawn from each dormitory with responsibility for seeing that minor rules, like quiet after lights out, whose breach could mean trouble, are properly kept and with the power to impose small fines and penalties.

The basic idea is that for the committee members this means learning self-restraint in not abusing powers; for those who offend against the common well-being, it means learning how to accept discipline from their fellows without rebelling, because if they do so the staff need not be involved and so no precious points for behaviour need be lost. All these committees are elected by a fortnightly camp meeting of all the boys, to which they are responsible. From the staff side this meeting is attended only by the Governor himself, who acts as chairman.

The second experiment at Pollington is group counselling, which as a penal method was first started in California and in 1959 was being tried out in half a dozen British penal institutions (including Dartmoor!). The assumption is that these boys who arrive at Pollington are usually suffering from particularly strong adolescent emotional disturbances, from subconscious grievances against parents, sensations of failure and the like, which could do with an airing. And so about eight to ten boys meet regularly once a week for a session with a particular officer, to talk on a footing of absolute equality about anything, but preferably about themselves and their problems. In fact, the more a group starts off as a grievance committee in which the boys shoot their mouths off, the better. In this way, deep-down grievances over which a boy may have been brooding to the point of obsession will at least be brought into the open and talked about to others. If a boy can see his troubles through the eyes of others, he may learn that they are not unique and perhaps not even as bad as he thinks. In any case, the hope is that they will seem to him diminished.

The whole of Pollington Camp is divided into such groups. (At the time of my visit it was still too soon for proper evaluation of the experiment.) The boys, including Johnnie, with whom I talked about group counselling, were evidently able to laugh about their plight – shut up in a camp and with no girls! – and the silliness that had led up to it. They appeared already conditioned: the eager cross-talk about themselves which made up our conversation sounded almost like another counselling session. Some of the chief topics which came up at the sessions, so the boys told me, were their grievances against 'them', the camp authorities, who opened parcels and did other unpleasant things. But I also caught deeper echoes. 'You see, this bloke, he says everyone's against him, so in the end all the fellows told him it's his own blank fault, it's him that's selfish, it's up to him to change.' The arguments seem to be drawn with fascination to the subject of fathers and their unjust attitude – almost as if the boys had read Freud. Johnnie put the opposite view. He remembered, he had once told another fellow it was no good going on and on about his own father, the blokes were sick of hearing about it, and besides, supposing his father had a good reason for doing what he did?

How important all this was I could not tell. In contrast to the Californian system, where the group counselling was to be conducted by trained psychologists, the men in charge at Pollington, after some preliminary coaching, were the ordinary officers, including the security officers. How highly the officers I talked to regarded its results I could not tell either – they probably had their own reservations. But the very fact that the counselling was done not by psychologists from outside but by officers who were actually living with the boys seemed to me to have its advantage too. As I drove away from Pollington in the twilight across the flat Yorkshire plain, I felt as if the whole camp was like an organization geared single-mindedly to the task of teaching these youngsters who had got into trouble the simple social lesson of today: learn to think and to conform.

More conformity

The methods used at Pollington are for the Borstal élite. Is it possible to apply them more widely? It seems quite likely. Penal reforms which seemed *avant-garde* ideas thirty years ago are today accepted without much trouble, and no doubt more far-reaching changes may be expected.

In the case of the approved schools, for those under seventeen years old, there has been a growing demand for their rationalization, for taking them over into a single State system which would fall into the administrative sphere of a single juvenile penal authority. This would be of help in raising conditions of work and salaries to a reasonable modern level. Under a single authority there would also be more flexibility in applying the various penal methods available to an offender under the age of seventeen and reviewing his case when necessary.

From the approved school representatives themselves, a strong demand has come that boys and girls should be sent to them at an earlier date. As things were, the Courts generally sent an offender to an approved school only as a last resort, after all other means had failed. This meant that in the eyes of parents and boys even the most permissive approved school, with small classes, excellent teaching, psychiatric facilities, had a penal look. It stood for the stiffest punishment in the juvenile code, a young offender being sent away 'for a stretch'. It also meant that when a boy went to approved school he might already have defied several other penal methods and be a tough little criminal.

In the view of approved school authorities, the modern classification technique made it quite possible to pick out likely candidates for re-education before they had been convicted several times over. If they were packed off earlier this would have several clear advantages. It would remove the historic stigma from approved school of being a last resort. Boys would be removed before they had been infected by the modern gang life. In addition it would give the approved schools a better chance to give a youngster from a bad background continued and intensive re-education to put him right.

As for the Borstals, I was given some current advanced ideas about their further reform from a critical young intellectual who had joined the penal service (one of the few who had done so recently).

He thought the basic Pollington ideas about self-education could be applied not only to a chosen minority but to the ordinary majority of Borstal boys though perhaps in not quite the same way. What he thought wrong in the system as a whole was the gap between the society 'inside' and the changing conditions in the outside world. The authority of the housemaster as father-figure was still of therapeutic value. But beyond this, the public school prefect system had seen its day. So had the historic emphasis on setting the boys to 'learn a trade' – in modern industry the widest range by now was of semi-skilled jobs which could be learned in a few weeks by anyone with some *general* technical training. Instead of all this stress on 'vocation', my young critic wanted to see the Borstal system as re-training in *choice*, not merely between behaviour and misbehaviour (as was the case even in Pollington) but of choice between positive alternatives with a chance for the offender of learning from mistakes.

In practice this would mean considerable changes. A boy might, for instance, start in a closed Borstal and on attaining a suitable standard of progress go on to an open one. As for training in work, instead of a boy being simply ordered on to this job or that, there should ideally be a series of jobs open to him, so that he could work his way up the ladder. Pay for these jobs should be on a scale which would enable a boy to learn with some purpose. For instance, a boy might have to make at least some payment for skilled vocational training. Instead of skilled training being something which was simply handed to the boy through his saying 'I want to be a mechanic' and being told 'Right, we'll put you in the machine shop', it should be something which, with proper advice, he could see as an aim – one for which he himself could decide to make some sacrifice. Similarly, a boy should be able to acquire some extras for his cell, like a picture, a rug, or a bookshelf – these would depend on his work and saving. An approximation like this of Borstal life to life outside, so my young informant thought, would in itself call for the general establishment of the sort of self-government by committees in practice at Pollington.

The new re-education

Advanced reforms of this kind may or may not be realized in the near future. But even visits to a few institutions are enough to show how the winds of change are blowing through the whole juvenile penal system of the 1960s. The broad trend in outlook is that stern legal morality is going out. The shift is away from the historic concept of the young offender as a lawbreaker who has to be punished for a moral wrong. It is towards seeing him or her as a young person who for various reasons has failed to conform to the demands of society and must therefore be re-educated to find new adjustment. Moreover, the reasons for the original failure are increasingly regarded as having their roots in the offender's childhood, in a defective early family background, so that it is felt they must be tackled by psychiatric methods, as is, indeed, often enough the case.

These changes in penal outlook (which are, of course, by no means confined to Britain) have already produced some of their own new problems. For instance, with the stress now all on re-education and psychiatry, penal officers, including security officers, have found themselves increasingly drawn into an 'active rehabilitation role', for which many have had inadequate training. What with the overcrowding of penal institutions and the simultaneous staff shortages, this means that re-education often remains theoretical, especially for adolescents not in the brightest intelligence grades. There has also been some criticism as to the whole direction of the new penal trend. In a special section of her *Social Science and Social Pathology,* Lady Wootton has expressed misgivings against the progressive advance of the psychiatrists into the penal realm, which to her mind involves a dangerous departure from some of 'the basic assumptions of ancient and honoured legal system' on the concept of the individual responsibility of the offender.

Already in many countries, among which England must now be included, the first steps down this slope have been taken; and the possibility cannot be dismissed that the relaxation of definitions of responsibility, which is already in progress, is the beginning of a process which, in the remoter future, is destined to result in the total destruction of the concept itself.[1]

While one can sympathize readily with Lady Wootton's misgivings, it seems, however, also apparent that this change in penal philosophy did not come by itself. Nor did it come solely through Freud and the psychiatrists. The classic concepts of right and wrong, lawful and unlawful, did after all not exist in a vacuum. They reflected the morality of an established ruling class, certain of its authority in its attitude not only to questions of law but also to the role of the individual and the state, to all issues of religion and property, sex and family life.

It is this traditional, bourgeois moral authority which is receding in our changing society. The young offender of today does not only hear the call urging him to be an obedient citizen. The loudest voices calling to him are anonymous. They are asking him to spend and to consume, to be a mass reader, a mass viewer and listener, a mass motorist and purchaser of gadgets, and always to fall into line with whoever and whatever is most up to date. This is the basic change. I have a feeling that in an affluent society dominated by mass advertising, the penal system also cannot be out of line. (After all, what is the authority of a magistrate or judge compared with the influence of the films, of television, and of magazines?) And so, in practice, I think it is inevitable that the penal system has also shifted its emphasis – away from the ideal of obedience to authority and towards the ideal of conformity, of re-educating young offenders to adjust, so that they, too, can enjoy the gifts of the new society. To be sure (and visits to institutions show this) here is where the new problems begin. The values of the affluent society to which the youngsters are to adjust

1. Barbara Wootton, *Social Science and Social Pathology*, Allen & Unwin, 1959.

are, to say the least, confused, and it may well be that whole new techniques of penal re-education will have to be learned.

This, that no miracles can be expected from the present juvenile penal system, is therefore the first conclusion. The second is the point, obvious indeed, that in spite of periodic public clamour that the penal system should find a cure for juvenile crime, any possible penal system, even the best, has in this respect its narrow limits. The measures it can take follow only after the event, after an offence has actually been committed. To attack the causes of crime, as in searching for them, one must look at society itself. And in the context of Britain today, this means that one must look beyond penal issues at the much larger question of education in the affluent society.

CHAPTER 15

Education in the Affluent Society

Correcting the unbalance

In what follows I have based myself on the assumption that
it is perfectly possible for any British Government to allocate
the division of the national income so that far more is spent
on essential public services. In a country like Britain, where
purchase tax is already well established, the fiscal mechan-
ism for transferring further funds to public use may not
even be so difficult to find, if only the will is there. In any
case, in the field of education this is something that just has
to be done. It was the clear recognition of this need, I felt,
which lent special interest to the Crowther and Albemarle
Reports of 1960. Neither document, it is true, recommended
immediate spectacular Government action. Yet here were
the reports of two major committees of inquiry which, for
the first time, accepted the arrival of the British affluent
society as a fact, pointed to the dislocation it had caused in
the lives of young people, and called for conscious public
intervention to correct this. From this standpoint, both
documents may be remembered as landmarks.

The Crowther Report was published by the Central
Advisory Council for Education (England), which at the re-
quest of the Minister of Education had for three years
examined the English system of State education for boys
and girls between fifteen and eighteen 'in relation to changing social and industrial needs'. In 1960 this system still had
its archaic features even in the case of the most privileged
and talented boys and girls who passed on with ease to university. However, the decisive conclusion of the Crowther
Report was its recognition of the needs of the majority of
adolescents, far too large a majority, who were *not* being
educated at all after fifteen. The report underlined that at
the age of seventeen only one boy and girl in eight was still

receiving full-time education; between fifteen and seventeen, only one boy in five and one girl in fifteen received any part-time education. That is, at the most suggestible stage of their lives, most boys and girls were pushed into a complex adult society without really adequate education or guidance.

The authors of the Crowther Report saw this not only as a waste of ability, which the country could ill afford, but as a moral wrong inflicted on youth: 'There seems to us to be no social injustice in our community more loudly crying out for reform than the condition in which scores of thousands of our children are released into the labour market.' To counteract this, the Report proposed that the leaving age should in the 1960s be raised from fifteen to sixteen (a somewhat conservative and limited increase, but in the right direction); that part-time education, especially technical, should be substantially increased; that, following this, County Colleges for further education should be established; and that the State should pay generously for these extensions of the school system.

The Albemarle Report was a slighter document, and rather more literary in its style. The Albemarle Committee had been appointed in 1959 to inquire into the Youth Services in England and Wales. These included a great variety of organizations, uniformed and non-uniformed, serving young people of all ages. But in practice the real subject of inquiry was the provision of leisure-time facilities for adolescents, that is, the state of the country's network of youth clubs, mainly boys' clubs and mixed clubs. What was right and what was wrong about these institutions in England was not really in very much doubt – they had the advantages and defects of their history. Most of them had been started back in the bourgeois age in a spirit of middle-class charity to keep working-class boys and girls 'off the street', a function they retained until well into the depression days of the thirties. Some of the most famous (and best-run) clubs for boys and girls had been established by bodies like Public Schools and Oxford and Cambridge Colleges in places like the old East End of London. Since that time, the youth clubs had, indeed, changed. They had become efficiently organized by bodies like the National Federation of Boys' Clubs and the National Association of Mixed and Girls' Clubs. Some grants from local authorites supplemented their private funds. Even so, and in spite of much dedicated effort and local success, it was felt that the whole organization of the youth clubs had itself become a problem. The traditional spirit of charitable effort, often reflected in the very look of the club premises, seemed as hard to shake off as it was unsuitable for the new age.

At any rate, the Albemarle Committee noted that in the fifties the majority of adolescents who had left school at fifteen to go into jobs were not members of any youth club at all. The authors of the Report stated that it was wrong – indeed socially harmful – to leave so much of the leisure time of these more affluent but often bewildered youngsters of today to exploitation by purely commercial interests. In somewhat general terms, the Report therefore proposed a ten-year plan by which the youth clubs were to be gradually remodelled. A national youth council was to be set up, better premises built, more youth leaders trained; and, again, the State was to make the main financial provision for these reforms.

Wanted: a sense of national purpose

All this made good sense. However, the British tradition of approaching problems through government-appointed committees of enquiry also has the drawback that the terms of reference of the enquiry are often limited to fit with the way official minds are already thinking, and a well-chosen committee is also not anxious to propose what its Minister is likely to reject. At any rate, in both the Crowther Report and in the Albemarle Report, the analysis of the defects of the new British affluent society went much further than the corrective steps which the committees thought it fit to suggest to a Conservative Government.

This was true especially of the Crowther Report. In fact, its main proposal, to raise the school-leaving age from fifteen to sixteen, had already been put forward by Sir Will Spens in 1938 and actually included in the 1944 Education Act, though never enforced. Moreover, had the Crowther Committee been simply bold enough to state that an affluent Britain could afford to spend not three per cent, but, like many other countries, nearer to five per cent of the national income on education, it could have done without some of its elaborate recommendations on the problems of educational finance. Even so, when one reads the pages of both these intelligently written reports, one common theme stands out. In Britain in 1960, the majority of middle-class boys and girls, plus those who were trained to become middle-class, . were educated up to the age of eighteen or beyond, while their social life during this period was also strenuously organized. By contrast, the majority of working-class boys and girls left school hardly educated at fifteen, to proceed at once into a pseudo-adult life of earning and spending, most of them without membership of any leisure-time organization.

It is interesting that both the Crowther and the Albemarle Reports emphasized that in the new British society this class contrast was socially harmful and no longer justifiable. It led to an undoubted waste of youthful ability, it led to renewed class distinctions, it engendered youthful malaise and played its part in spreading juvenile delinquency. To lessen this discrepancy, both Reports – and this is the crucial point – proposed State intervention to arrest some of the dangerous trends of the affluent society. The basic recommendation was that the outlook of the country's teenagers should be shaped much more directly through the conscious endeavours of the community and not merely left to the combined persuasions of the advertisers, the press, and the record industry.

Within the English tradition of *laissez-faire*, this was quite an innovation in official thinking. One might have imagined that in a world grown so highly competitive as that of the present day, any proposals to raise the standards of British State education would have aroused special interest. In fact, almost the opposite was the case. Though both the Crowther and the Albemarle Reports had a good press, the general public interest in their recommendations was not profound. Not even at Westminster. When the Government in April 1960 rejected the Crowther Committee's proposals for raising the school-leaving age during the sixties – a bad and timid decision, though fortunately not irretrievable – less than one-tenth of the Members of Parliament attended the debate in the Chamber.

To go into the specific reasons for this indifference among both Conservative and Labour members towards educational issues which could shape the future of the country would bring me into the field of party politics, which is here outside my subject. But I think one generalization is relevant, that in Britain in 1960 what one might call the sense of national purpose had become unusually dimmed. Perhaps I should define this generalization. As a democratic country with a *laissez-faire* tradition, Britain can, of course, have no official imposed philosophy, like a Communist country, and it would also have been too much to expect British life in the fifties to have that overall sense of purpose, in which every citizen is aware of over-riding national aims, which one can find today in new countries like Israel, Ghana, Egypt, or Cuba; nor even that same purposefulness one met in Britain during the war. But instead, Britain, more than most countries, has something which can be called a national way of life, something very insular and liberal and unique. If it is accepted that maintaining this British way of life and developing it and building on it could be called the national purpose, then I would say that the active sense of such purpose had in the 1950s noticeably waned. Democracies can grow tired, as was shown in the U.S.A. after Roosevelt. Similarly, in Britain, the forties had been a time for greatness and creativeness: the decade saw Churchill, the R.A.F., the convoys going through, the Grand Alliance, the Attlee Labour Government, the Health Service, the new pattern of public housing, the achievement of independence within the Commonwealth for India, Pakistan,

Ceylon. By reaction, the fifties looked like a decade of dull fatigue. British leadership of Europe fell apart; the Conservatives cut a sorry figure over Suez; at home, the Labour Party floundered, exhausted. The Welfare State became prosaic, the ideal of Commonwealth a shadow; political issues grew remote from the ordinary man and especially from the young. All in all, the sense of national purpose, any national purpose beyond material consumption, receded into the background.

I think this intellectual confusion was linked not only to the relative decline of Britain in terms of world power and a consequent loss of political direction. For the ordinary man, another cause was the suddenly accelerated shift towards the new life of the affluent society, the increase in the consumption drive, the more strident note one could notice in popular newspapers, in magazines, in television advertisements. Even if the politicians did not know what to make of it, the advertisers, the magazine publishers, the gossip writers and publicity agents, who went from strength to strength in the new society, knew well what its dominant forces were.

For that matter, so did any secondary school teacher, struggling with a class of indifferent adolescents in trying to compete with the lure of commercial youth culture. It was the acknowledgement of these new trends, and of the general need for counter-measures to create a new sense of purpose, which made the Crowther Report and Albemarle Report significant documents of the new age – even if the government actions they recommended are to my mind inadequate and likely soon to be superseded.

Social advance and education

To look ahead in terms of education. Since British society is for better or worse considerably stratified, already something of a 'meritocracy', any movement for educational reform will have to take place on two levels. There are the organization men and women: to compete today, Britain must have a class of administrators, scientists, and technicians who will be as efficient and purposeful as their equivalents anywhere else; and, as the unceasing newspaper advertisements of situations vacant show, this is going to be a considerably larger class than the old middle class. How this class will be recruited from public schools, grammar schools, and technical colleges does not belong to the subject of this book. It does, however, touch on it indirectly, because for one thing the doors through which working-class boys and girls can rise into this new middle class should clearly be as wide open as possible; and furthermore, provided these doors are open wide enough, because a more purposeful educational drive at the higher levels must affect the tone of the British education system all the way down.

Even so, the more important task is that of giving the seventy to eighty per cent majority of British boys and girls who are early school leavers a more appropriate and modern education than many of them are getting today. Indeed, it may well be the most important task of social reform facing the country. After all, the really revolutionary social change in the British scene of today is the steady *embourgeoisement* of the working-class. In material terms, in such things as housing, cars, and television, this is easy to see. But public opinion has not yet caught up with the educational and other changes which must surely go with this social revolution. Here I come back to the picture at the starting-point of this book – that of my little group of confused Teds, hanging about aimlessly on their new London County Council Estate, defiant of society, not knowing what to do with themselves. Their confusion may represent an extreme predicament, but I think it throws light on a general and urgent British education need of today, which is simply this: that the material advance of British working-class youth should be accompanied by an equivalent cultural advance. Just as in the mid-fifties there was a 'break-through' in material consumption, so there has now to be a 'break-through' in education, because it is evident that the present secondary modern school system, the system for the seventy to eighty per cent majority, is not adequate in preparing boys and girls for the new society.

There is already an extensive literature on its inadequacies. For present-day needs, the system falls short in that the majority of boys and girls leave far too early. A good many of the jobs into which they are drawn are from their nature tedious, mechanical, monotonous, offering little outlet for natural adolescent emotions and so creating a sense of frustration – this phenomenon has been noted in German and American studies as well as in this country. Perhaps much of this emotional frustration during the working day cannot be helped: all the more reason, therefore, for not exposing adolescents to it at the immature age of fifteen.

In the second place, there is a fair measure of agreement among teachers that the secondary modern school system with its present-day curriculum is inadequate as a 'bridge' to working life. The shock when young teenagers encounter the different morality and temptations of working life is often an acute one.

However, to my mind the main defect of the present State school system lies in the way in which it still perpetuates outworn class distinctions. Under the tripartite secondary school structure set up in 1944, by which abler boys and girls are 'creamed off' at eleven, not merely to go to different schools, but, in effect, into a different social life, cultural class distinctions are being preserved and even intensified which are inappropriate to the affluent society. And this is not merely a matter of different education within the school walls. The exaggerated difference in school-leaving age plays an equal part. The authors of the Albemarle Report noted that those teenagers who at fifteen had gone into easy jobs with good money, were spending most of their earnings on a surprisingly narrow range of mass-produced consumption goods and entertainments; for instance, not merely on pop records in general, but each month on a very few records which the industry plugs as top-of-the-month hits. In view of the increased power and skill of advertising techniques, this need surprise nobody. The trouble is, however, that the whole outlook of such teenagers also becomes shaped and narrowed by the advertisers' culture which is projected at them in order to promote the sale of the products. A working-class girl who is induced to spend a pound a week on pop records and another pound a week on hairstyling and cosmetics – which is common enough – is through her very preoccupation with this expenditure isolated in class terms from other girls of her age who at grammar school and technical colleges are being taught quite different cultural values.

This excessively class-orientated system of education, whereby the majority of boys and girls are pushed (or lured) far too early into the racket of the teenage market, is harmful in a number of ways. There is little need to stress the waste of abilities among early leavers which is involved. There is, however, one special piece of evidence of a sort of cultural 'downward pull' at work in the affluent society which ought to receive attention.

To judge from the regular complaints of certain teachers, something like a genuine breakdown of discipline has in recent years occurred in a number of the more difficult secondary modern schools in various parts of the country. In most cases, these schools are found in areas like the traffic-filled inner working-class districts of London, where the population tends to be unorganized and shifting and there is little, if any, local community spirit. Often enough, these are also among the schools worst affected by the persistent shortage of teaching staff. But the problem goes further than this. As teachers see it, many boys and girls of thirteen and fourteen in these schools have their minds already so firmly fixed on the world of jobs and money and the glittering attractions of the commercial youth culture that they regard their last years of school as a mere senseless waste of time, and react accordingly. Conversely, a good many unhappy teachers have been made to feel it to be a complete waste of time and effort to keep such teenage and worldly-wise boys and girls, who contemptuously refuse to be taught, at school at all. It was significant that the publication of the

Crowther Report, advocating raising the school age to sixteen, led to a number of letters to the press from secondary modern school teachers who opposed this move, and mostly they were teachers who, after entering the profession as idealists, had simply thrown in their hand. Now, even if this breakdown in discipline is marginal, the significant thing is that, as far as I know, it has no parallel in any country on the Continent, where the authority of secondary schools has nowhere declined so sharply. Since one cannot assume innate mental characteristics which make British teenagers more unteachable, the reason for the difference, it seems to me, is that in Britain the teenage market is more developed, while the commercial mass attack directed against youthful minds has also been going on for a rather longer time.

This breakdown of discipline in a number of marginal schools is one danger sign of a sort of cultural 'downward pull' as one of the trends of the affluent society. The other is, of course, the rise in actual juvenile delinquency – it is noteworthy that in 1959 this was already so marked that both the Crowther Report on secondary education and the Albemarle Report on the youth services mentioned it definitely as a problem to be attacked by educational and recreational reform. And quite rightly – this is the heart of the matter.

Schools for the affluent society

What, then, should be done?

The ideas put forward below should not be regarded as cut-and-dried proposals for educational reform – this would not be within my competence. My approach throughout has been to treat the rise of juvenile delinquency in Britain from 1955 onwards as a danger signal throwing light on much broader changes in the social life of today. But what these changes in turn suggest is that a much stronger 'upward pull' has somehow to be infused into the whole British State education system, to counter the opposite pulls of the new affluent life. Both for social reasons and other obvious reasons, such as Britain's competitive future in a technological age, the drive for British boys and girls to 'get on' has to be given a new moral force – larger numbers than hitherto have to be enrolled in it. And since the old bourgeois values to which one could formerly appeal have lost impact, this means that a new educational framework for such a drive to 'get on' has to be provided. If this reasoning stands, a number of practical measures appear to me to follow:

1. In order that the level of the majority of secondary school boys and girls should be raised, not only in classroom attainment, but by enlarging their whole range of interests, the State school system must be less class-divided. That is, the 1944 Education Act with its tripartite system of social as well as educational separation of children at the age of eleven should by now be seen as reflecting the superseded class differences of the bourgeois age – and relegated to the past as such. The top stream of boys and girls, who should be the natural leaders in secondary schools, must no longer be so quickly separated from the majority, to leave the latter leaderless. It is perfectly true that the country has to train its specialist class of organization men and technicians, and from this standpoint it would probably be all wrong to tamper with such traditions as Manchester Grammar School's capacity to turn out a hundred efficient young scientists every year. Indeed, at this level, the peculiarities of English educational history have made any change rather complicated. One can see this from the dilemma of the comprehensive schools. Under the new competitive stress, the English system of university entrance has led to an unforeseen and often criticized degree of 'sixth-form specialization'. In turn, the need to provide for a sufficiently large specialist sixth form has led to the vast size of comprehensive schools, which has aroused opposition and so limited their numbers. But without going into the pros and cons of the existing comprehensive schools, I feel there is a much broader proposition to be made. In looking to the future, I feel that the whole problem of specialist education for the new administrative-technical middle class can be solved without introducing *social* separation within the secondary

school system at a point where children are only eleven years old. As in other countries, such educational separation could well take place only at the age of fourteen, fifteen, or sixteen years.

2. This could be achieved more easily if the age of compulsory school attendance were to be substantially raised throughout the country – not merely to the age of sixteen *after* 1970, as the present Conservative Government proposes, but at a much earlier date to the age of seventeen. Perhaps one might qualify – not for *every* boy and girl but, say, for all *except* those in the lowest streams for whom prolonged schooling is judged unsuitable. Even if this is not clearly seen today, I believe it will rapidly become apparent that a much longer secondary school period is needed to train youngsters to cope with the demands of our technological age, and one argument is compelling: if other countries, and especially Soviet Russia, are aiming at far more ambitious educational targets, Britain cannot afford to remain out of step. In fact, here the Soviet challenge may become a decisive factor. This challenge has been talked about in terms of export trade, or of arms, but one feels inclined to say: 'Forget this, the primary Soviet challenge is in education.' That is, if the Russians establish a strenuous polytechnic type of education for the majority of their children to the age of seventeen, as they probably will do in the course of the sixties, Britain cannot continue with her present class-divided and old-fashioned education system, by which training after fifteen is only for the minority, and still hope to compete. While this may soon become clear, I believe the social argument for raising the school-leaving age is equally strong – namely simply to enable all boys and girls to grow up more naturally within an organized life appropriate to their age-group (as middle-class children already do) instead of being thrust out as psuedo-adults – to sink or swim in the affluent society.

3. Such a decisive expansion of secondary school life would naturally pose major problems. It might create difficulties for industries which at present rely very much on

juvenile labour, but automation may in any case take care of this. It would also be a blow to the various cruder commercial interests which at present exploit the teenage market, but as for them, *tant pis*. A more serious objection against a substantial raising of the school age is that it would involve vast new expenditure on school buildings and equipment and an even greater increase on teachers' training facilities. So it would, of course, but greater than the nation could afford? Even a crash programme to step up education would only mean that instead of an inadequate three or four per cent, as now, Britain would devote perhaps five to six per cent of the national income to education, which some other countries are already doing. Basically, the question is not one of the means but of the will.

A more important objection has sometimes come from the teaching profession, namely that at present a large number of boys and girls in the lower intelligence groups seem unable to profit from being kept at school, even up to the age of fourteen or fifteen: trying to teach them only drives teachers to despair and they would therefore be much better off if put earlier to some practical work. From time to time this argument has been advanced forcefully by teachers from bad schools who, term after term, have struggled in vain to inject pitiful fragments of an academic curriculum into classes of hostile, unresponsive, but already fully fashion-conscious and sex-conscious louts and hussies – or so the dismal picture looks. For the schools and the teachers concerned, the problem of such apparently unteachable fourteen-year-olds is today serious enough, but I suspect strongly that the resistance of these particular working-class boys and girls to school is due far less to inbred low intelligence, as is often alleged, than it is a cultural problem; if one likes, a peculiarly English class problem. The resistance seems like a survival of historic class differences, a hangover from past generations of degraded English working-class life, in which these boys and girls still display the defensive hostility of the old slums against a middle-class institution like secondary school. The lure of the crude commercial youth culture, whose standards are so much more easily attained than school knowledge, has now evidently helped to increase this resistance. But, just because I believe the problem posed by these obstructive teenagers to be largely cultural, I also feel that it is one which longer compulsory school attendance, more individual attention in teaching, and a keener sense of purpose in school life could go far to solve, especially in more democratic schools where the natural leaders are not 'creamed off' but are present to set the tone.

4. At this point one also touches on the problem of the young delinquents. 'Delinquency starts not at schools but in the home' – true enough. But there is one important point to be made. If we have to accept that in the changed climate of the affluent society adolescents will tend to have weaker family ties, it is important that this should be compensated by a school life in which there is a stronger sense of guidance and where a youngster can feel that he belongs to a purposeful group of his own age, which is not that of the street corner. Altogether, I feel that if it becomes possible by means of a longer period at school and more stimulating teaching, to infuse a new outlook into the schools with greater emphasis on 'getting on', this sort of *embourgeoisement* would be a powerful means of drawing adolescents away from the Teddy-boy society and its haunts, and so of reducing the delinquency figures. *Better and more purposeful education may mean less need for purposeful re-education.* This may sound a prosaic answer to the problem on which I have in this book spent so much time, but I am sure the answer lies in this direction.

To make another minor but not unimportant point, the raising of the compulsory school age to seventeen would also make it easier to effect long-envisaged reforms of the present system of juvenile courts and approved schools. The treatment, or rather the re-education, of young offenders under seventeen could simply be integrated into the structure of general education. The juvenile courts could be transformed into juvenile welfare tribunals on which headmasters and teachers would be represented, while the approved schools could also be brought into line, as State schools with special disciplinary features but part of the general school system, just as the E.S.N. schools, the schools for educationally sub-normal children, form such a part today. After all, where is the basic difference?

5. However, these are subsidiary issues. The main purpose of raising the school-leaving age would be to raise the whole level of knowledge and attainment of the working-class majority of boys and girls in English State schools, to give them new interests and a better view of the world they live in, and for this a good many changes would also be required in the curriculum. Some of these one can already see being introduced here and there. A significant passage in the Crowther Report stated that a boy leaving school in the sixties was likely in his lifetime to witness at least one complete technological revolution in his occupation. The job he worked in as a youth might not exist any more by the time he reached forty, when he might be working on processes and with machinery not even devised today; and this might well be the case not only in new industries but in transport, in agriculture or in distributive retail trade. 'To cope with such a world,' said the Report, 'the first quality that is needed is adaptability.' And the new fact is that this no longer applies only to a minority trained in special skill. After remarking that the rapidity of technological changes requires the production of a larger number of qualified scientists, technologists and technicians from the schools, the Crowther Report goes on to say that though these will remain a minority, for the great mass of ordinary boys and girls, too, the advent of a new technological age has created altered needs:

To be able to comprehend something of the language of science and technology; to be at home in a world of machines; and to be able to adjust to a rapidly changing environment. There will be less need in the future for 'skill' in the old-fashioned sense of the word; what will be needed in ever-growing volume will be the quality that can perhaps be described as 'general mechanical intelligence'. . . .

One can go further. What is needed is education much more purposefully designed to produce not only technological adaptability but also social adaptability – to prepare young peope both for their working life and their social life in the new affluent society that lies ahead of them. This sort of purposeful education for every pupil is the aim of the Soviet school system, in theory, at least, though in practice very much distorted by Communist dogma: but there are useful lessons to be learned from the theory.

Of course, with due differences. In a free country like Britain, if boys and girls are to appreciate an extended school period, they could not be forced to do this, nor subjected to mass propaganda. They would, above all, themselves have to feel that the extra school years made sense as profitable preparation for their own adult life. Without going into detail, I believe this would mean fairly drastic changes in the curriculum. The burden of the likely change is that the slant of the later secondary school years would have to be made more deliberately vocational. To my thinking, the weight of argument in the current educational debate lies with those who maintain that as British boys and girls are growing up in a highly industrialized country which must export in order to live, this fact should somehow already be brought home to them at school – for instance, industry ought to be brought nearer to the schools and the schools into closer contact with industry. To this end, the practice of visits to industrial and commercial firms, already introduced by enterprising secondary modern schools, could be made more regular and systematic. Youth Employment Officers, whose numbers should be increased, could be brought into contact with school life at an earlier stage. The actual school curriculum during the additional years could also without much harm be made more directly practical. For instance, adolescent girls could learn domestic science or take typing and secretarial courses while still taking part in the organized social life of school. In the same way, for boys, pre-apprenticeship courses could be made part of the secondary school life, though this would depend on the much-needed extension of the individual apprenticeship system itself.

The future schools

Something like this trend towards adjusting education to new needs in a changing society can certainly be seen in the new and vast comprehensive schools. These, however, have remained few in number. What is more important, therefore, is that the trend is also noticeable in many secondary modern schools where the majority of pupils are working class, but the atmosphere of the school is distinctly more middle class than ten years ago. I saw a good illustration of this at a big secondary modern school for boys in Middlesex, on the very outermost fringe of London. True, this was a new school, a showpiece of the Middlesex County Council, with everything in favour of experiment. The school was equipped with facilities for handicraft and machine workshops which an expensive public school might envy. Its spread-out, functional buildings stood in an expanse of open green space, large enough for several association and rugby football pitches. Most of the boys were the sons of artisans and skilled and semi-skilled workers who were earning high wages in the new modern factories west of London and who were living on new modern housing estates – a working-class population rapidly going up in the world (and which, in fact, in 1959 elected a Conservative to Parliament).

This naturally made experiment easier. I was interested to learn from the headmaster that special arrangements had been made with some of the large firms in the area for boys to start on actual apprenticeship courses while still remaining at school, and a good proportion of the boys were in fact staying on a voluntary extra year or more for this purpose. And their continued presence as a school leadership, said the headmaster, had led to something like a general upgrading. I saw, for instance, boys in the c and d streams (apt to be neglected in bad schools) who were performing tasks such as running the lending library. Outwardly, too, the school had a middle-class look. Boys wore blazers with school badges; I saw some of them going out to play rugby football on well-prepared pitches; for all I knew, England being England, there might already be a school song. Perhaps all this up-grading was a shade self-conscious, but, as the headmaster said, the most important aim was that boys should be able to start on their technical training while still at school, while playing team games and playing a role in the organized social life of the school, instead of spending their free time in standing about aimlessly at street corners, as many of them would otherwise have done. And this seemed to me the essence of the matter.

True, this particular local authority school, standing among green fields and brand-new housing estates, looked specially favoured for this sort of social upgrading. One could not quite expect this atmosphere to be reproduced amidst the traffic din and temptations of inner London. Yet I felt that this particular school did point to the desirable pattern of English education of the future. The addition of another two years of obligatory school attendance could probably make it easier to make the pattern universal. At any rate, as I wandered through this new secondary modern school in Middlesex, which seemed so expressly designed to turn out the technicians of today, I felt that it was much more like a Soviet school than any English school would have looked fifteen or twenty years ago. Reflecting on this as I drove back to London past new factories, traffic roundabouts with a background of occasional fields, advertising posters for soft drinks, shopping arcades, suburban cinemas, through the raw emergent landscape of a new England, it came to me that the point of resemblance was not that both in the school I had just seen and in a Soviet school the stress was on technical training. It was rather that in this school in Middlesex, too, rather as in a Soviet school, one had the feeling that a whole stratum of the population had put 'lower-class' status aside and was advancing into a new life.

Can the example of such a leading school be followed fairly rapidly throughout the secondary school system? A group of young teachers I talked to told me that I need not worry. Under the pressure from the teaching staff, or from parents who felt that they had made good in life, and because there was really no other possibility, the whole spontaneous trend in the secondary modern schools was in the direction of middle-class values, ways and speech – the effect was already especially noticeable among the girls. My young informants felt that in this process something was also lost – a traditional quality of working-class spontaneity in speech and manner, a directness and lack of emotional inhibitions, which could be very attractive.

Perhaps there is this loss. But since there is no alternative, could this advance towards middle-class standards in the State school system not be made altogether more *dynamic*, so that boys and girls again felt conscious of direction and authority in the society they lived in, and so that their imaginations were stirred? At any rate, I feel that the secondary school system, more than anywhere else, is the place where a greater sense of purpose and drive can be brought into British life. A greater sense of national purpose, too. There should be no doubt that if what is today fashionably called a 'crash programme' could be introduced to step up British State education, not only the actual standards of attainment in secondary schools would be transformed, but the consequent social 'upward pull' would be felt among adolescents throughout society – all the way down to the groups of Teds and Drifters in their juke-box cafés.

What sort of youth services?

Much the same could be said about the youth services. Their chief need is to provide far better social and recreation facilities for the majority of working-class fifteen- to eighteen-year-olds, who are in this respect still badly under-privileged.

Here, too, there is a class barrier to be breached. To any-one from abroad, English class distinctions still appear as sharply drawn in leisure time as in schools. Middle-class teenagers have sports and social life organized for them at schools and colleges. Working-class teenagers have little of the sort. This statement has to be qualified. There are also the youth clubs, available to early school-leavers in most parts of England at least on one or two evenings a week, yet here a problem of outdated class outlook has to be solved. The youth clubs have changed since the time when they were started as moral rescue efforts in the slums, yet many of them have not changed enough – they are still only *half-modern*. My own composite impression left from visits to many London youth clubs is of strenuous activity in a gym; of rather dressed-up youths playing billiards or ping-pong; of rather self-conscious teenage girls; of a fre-quent undertone of defiance contrasting with the middle-class voices of club leaders and student helpers; and, nearly always, the picture of one particular room where a gramo-phone was turned on to top volume and scores of younger boys and girls crowded the floor, a few jiving, the majority just standing and listening to the appalling blare.

This is not meant disparagingly. Some clubs, with devoted and selfless workers, have done admirable work for difficult youngsters. Other clubs, rather more numerous, where the youngsters are not at all difficult, but only keen, can show the visitor an impressive and expanding range of activities – sports, amateur dramatics, motor-cycle clubs, foreign holi-days. But the one thing I felt was wrong with the whole club structure (and this view was shared by many youth workers) was that most youth clubs have remained segre-gated class institutions. It was really extraordinary that in 1960 one might not find a single middle-class youngster in a typical youth club in the London area. (In the outer suburbs, the reverse might be the case. The members of a youth club would all be from grammar schools or the A stream from secondary modern schools, with those lower down somehow excluded.) Consequently, the ordinary urban youth clubs do not give their young people enough of a chance to meet their contemporaries from different walks of life, to rise socially, to 'get on'.

This may be a reason for the feeling that the youth clubs, as they are, have been left far behind by the changes in the affluent society. The proof, at any rate, is that the majority, and when one reaches the age of sixteen to seventeen age-groups the great majority, of early school-leavers are today not regular members of any youth organization. Instead, they are drawn away into the world of the commercial youth culture, even though this often means frustration, insecurity, and drift.

It was this problem of the untouched majority that the Albemarle Report tried to resolve. The authors were aware of something old-fashioned in the whole structure of the youth clubs. Implicit in their recommendations for a National Youth Council, for better club premises, for training professional youth leaders and paying them proper salaries and for generous grants from public funds, was the idea that the clubs should be re-modelled in order somehow to be brought up to date, to catch the elusive mood of the young of today, to overcome their resistance and meet their real desires.

And here, no doubt, lies a great difficulty. It is never easy to find the right form of organization for the young, and the result is often quite unexpected. As example one can take the Boy Scout movement, which was surely one of the oddest and yet subtlest inventions of the twentieth century. Baden-Powell took certain ceremonials from primitive societies, the Zulus, the Iroquois, blended them with late-Victorian morality, added some elements from merchant marine and sailing-ship life, discovered intuitively a good deal of what we know of group dynamics and provided the uniform of the Boer War heroes – and the result became a major invention. Through the international scout movement, millions of young people made a better adjustment to life. By now, the Scout movement has probably had its day among boys and girls over thirteen or fourteen. Yet, at the time when it was launched, who could have foreseen in turn that the esoteric jazz from a corner of New Orleans would one day provide youth with one of its main preoccupations, with a new international language – almost a new youth world of its own?

Still, if it is accepted that large numbers of young people are today more active than ever before (more sailing, rowing, jazz, dancing, motor-cycling, etc.) and many more want in a confused way to be active but do not know how, the preliminary proposals of the Albemarle Committee to re-equip the youth clubs made good sense, especially the financial recommendations for proper State aid. It seems anomalous, to put it mildly, that in 1960 the sum total of Government and Local Authority grants to the entire Youth Services was less than the cost of the Approved Schools. If the Albemarle Committee's recommendations for multiplying this total several times over, for a 'generous and imaginative' building programme, for doubling the force of trained youth leaders, and so on, are implemented, no doubt this could give the Youth Services at least emergency aid.

Centres of animation

However, on a long-term view one can go much further. The demand of the teenagers of today for a social life all of their own and for places where they can lead this social life undisturbed may be nothing novel. What is quite new, however, is the scale, the intensity of this demand, clearly connected with the present changes in family life and the earlier maturity of adolescents. In this respect, I found the same views on the Continent. The complaints by and about adolescents who were too much 'in the street' because they had 'nowhere to go' sounded exactly alike. As in England, I found also that current ideas of town planning had not yet caught up with the needs of youth. The usual standardized design of blocks of labour-saving flats (or small houses) with shopping streets, perhaps a playground for small children, and nothing much else, reflected the fact that the average family had grown smaller, its ties looser, while its members looked for more of their entertainment outside: but within this design, the special needs of adolescents were simply left out.

One could see this deficiency perhaps most directly – and visually – on the average London housing estate, as a rule consisting of rows of blocks of flats and nothing else. For the adolescents who have been moved to such estates, home has become a smaller and more impersonal place; at the same time, the old familiar meeting places on doorsteps and under the lights at street corners have gone, with nothing put in their place. A good example of this could be seen at the L.C.C. estate at Woodberry Down, in North London. Here, in what was practically a self-contained area, impressively designed complexes of flats housed upwards of 7,000 people, or the population of a small town, yet for years after the estate had gone up, the youth club provision still consisted only of a temporary hut. Something in this state of affairs is surely wrong. It is not surprising that many new estates have become breeding-grounds for groups of adolescent Teds and Drifters. It is also significant that several of the New Towns around London, where the combination of elaborate planning and financial stringency has produced a rather arid landscape of monotonous rows of small houses and gardens – arid, that is, when seen through the eager eyes of youth – should already have produced sizeable 'youth problems'.

These problems may well continue to grow. If, as looks likely, the majority of the population will from now on live in this rather 'classless' new landscape of blocks of flats, sprawling suburban estates, New Towns, arterial roads, with cars and television aerials everywhere, we must realize that to the young this new landscape can seem something of a wilderness, with few landmarks to which they can feel emotionally attached. To this new landscape one new amenity must therefore be added. Each locality should by design include properly planned provision for the leisure time of its adolescents. This might be a well-organized local youth club, or on a larger scale a real centre for sport, music, dancing, or in a smaller area even a properly run café – but above all a place where the young can meet, preferably with adult guidance well in the background. How such places should be run, whether, as may be best, by the remodelled existing youth organizations, is something experience would show.

A second point is equally important. Just as in the interest of a more balanced society the remodelled English secondary schools of the future should display much less class divisions, so I think it essential that the Youth Services should at least to some extent (one mustn't be Utopian) break through the existing class barriers. As far as future major ventures go, my inclination is therefore for the larger type of youth centre, on the Scandinavian model. In one respect, namely the important visual one, I think the architecture of the new secondary school already provides a basic design for the future. Just as a traveller returning to England in 1960 would certainly be struck by one change – the architecturally dominant and often striking-looking school in each new area, so I believe that in 1970, say, each medium-sized town should have its equally prominent youth centre; also an essentially modern building, with imaginative facilities for music, dancing, and play; for more elaborate hobbies like a ciné-photography club, real jazz, amateur acting, or boat-building; the complex might be geographically linked with the local public library or swimming pool, it might be administratively run by the local youth clubs – these are details. In France, a chief organizer of the new youth movement of the Maisons de la Culture et de la Jeunesse told me that he liked to see each such centre (of which there are some excellent ones in France, but, of course, still far too few) as a true *centre d'animation* – a busy recognized meeting-place for the young which would bring new animation to the social life of its whole area, and this seems to me just the right definition.

New animation to what end? In England today one hears

much talk about the need for the Youth Services to present a new 'challenge to youth'. The nature of this challenge is sometimes still oddly looked for in such things as mountaineering; there is nothing wrong in introducing working-class boys to mountaineering, or for that matter to sailing, ski-ing, or other such sports, but to equate this with a major challenge to youth seems curiously old-fashioned, as though we were still at the day when Mallory and Irvine stood on the North Ridge of Everest. The Albemarle Report comes nearer when saying that the Youth Services should encourage and challenge boys and girls to run their own activities as much as possible by themselves. But I think one can be much more precise. First of all, when people speak of 'presenting a challenge to youth', the reference is, in fact, to working-class youth, the great mass of early school leavers who today go into dull yet well-paid routine jobs. (Nobody, for instance, worries much about finding a 'challenge' for the students at Colleges of Advanced Technology!) And this defines the real challenge, not to youth, but to the Youth Services themselves. In material terms, the young people they are concerned with have been caught up in a rapid process of *embourgeoisement* – they have plenty of money in their pockets – but this is not enough. Indeed, culturally many of these boys and girls are today being exploited and downgraded, involved in a drift towards purposelessness. And the main task of the Youth Services is, quite simply, to oppose this drift; to help the majority of newly affluent young people to lead a fuller social life, to widen their interests and activities, to acquire greater urbanity, take keener interest in further education, in short, to 'get on'.

It is, in fact, the same urgent task which faces the secondary school system and which should be pursued by the Youth Services in close cooperation.

The case for action

There is a time to end. My argument has carried me a long way from the starting-point of this book, namely the plight of a little group of Teds on a London housing estate; and, as the reader who has borne patiently with me may feel, after all the topics upon which I have touched, the concluding proposals for expanding British secondary education and Youth Services may not look very imposing (and some are directed at specifically British problems only). Yet my basic point – and the justification for this book – rests in my belief that at the present day these problems of educational reform have taken on a new urgency.

The affluent society: perhaps it has been the chief virtue of Professor Galbraith's term, much misused as a cliché, to emphasize that with the contemporary break-through into mass consumption and mass communication we have indeed progressed into a new *kind* of society. And raw and recent though this society may be, we can already discern in it the lines of a disturbing conflict between opposed trends of expansion and aimlessness.

If it is argued that I have in my analysis not made enough of the advance of British post-war youth, the answer is that this change is surely in the foreground of our awareness. The fact is that by almost any index of actual measurement, the boys and girls of the last ten years have been a more active, more successful, and more self-reliant British generation than any before. More of them stayed on voluntarily at secondary modern schools after fifteen, more went to grammar schools and technical colleges; official plans for the sixties (even by a slow-moving Conservative Government) were for the number of university students and advanced technologists to be doubled: and of these many were coming from working-class backgrounds where such careers had previously scarcely been thought of. In addition, the young seemed also strikingly more energetic and enterprising in the way they conducted their affairs. They matured earlier, they married earlier; they participated in greater numbers in the arts and sports. Many of them, indeed, looked to be far more at home in the affluent society than their elders, and not only in coping with the new scientific knowledge and techniques. For the first time in

Britain, I think, one was aware of a continuous upsurge of working class young people who were no longer content to be regarded as culturally of another nation, but on the contrary brought their own more spontaneous outlook with them into English middle-class culture, making it more democratic, livelier, more unforced. It was this break-through which has already been so effectively mirrored in the rather striking 'new movements' in the British theatre and film.

However, equally clearly, this advance has been only one of several contrasting trends in the British affluent society. Against this picture of bustling youth one had also, in looking at British life at the start of the sixties, to set its precise opposite. It was evident that the whole expansion of State education was still only fragmentary, and far too many boys and girls were left right outside. There was undeniable evidence that a large section of British youth felt frustrated, angry, bored, and adrift without guidance and that in places this *malaise* was actually on the increase. Employers in places complained more frequently about the indifference of the young towards their work; teachers spoke of a bored or disaffected generation of teenagers at schools, and there was of course the increase in the number of actual young delinquents. All these things seemed symptoms of the other side of the affluent society – a new and disturbing drift into purposelessness.

As I have tried to show in earlier chapters, this conflict between expansion and purposelessness seems inherent in the present stages of the affluent society. In one form or another, it has been revealed in many countries, East and West, and certainly in striking form in Britain. Whatever the result of this tug-of-war, it seems obvious what is desirable: to encourage the forces of progress, of social emancipation among youth, and to discourage the downward trend. But this cannot come about by itself, only through purposeful action, that is, public action. Writing at the outset of the 1960s, after a decade in which Britain has steadily lost ground in industry and trade relative to other countries,

I have no doubt of the form which this action must take. What is required is basically simple – namely for a slightly larger percentage of the national income to be diverted from personal consumption and transferred to investment for the future, above all to a plan to bring the mass education of adolescents up to quite a new level.

This brings up the question of the cost: in 1962, during one of its *laissez-faire* crises, the Conservative Government was, in fact, stumbling in the opposite direction by slowing the expansion of State aid to education all the way from the university level downwards. Yet, fundamentally, it seems to me beyond argument that this question is not one of what the country can in absolute terms afford. In the long run, if one were to suggest that a rich country like Britain cannot *afford* to pay reasonable salaries to such key workers as probation officers, or to raise the school-leaving age beyond fifteen and run youth clubs on more than shoestring finance, in short, to spend as large a proportion of the national income on education as much poorer countries do – in the long run this would seem as absurd as to suggest that Britain cannot *afford* to build the roads for the million motor-cars it turns out each year.

Seen in this light, the question is not really a fiscal one but one of political priorities, that is, of will; and educational reform seems to me such a priority for two most obvious reasons. The need to strengthen Britain's competitive position in a technological age is an argument few would quarrel with. But I believe that in the new circumstances of the affluent society, such educational reform should also be carried out quite explicitly for a second reason, for after all this society does not look as stable as its advertisers make out (and, to say it at last, one should not forget that the adolescents of today have been growing up in a world under threat of nuclear catastrophe). This second reason is the need to keep the country's adolescents until a much later age away from the racket of dead-end jobs and the commercial youth culture, to protect them against the undue influence of the mass media, in fact to provide them with a framework of more purposeful educational and social discipline which can prepare them for life in the affluent society rather better than so many are prepared today.

Educational reform on such lines is to my mind an essential British task for the sixties. It would, I believe, also be the way to reduce the problem of juvenile delinquency to manageable proportions.

Index

261

Index

Index

*Some other Pelican and Penguin
books are described on the
following pages*

BRITAIN IN THE SIXTIES

Britain in the Sixties is a new series within a series. The books issued under this general title are Penguin Specials which are broader in subject and, therefore, less closely tied to the immediate topics which fill the headlines of the newspapers. In them specialists discuss some of the major social issues in Britain, as they present themselves in this decade, and indicate the lines along which reforms are required.

Titles so far published in this series are:

COMMUNICATIONS s207 *Raymond Williams*

EDUCATION FOR TOMORROW s208 *John Vaizey*

THE FAMILY AND MARRIAGE s210 *Ronald Fletcher*

HOUSING s211 *Stanley Alderson*

Coming shortly:

Kingsley Martin
THE CROWN AND THE ESTABLISHMENT s217

EDUCATING THE INTELLIGENT

Michael Hutchinson and Christopher Young

A566

If the Battle of Waterloo was won on the playing-fields of Eton, it is equally true that Britain's destiny is today being hammered out in the classrooms of secondary schools all over the country. Recent controversies have raised many questions about the direction which is being taken by secondary education. Is it correctly orientated for the needs of modern society or does it tend to 'level downwards'? Should more encouragement be given to pupils who are above the average intelligence? Ought we deliberately to train an élite?

The two authors of this constructive and absorbing book have had many years' experience as teachers. After exposing some of the serious inadequacies of the present curriculum in secondary schools, they go on to analyse the basic educational needs of the intelligent child. They then outline an alternative curriculum which would both meet these needs and be practicable within the average secondary school. In addition they discuss fully the sixth-form syllabus, the examination system, university selection, and the choice, training, and remuneration of teachers.

THE COMPREHENSIVE SCHOOL

Robin Pedley

A613

Nearly everyone interested in education today wants to abolish the '11+' examination, but few people are clear what the alternatives are.

The best alternative is the comprehensive school, and in this new appraisal the Reader in Education at the Leicester University School of Education gives a clear and critical picture of the comprehensive school as it exists in England and Wales today. Dr Pedley first describes just what the '11+' is and does. Then, after dispelling the bogey that comprehensive schools need at least two thousand pupils in order to function, he goes on to demonstrate, by statistics, that those in existence are already rivalling the grammar schools in academic achievements. Finally, and most important, he argues that a good comprehensive school can both focus and mirror a community as can no other school.

Of all our educational establishments the comprehensive school is the least understood. This book, which contains a glossary of educational terms and a list of comprehensive schools, offers to interested readers – especially parents – all the facts.

FAMILY AND KINSHIP IN
EAST LONDON

Michael Young and Peter Willmott

A595

The two authors of this most human of surveys are sociologists. They spent three years on 'field work' in Bethnal Green and on a new housing estate in Essex. The result is a fascinating study, made during a period of extensive rehousing, of family and community ties and the pull of the 'wider family' on working-class people.

'Probably not only the fullest, but virtually the only account of working-class family relationships in any country. The general reader will find it full of meat and free of jargon' – *New Statesman*

'This shrewd – and in places extremely amusing – book combines warmth of feeling with careful sociological method' – *Financial Times*

'Observant, tactful, sympathetic, humorous ... I really feel that nobody who wants to know how our society is changing can afford not to read Young and Willmott' – Kingsley Amis in the *Spectator*

'No short account can do justice to this book, charmingly written, engaging, absorbing' – *British Medical Journal*

Obviously there have been changes in the two districts under survey during the last five years. This edition in Pelicans, with its fresh introduction and simplified appendices, is justified by the standing the report has achieved as a modern classic of sociology.